W9-CBA-097

WEARSIDE BATTALION

WEARSIDE BATTALION

20th (Service) Battalion of
the Durham Light Infantry

**A HISTORY OF THE BATTALION RAISED BY LOCAL
COMMITTEE IN SUNDERLAND**

John Sheen

Pen & Sword
MILITARY

This book is dedicated to the memory of the Officers, Warrant Officers, Non Commissioned Officers and men of the

20th (Service) Battalion Durham Light Infantry (Wearside)

First published in Great Britain in 2007 by
Pen & Sword Military
an imprint of
Pen & Sword Books Ltd
47 Church Street
Barnsley
South Yorkshire
S70 2AS

Copyright © John Sheen, 2007

ISBN 9781844156405

The right of John Sheen to be identified as Author of the Work
has been asserted by him in accordance with the Copyright, Designs and
Patents Act 1988.

A CIP catalogue record for this book is
available from the British Library.

All rights reserved. No part of this book may be reproduced or transmitted in any form or by
any means, electronic or mechanical including photocopying, recording or by any information
storage and retrieval system, without permission from the Publisher in writing.

Typeset in Palatino 9pt

Printed and bound in the United Kingdom by CPI

Pen & Sword Books Ltd incorporates the imprints of Pen & Sword Aviation, Pen & Sword
Maritime, Pen & Sword Military, Wharncliffe Local History, Pen and Sword Select, Pen and
Sword Military Classics and Leo Cooper.
For a complete list of Pen & Sword titles, please contact
Pen & Sword Books Limited
47 Church Street, Barnsley, South Yorkshire, S70 2AS, England
E-mail: enquiries@pen-and-sword.co.uk
Website: www.pen-and-sword.co.uk

Contents

Foreword

It was a privilege to be asked by John to write this foreword having known him for many years now. His passion for bringing the histories of our local North East regiments to life, especially for the relatives of those who served in them, has resulted in a valuable contribution to the history of the north east.

Eighty-two years after its raising, this new history of the 20th (Service) Battalion, Durham Light Infantry (Wearside) will not disappoint the relatives of those who served with the Battalion, or those who enjoy reading military history, as once again he has brought the memory of a fine D.L.I. battalion back to life for us all to enjoy.

From its raising to its disbandment John resurrects the Wearside Battalion through his meticulous research using, once again, previously unpublished material, including personal memoirs and the Battalion War Diaries. The book ends with another well researched battalion nominal Roll which has become one of the outstanding trademarks of his research, a feature which enhances his authorship.

Further to this the book has, with the permission of the regimental trustees, what I consider to be one of the largest selections of battalion photographs that have ever been seen in this, the Pals series. Of great value to the reader and researcher, is the amount of named individuals that are given in the photograph captions. For those whose relatives served with the original Wearside Battalion this will not just be the icing on the cake, but will fill them with pride as they come face to face with those men who never failed in their duty during those terrible years of sacrifice.

Graham Stewart,
Darlington,
August 2007.

Top: A Company.
Bottom: D Company.
20/Durham LI, at Aldershot 1916 prior to embarkation for France.

ACKNOWLEDGEMENTS

Thanks are due to many people, and this work could not have been completed without the support of the Trustees of The Durham Light Infantry Museum and the advice and help of Steve Shannon and the late George Fraser at The Durham Light Infantry Museum.

The staff at Durham City Library, Darlington Library, the staff of the Durham County Archives in particular Gill Parkes for her help and assistance with photographs of the battalion. Sunderland Library.

The late Mr Malcolm MacGregor for assistance with Honours and Gallantry Awards to members of the 20th Battalion.

Graham Stewart, Clive Dunn, Andrew Brookes, Fred Bromilow, Simon Jervis, Stewart Couper and Sid Patterson all who loaned material from their collections.

My son, James, assisted with the research in the early stages, now a serving 'Tommy' or 'Squaddie' as they say today, in the Royal Electrical & Mechanical Engineers, I owe him thanks for his work at the National Archives.

Photograph of the regimental staff of the 20/Durham LI, 1916. Left to right: Sergeant A. James, Sergeant F.A. Bertram, Company Quartermaster-Sergeant Clark, Regimental Sergeant-Major Hicks, Captain and Adjutant P. Spencer, Lieutenant-Colonel K.J.W. Leather, Major J.W. Hills, Lieutenant and Quartermaster S. Simpkin, Regimental Quartermaster-Sergeant Coxon, Sergeant-Bugler Davison, Sergeant A.E. Miller.

Chapter One

Sunderland
The biggest shipbuilding town in the world

SUNDERLAND STANDS on either side of the mouth of the River Wear on the east coast of County Durham, it was in 1914 a large seaport, importing and exporting all nature of goods from and to the rest of the world. The main imports were wheat, barley, iron ore, petroleum, timber and paper-making material. The main export was of course coal and coal-based products, of which annually over two million tons was exported. Also machinery and from Sunderland itself ships, that is to say vessels made for other countries, those that were not registered as British vessels. In 1912 almost two thousand foreign ships, both steamers and sailing vessels, loaded or unloaded in the port. Over three thousand ships engaged in the coastal trade came and went as well as many small fishing boats. As many as 201 steamships were registered in the port at the beginning of 1912.

The port was formed and protected by two piers which reach out into the North Sea some 456 yards. The North Pier was commenced in 1706 and wasn't finally completed until 1840. Originally it had a lighthouse about 500 feet from its end but this was removed in 1906. The South Pier is a

Sunderland High Street at the turn of the century – the old Town Hall is seen in the centre of the photograph.

The harbour: from here ships were sent worldwide whilst further up river the shipyards turned out many merchant ships.

substantial structure which is 16 feet wide and stands eleven feet above high water in a spring tide. A new pier was added in 1903 when the Roker Pier was completed. This had a new lighthouse constructed at its end, the pier curved out from Roker across Roker rocks in a southerly direction for 2,800 feet. Almost complete in 1914 was the new South Pier which curved northwards to form a harbour of around 150 acres. Both these outer piers are constructed of massive granite-faced concrete blocks. Inside the harbour situated on the south side was South Docks which opened in 1850 and was probably at that time the most important dock on the north-east coast; consisting of tidal and half tidal basins, there were also three deep water docks, Hudson Dock North, Hudson Dock South and Hendon Dock. Here there were grain warehouses number one and number two, number three or Laing's warehouse and on the western side a coal staithe, also good covered buildings for the fishing trade. Wearmouth or North Dock opened in 1840 and was owned by the North East Railway Company and it had a capacity to hold up to fifty vessels of heavy tonnage.

However the origins of the town can be traced back many centuries, in 674, King Ecgfrith of Northumbria granted a large tract of land to Benedict Biscop to set up the monastery of Wearmouth – Jarrow, its most famous son being the Venerable Bede, the greatest scholar and writer of his age. The formation of the monastry led to the land on the north of the river being known as Monkwearmouth and the land on the south bank, which was still controlled by the Bishop of Durham, being known as Bishopwearmouth. This could well have given rise to the name of the town for the land was 'sundered land' or separated or parted land, eventually shortened to Sunderland. Biscop brought glass-makers and masons from France to build his church of St Peter's. They established a glass making workshop at Monkwearmouth, where stained glass was made, a skill that had been forgotten since the Romans had left, this led to the re-introduction of the trade to Britain and Sunderland became known as a centre for making glass and a number of bottle and glass works lined the river bank. Brewing was also carried out in the town, the most well known brand being Vaux's. Captain Vaux, the son of the brewery owner commanded the machine-gun section of the Northumberland and Durham Yeomanry in South Africa during the Boer War. The section was armed with two Maxim machine guns and afterwards to commemorate this they brewed a beer that became the world famous Vaux Double Maxim.

In 1851 there were no less than seventy firms building ships along both banks of the river and by the time war broke out in 1914 the majority of households in Sunderland depended on men who were employed in the yards or relied on the shipyards for work. When war broke out in 1914 there were fourteen shipyards on the Wear. Laing's yard at Deptford had launched their first iron-built ship, the *Amity*, in the 1850s. William Doxford started his yard up river at Cox Green but in 1857 he moved down river to Pallion. In the early 1900s when the East yard was built Doxford's was one of the greatest names in shipbuilding. Robert Thompson started building ships on the Wear in the early 1800s and with his three sons opened a yard at North Sands; eventually his son Joseph Lowes Thompson took over and the firm remained there until the yard closed in 1933. Other well known names were Short's, Priestman's, Pickersgill's, Blumer's, Bartram's, Austin's,

Platers at Blumer's yard in 1914. Many of the younger men enlisted but were discharged and sent back to the yards as munitions workers to keep the yards working.

Osbourne Graham's, Crown's, R. Thompson's, Sunderland Ship Building and Swan Hunter's.

The town was supplied with electricity by Sunderland Corporation and gas by the Sunderland Gas Company, the electricity not only provided lighting but also ran the trams on the city streets and powered lifts and pumps in the docks, bottling plants and printing presses and many other applications throughout the town. Water was supplied by the Sunderland and South Shields Water Company with huge bore holes at Stoney Gate and Dalton and Ryhope where huge steam-driven pumps brought the water to the surface to be pumped up to the reservoir on Humbledon Hill. Although most of the town's connections are with the sea and maritime trade, the town did have military links. Prior to 1881, the 106th Bombay European Light Infantry had its depot in Sunderland, right down at the mouth of the river on the south bank. When the regiment amalgamated with the 68th to form the Durham Light Infantry in 1881 the depot moved to Newcastle. The Territorial Army was well established in the town, the Royal Garrison Artillery had a 'Heavy' Battery commanded by Major J. C. Marr with its headquarters at The Green and the Durham Light Infantry Brigade Company of the Army Service Corps was also located in the same drill hall. In Livingstone Road, 7th Durham Light Infantry commanded by Lieutenant Colonel E. Vaux DSO CB, had its headquarters.

This then is a brief description of the town that was to raise the 20th (Service) Battalion, the Durham Light Infantry (Wearside) in 1915.

FAITHFUL – THE COUNTY REGIMENT

The County of Durham has produced for the British Army some of the finest soldiers ever to set foot on a battlefield, not only the county regiment, the Durham Light Infantry, but many other regiments have drawn large numbers of Durham men to their colours. The Northumberland Fusiliers, the East Yorkshire Regiment, the West Yorkshire Regiment and the Green Howards all had large contingents of Durham men in their ranks during the First World War. The Durham pitman, small, stocky and hard, used to hard work and danger, had all the attributes needed by the front-line infantryman, but even in peacetime many men escaped the drudgery of the mine by joining the army: regular meals, a bed, a uniform and fresh air to breathe would seem quite attractive during a prolonged dispute with the colliery owners.

The Durham Light Infantry first came into being on 29 September 1756 as the second battalion of Lieutenant General Huske's Regiment, or the 23rd Regiment of Foot, later the Royal Welch Fusiliers. At that time fifteen regiments of infantry were authorised to raise second battalions. In 1758 these second battalions became separate regiments and were numbered between 61 and 75, thus the second battalion of the 23rd Regiment, Lieutenant General Huske's, became the 68th Regiment. The battalion was raised in the Leicester area where it remained until the end of April 1757, when a move was

General John Lambton 1710 - 1794, the founder of the regiment.

12

made to Berkshire, followed by further moves made to Chatham and Dover. Then both battalions of the 23rd marched to the Isle of Wight in 1758, and it was here that the two regiments separated and the 2nd Battalion 23rd Regiment became the 68th Regiment of Foot.

It was on 13 May 1758 that Lieutenant Colonel John Lambton, of the Coldstream Guards was authorised to raise recruits, 'by beat of drum or otherwise in any county or part of our kingdom'. In 1782, Lambton had the 68th linked to his home county of Durham, although not many of the men were recruited from the county at that time, indeed there were probably more Irishmen than English. The Regiment saw its first action in a raid on the French coast, at Cancale on the coast of Brittany. A few days were spent ashore, before withdrawing to the ships and sailing back to the Isle of Wight. In July another successful raid took place but in September a third raid went wrong and the Grenadier Company of the 68th along with the grenadiers of the other regiments involved, suffered casualties when covering the retreat to the ships.

The next posting for the regiment was to the West Indies, in 1764 the regiment sailed to the island of Antigua. Here they lost 150 men to fever and still more were lost to disease in St Vincent before returning to Britain. They were posted back to the West Indies in 1794, to St Lucia and then to Grenada, where fever took its toll of all ranks. By the middle of 1796 there were only sixty men fit for duty. After being sent back to England and reformed they returned to St Lucia for a number of years and again lost many men to disease. Returning to England again the regiment was selected to train as light infantry, skirmishers who used their initiative, using the tactics of fire and manoeuvre and carrying out orders by bugle call. Armed with an improved musket, with better sights and a dull or browned barrel, the regiment was soon called to action. Its first action as a regiment of light infantry was as part of the invasion of the island of Walcheren on the Dutch coast. After taking part in the capture of Flushing the 68th joined the garrison of South Beveland. For six months they remained here losing men daily to the 'Walcheren Fever', a kind of malaria that even after the regiment returned to England was rife among the ranks. Refitted and reorganised, the regiment's next posting was to General Wellington's army in Spain. Here they took part in the battles of Salamanca and Vittoria and the fighting in the Pyrenees. They didn't play any part in the final defeat of Napoleon at Waterloo and over the next forty years in postings to Canada, Jamaica and Gibraltar established a reputation as a smart regiment.

The year 1854 was the next time the regiment would see action, from their base in Malta the 68th joined the 4th Division and sailed for the Crimea to fight the Russsians. Although they were present at the Battle of the Alma on 20 September, the regiment saw little action, however on 5 November at the Battle of Inkerman, Private John Byrne won the regiment's first Victoria Cross, when he rescued a wounded man under enemy fire. A second Victoria Cross was awarded to the regiment in May 1855 to Captain T. de C. Hamilton for action at Sebastopol. The force he commanded was attacked by the Russians, at midnight; in a howling gale they managed to enter the trench held by the 68th and spike one of the regiment's guns. Captain Hamilton immediately led a counter-attack and recovered the weapon, during which time they killed two Russian officers and a number of their men. The conditions in the Crimea were miserable but the regiment remained until the end. This was the first war to have a photographer with the army in the field and the outstanding thing to emerge was the bravery of the soldiers and the conditions that they endured, whilst the Generals displayed a total mismanagement and indifference to their suffering. It is largely due to the war correspondents that changes to the army were brought about.

There followed a few pleasant years in stations around the Mediterranean, before the regiment finally arrived back in England in 1857. However the Government didn't keep the 68th sitting

Soldiers of the 68th Light Infantry in summer dress April 1855 during the Crimean War. Standing third from the right is Sergeant Henry Sladden wearing his recently awarded DCM.

The same group of men of the 68th wearing their winter dress during the Crimean War.

about at home, within three months the regiment was on its way to Burma and afterwards in 1863 to New Zealand. In one of Queen Victoria's little wars a fierce conflict took place in those South Sea Islands, where the Maoris, the native people of New Zealand, resented the fact their lands were being stolen. The Maori, a brave and resourceful warrior, fought hard and was a difficult opponent. The 68th had to take them on hand to hand and on 21 June 1864, Sergeant John Murray won the regiment's third Victoria Cross leading a bayonet charge, in which he saved the life of Private Byrne VC, by killing a Maori who was just about to kill Byrne. The war ended and by 1866 the regiment was back in England. After six years at home the regiment was posted to India.

In 1881, Cardwell, the Secretary of State for War in the Liberal Government, brought in some sweeping changes to the army. He linked all infantry regiments to a county and for all those without a second battalion he linked them to another regiment. The 68th already with Durham in its title became linked with the 106th Bombay Light Infantry.

The 106th started life in 1839 as the 2nd Bombay Europeans in the Honourable East India Company's forces. They saw action in Persia, at the battles of Reshire and Bushire in 1856

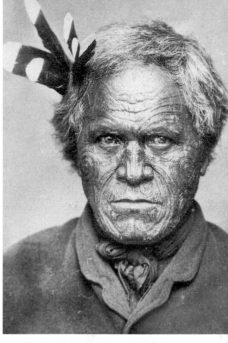

Tomika Te Mutu, a Maori chief, famous for the tattoos on his face.

Officers and men of the 68th Light Infantry at Te Papa Camp in Tauranga, New Zealand in April 1865. Seated fourth from the left is the Commanding Officer Colonel Henry Greer.

James Francis Durham, an abandoned Arab baby found by the 2nd Battalion after the Battle of Ginnis. He was rescued and brought up by the regiment, which he eventually joined.

and when taken onto the British Army establishment became the 106th Bombay European Light Infantry. From 1881 the two regiments became 1st and 2nd Battalions of the Durham Light Infantry. One of the other ideas of the reforms was that a regiment would always have one battalion overseas and one battalion stationed in the United Kingdom, the home battalion supplying drafts of men to the overseas battalion. The regiment next saw action in 1885 in the Sudan, where 2/Durham LI fought at the Battle of Ginnis against the wild Dervishes of the Mahdi's Forces who had taken Khartoum and killed General Gordon and the Garrison.

Whilst clearing the battlefield after the battle the regiment

The 2/Durham LI polo team that won the Inter Regimental Polo Cup in India 1896 and 1897. Left to right: H de Lisle, H D V Wilkinson, Dr Mander, J W Ainsworth and C C Luard.

24 October 1899: NCOs of 1/Durham LI en route to South Africa on board the Cunard steamship Cephalonia.

found an abandoned Arab toddler. He was rescued and brought up by the battalion, christened James Francis Durham and as soon as he was old enough, at about the age of fourteen in 1899, he was enlisted as a band boy into 2/Durham LI. He served with them in England and Ireland until he died at Fermoy in August 1910.

Throughout the 1890s 2/Durham LI served in India, where they excelled on the polo field: training their own ponies, they won many cups, beating and upsetting many rich cavalry regiments along the way. In his memoirs Sir Hubert Gough who served in the 16th Lancers recalled playing polo against the Durhams:

'The regiment [the 16th Lancers] never managed to win the Regimental Cup though we were

A fortified blockhouse guarding a bridge over the Orange River in South Africa. This was manned by E Company of 4(Militia) battalion Durham LI between February and May 1902.

always runners-up. The nearest to winning in my time was when the Durham Light Infantry only just beat us in the final. I think they won the Regimental Cup three years running. It was a wonderfully fine effort for they were not at all a rich regiment, but they trained their ponies themselves.'

The next time the regiment went into action was in South Africa during the Boer War. Ordered out in October 1899 as part of the Army Corps under the command of Sir Redvers Buller, 1/Durham LI sailed from Southampton on board the Cunard steamship *Cephalonia* on 24 October 1899 and by December they were in South Africa marching towards the battle front on the Tugela River.

1/Durham LI won fame on 5 February 1900, when they stormed the hill at Vaal-krantz. With 3/King's Royal Rifle Corps on their right, in extended line the two battalions advanced, taking casualties from enfilading rifle fire from a hill known as Doorn Kloof. They pressed on up Vaal-krantz and took the crest at bayonet point. As they advanced up the steep hill, the regiment left a large number of dead and wounded along the way, from the rifle fire of the Boer marksmen,

1 May 1903: General Wolseley presents Queen's South Africa medals to men of 1/Durham LI at Wellington Barracks in India.

Led by a Lieutenant, men of 2/Durham LI take part in the Evelyn Wood march and shoot competition at Aldershot 1904, note the wearing of the 'Broderick Cap'.

armed with their Mauser rifles. On 6 February the Boers launched a counter-attack which retook some of the ground they had lost the previous day, however, the British troops were rallied and a brilliant bayonet charge by the Durhams and KRRC regained all the ground that the Boers had recaptured. After the Relief of Ladymith the regiment was employed guarding blockhouses along the railway and patrolling the countryside. They were joined by the Volunteer Company formed from the Volunteer Battalions of the Durham Light Infantry, the Territorials of their day.

In 1908, Lord Haldane brought about changes to the Volunteer movement and created the Territorial Force, all the Rifle Volunteer Battalions were renumbered and became battalions in the

8/Durham LI at summer camp in 1913.

new force, thus the 5th Stockton, 6th Bishop Auckland, 7th Sunderland, 8th Durham City and 9th Gateshead battalions of the regiment came into being, the 3rd (Reserve) and 4th (Extra Reserve) Battalions being draft-finding units for the two regular battalions.

By 1914 1/Durham LI was back in India, on the North West Frontier. 2/Durham LI spent the early part of the century at Aldershot and in Ireland: as the home service battalion many young Durhams passed through its ranks before being posted to 1/Durham LI in India. Having served their time in India, 'seven with the colours', many were still on the reserve when war broke out and rejoined the battalion which was stationed at Lichfield in Staffordshire, with one company detached at South Shields. The Territorials were well up to strength, in some cases over strength, the Durham County Territorial Force Association reported in *The Durham Advertiser*, in July 1914 the strengths of all units in the county as follows:

UNIT	ESTABLISHMENT		ACTUAL	
	OFFICERS	MEN	OFFICERS	MEN
NORTHUMBERLAND HUSSARS SQUADRON	5	100	4	101
3rd NORTHUMBRIAN BRIGADE RFA	25	595	21	606
4th NORTHUMBRIAN HOWITZER BDE RFA	18	309	14	341
DURHAM RGA	14	312	12	273
DURHAM HEAVY BATTERY RGA	5	125	6	131
DURHAM FORTRESS R ENGINEERS	13	291	11	274
5 DURHAM LI	30	981	25	916
6 DURHAM LI	30	985	29	979
7 DURHAMLI	30	976	28	949
8 DURHAM LI	30	980	31	1008
9 DURHAM LI	30	975	28	990
4th SIGNAL SECTION R ENGINEERS	1	18	0	18
NORTHERN CYCLIST BN	8	215	6	202
HQ ARMY SERVICE CORPS	9	201	7	184
DLI BDE COY ARMY SERVICE CORPS	4	97	4	103
2nd NORTHUMBRIAN FLD AMB RAMC	10	273	10	278
TOTAL STRENGTH	**262**	**7433**	**236**	**7353**

As war clouds drew nearer the Durham Brigade and their supporting arms went away to their annual camp in Conway, North Wales at the end of July, but on 3 August orders were received that mobilisation was expected and they hurriedly returned to their home drill halls, where at around 1700 hours on 4 August the telegram ordering mobilisation arrived.

THE OUTBREAK OF WAR – THE CALL TO ARMS
On the bright sunny morning of Sunday 28 June 1914, the visit of the Archduke Franz Ferdinand and his wife, the Duchess Sophie, to Sarajevo, the capital of the Austrian province of Bosnia-

Archduke Franz Ferdinand arrives in Sarajevo by Royal Train.

Herzegovina was to set Europe alight. It was a National Fête Day and the streets were decked with flags and thronged with people as the Royal Train arrived at the station. Security arrangements began to go wrong almost immediately, when the royal cars left the railway station, the security detectives were left behind and only three local policemen were present with the royal party. The Archduke with the Military Governor, General Oskar Potiorek, travelled in an open-top sports car, which, at the Archduke's request, travelled slowly so he could have a good look at the town.

As the car drove along the Appel Quay, near the Central Police Station a tall young man named Cabrinovic threw a hand grenade at the car. The grenade bounced off the folded roof and exploded under the following car wounding several officers. Despite the threat Archduke Ferdinand ordered a halt to find out who had been injured and it was now that it was discovered that a grenade fragment had grazed the Duchess. Archduke Franz Ferdinand arrived at the town hall in an outrage and decided to visit one of the wounded officers who had been taken to a nearby military hospital, he would then continue with the visit to a local museum as arranged. The cars left the town hall and went back along the Appel Quay, this time at high speed, but the drivers had not been told of the unplanned visit to the military hospital. The first two cars turned right at the corner of Appel Quay and Franz Josef Street but General Potiorek shouted at the driver of the third car that he was making a mistake. The driver, obviously confused, braked sharply and brought the car to a halt, in the worst possible place. Standing right at the spot was a young Bosnian, Gavrilo Princip, who emerged from the crowd only some three or four paces from the Archduke's vehicle. Drawing a pistol he fired two shots into the car, the first mortally wounded the Archduke and the second struck the Duchess Sophie in the abdomen. The car raced to the Governor's official residence but the bumpy ride only made matters worse and the royal couple were pronounced dead shortly after arrival.

Having carried out his mission Princip is arrested and taken to the police station in Sarajevo.

If Austria-Hungary was to continue as a world power this outrage could not go unchallenged.

Should Austria-Hungary declare war on Serbia, this would bring in the Russians, but Austria was allied to Germany and as early as the beginning of July the Kaiser, who was a personal friend of the Archduke, is reported to have said 'The Serbs must be disposed of.' Then on 23 July the Austrian Government sent a strong memorandum to the Serbs listing ten demands, the strongest of which was that Serbia allow Austria to suppress local agitation and subversion directed against Austria. Although the Serbs accepted most of Austria's conditions Austria deemed it inadequate and declared war. The nations of Europe rushed to mobilise, the Tsar, Nicholas II of Russia tried to maintain peace but the Russian Army mobilised on 31 July. To counter this, Germany declared war on Russia, having first offered France the chance to stay out of the conflict and remain neutral. The French however remained true to their treaties and refused the German offer, the Germans therefore declared war on France. Having declared war on France, on 3 August the Imperial German Army crossed the border into Luxembourg and threatened to move into Belgium. Belgium had mobilised on 2 August and the Germans sent an ultimatum on the pretext that the French had crossed the border into Belgium. The French in fact had retired so that they could not give any cause for such an accusation. The note said that if the Belgian Army could not stop the French the Germans would and if the Belgians resisted then it would be considered an act of war. The Belgian border with Germany was covered by a line of forts and the key to these was the fort at Liège on the river Meuse. The main invasion of Belgium began on 4 August although a cavalry patrol had crossed the previous day. The German Cavalry moved quickly through the frontier towns and villages, their task was to capture the bridges over the Meuse before the defenders could blow them up. They also had the job of providing a screen in front of the advancing infantry and carrying out advance reconnaissance.

Meanwhile in England mobilisation had been ordered. On 30 July, more by luck than planning the majority of the Territorial Army were on their annual camp and were quickly moved to their war stations guarding vulnerable points on the coast and along railway lines and docks. The Belgians had a treaty with England and when the German Army crossed the frontier, Britain sent an ultimatum to Berlin. No reply was received so the British Empire declared war on Germany on 4 August 1914. The British Army at home in England and Ireland had been organised as an Expeditionary Force of six infantry and one cavalry divisions and at a meeting of the principal Ministers, including Lord Kitchener, who became Secretary of State for War on 6 August, the decision was taken to send four infantry divisions and the cavalry division to France on 9 August. The other decision taken by Kitchener was to raise New Armies, each army of six more divisions of civilian volunteers and on 7 August, he appealed for the first hundred thousand. He launched his poster 'Your Country Needs You', the recruiting offices were packed with recruits, over 10,000 men enlisting in five days.

German troops mobilise, here Number 5 Kompanie Wurttemburgische Infantry Regiment 121 parade in front of their divisional commander.

The 5/Durham LI from Stockton were mobilised and moved to Ravensworth Park near Gateshead.

The gallant Forty Two march away to the war, here the 1st Battalion, the Black Watch leave Aldershot.

But meanwhile the war was to be fought by the regular army. In the barracks and depots throughout the country, reservists rejoined their battalions, batteries and squadrons, for although the British Expeditionary Force is always described as a Regular Army, the majority of the men had left the Regular Army and when mobilisation was ordered they were recalled to the colours. They were hastily issued with their equipment, cap, tunic, trousers, boots, puttees, webbing and rifle and a hundred other small items like boot brushes and mess tins, and before long they were moving to their war station.

In Lichfield 2/Durham LI were part of 18 Brigade of the 6th Division, the Brigade was ordered north to Edinburgh to the Forth Defences, for 6th Division was not to go out to France immediately. But in other barracks the men were made ready and marched, in newly fitted army boots, down to railway sidings, where trains were waiting to take them to unknown destinations. The programme was worked out to the minute and in five days of hectic preparation 1,800 special trains ran in Great Britain and Ireland. At Southampton Docks almost the equivalent of a division a day was arriving at the docks. Up to thirteen ships daily carried

Embarkation of the BEF for France, here artillery horses are winched aboard a transport ship.

the BEF across the Channel to the French ports of Boulogne and Le Havre. On 12 August General Headquarters of the BEF left London for Southampton and crossed to Le Havre, having landed they moved by rail and by the night of 16 August had reached Le Cateau. All arms moved quickly across the Channel and inland to the concentration area, between Maubeuge and Le Cateau, the task of the BEF was to move northward and form the left flank of the French Army.

On 20 August GHQ issued orders for a general movement northward and the various Corps and Divisions began moving. The British Cavalry screen moved northwards early and patrols of both 9/Lancers and 4/Dragoon Guards sighted German Cavalry but had no contact. Then at dawn on 22 August, 4/Dragoon Guards sent out two officer patrols from their C Squadron. One of these came across a German piquet and opened fire on the enemy who made off. Later in the morning a troop from the same squadron came across a German Cavalry unit moving south, they immediately attacked the enemy and then chased them until checked by fire from enemy infantry. Further east the Scots Greys of 5 Cavalry Brigade were holding two bridges over the River Somme, they came under fire from enemy artillery, but the enemy infantry kept up rifle fire; it had little effect on the Greys who only had one officer wounded, in return they inflicted some thirty to forty casualties on the enemy. A troop from 16/Lancers was sent up to support the Scots Greys,

The Germans quickly crossed the French border, here men of Bavarian Landwehr Regiment 123 are stood in a French village in the Vosges. Note the Medical Orderly has already won an Iron Cross for bravery under fire, the ribbon is on his button hole.

as they rode up they came across an enemy patrol, these they chased and as they followed them they came very suddenly upon some German 'Jäger', the Lancers formed line and charged, riding straight over the enemy, turning round they again went straight through them, with only three horses killed and one man wounded.

The British cavalry commanders were now able to report to Headquarters that German infantry in great force was in front of the BEF. Both I and II British Corps were still advancing northwards and eventually they were in the positions worked out for them in GHQ's order of 20 August holding a line along the Mons canal. However the Germans were unsure of the actual location of the British troops and were advancing towards the British. Eventually the Germans met the British Regular Army, trained to fire ten rounds a minute; they thought every man was armed with a machine gun. Even though the British inflicted heavy casualties on the enemy they were forced to fall back from Mons. Then in turn from Le Cateau, they fell back and fought their way to the Aisne where the BEF turned and drove the enemy back. By now 6th Division with 2/Durham LI under command had arrived in France in time to join in the Aisne battle. The next battalions of the regiment to arrive in the theatre of war were the Territorials of the Northumbrian Division; arriving in France in April 1915 they were rushed up to Ypres, where the Germans had just launched the first gas attack against French Territorial troops. With the casualty lists getting longer by the day more men were urgently needed and it would be soon time for the volunteers of Lord Kitchener's New Armies to take the field.

Chapter Two

Raising and Training the Wearside Battalion

IN JUNE 1915 THE WAR OFFICE once again approached the Durham County Recruiting Committee and asked if another battalion could be raised; the general feeling was that the county was already short of men, the mines and the heavy industry of the region were short on manpower and some soldiers had been discharged and sent back to work in industry. The War Office were not to be put off that easily and they turned to Sunderland where the Recruiting Committee headed by the Lord Mayor had raised and equipped 160 (Wearside) Brigade, Royal Field Artillery. The Mayor of Sunderland, Alderman Stansfield Richardson JP and his committee met to consider the proposal and agreed that the work of raising the battalion could be undertaken. On 20 June 1915 under the authority of War Office letter 20/3343 the 20th (Service) Battalion The Durham Light Infantry (Wearside) came into being. On 11 August command of the battalion was given to Major K J W Leather of 4 (Extra Reserve) Battalion Durham Light Infantry. He was one of seven brothers who served during the war, two being killed and one severely wounded. A Colour Sergeant from 4/Yorkshire Regiment was initially appointed as Regimental Sergeant Major. Recruiting for the battalion commenced on 19 August and some fifty men enlisted, these were sent home and told to report on Monday 23 August when they were moved into billets in

> **WEARSIDE**
> **INFANTRY BATTALION**
>
> The 20th DURHAM LIGHT INFANTRY
>
> **RECRUITING NOW OPEN**
> AT ALL RECRUITING OFFICES.
>
> The Battalion will be under canvas in the Beautiful Valley of Wensleydale, and close to Wensley Village and Station.

St John's Weslyan School. Once settled drill took place on the Ashbrooke Cricket Ground, Lieutenant and Quartermaster J S Simpkin and Lieutenant J D Grubb joined from the Durham Territorial Association and during the week recruiting continued so that by 28 August

Left: *Major K J W Leather was appointed to command 20/Durham Light Infantry 11 August 1915.*

Rigt: *Lieutenant and Quartermaster Joseph Samuel Simpkin commissioned into the battalion on 18 August 1915.*

20/1 Private M. Oliver, the first recruit of the battalion.

there were well over one hundred men enlisted. Although the bulk of the men recruited came from Sunderland, the rest of the county was well represented in the battalion; men joined from as far away as Daddry Shield and Rookhope in Weardale, Darlington in the south, with others from Consett and Newcastle upon Tyne in the north. When the recruiting campaign opened it was proposed that a Darlington Company be raised for the Wearside Battalion and notices in the local press invited men to send their names forward and to be called up when the arrangements to accommodate the battalion were completed. The Darlington campaign however ran into difficulties on 25 August: it was reported that a sudden stoppage in recruits had occurred which was rather difficult to account for given the numbers of eligible young men in the town and district. More appeals in the press were put forward to try to obtain recruits. One local reporter for the *Northern Echo* wrote:

The tented camp in Wensleydale, the battalion's first home.

20/Durham Light Infantry football team. Standing right rear is 20/168 Sergeant J. Hanlon from Sunderland.

There are special inducements for local men to join the 20th DLI. Friends who enlist in that battalion will be kept together. It is in effect another "Pals". Non commissioned officers will be chosen from the men and this is an opportunity which the keen will readily seize on, and thirdly the camp will be in the beautiful Wensleydale district.

In the Bishop Auckland district of County Durham, Captain Shearwood took charge of the recruiting arrangements for the Wearside Battalion. He intended to raise a company of Bishop Auckland and Shildon men so that it might encourage 'pals' to join. Meanwhile in Darlington meetings were arranged to take place at the Whessoe Factory gates and in the Park at Albert Hill; both these meetings were addressed by Alderman T Bates. Other speakers were Major G M James, Chief Recruiting Officer of No 5 Regimental District and Colonel Capper who commanded No 5 Regimental District. Both these officers spoke of the need for more men to fill the gaps in the ranks.

On 26 August an advance party of fourteen NCOs and men under Lieutenant Grubb left Sunderland to prepare a tented camp at Wensley. Two days later the battalion, now 135 strong and headed by the band of 3/DLI, marched to the Town Hall where they were addressed by the Mayor. After the address they marched through Sunderland to Pallion railway station and entrained for Wensley. This latter station was reached in the late afternoon and the men quickly detrained and marched about one mile to where the camp had been erected on the outskirts of Bolton Hall. Two senior NCOs were appointed, Sergeant Jones, an ex-regular of the King's Shropshire Light Infantry and Sergeant Glover who had previous service with 2/DLI; within

Group photograph of the officers of the 20/Durham LI, in the United Kingdom, c.1916. Back row: Captain W.C. Brown, Second-Lieutenant Rasche, Lieutenant Scott, Captain A. Pumphrey, Lieutenants A.F. Collins, W.A. Rodwell, W.W. Brewer, and J.H. Barker, Second-Lieutenant J.E. Dixon. Second row: Captain F.C. Chatt, Second-Lieutenant R.D. Green, Captain F. Wayman, Second-Lieutenant J.W. Butterfield, Lieutenant C.E. Hopkinson, Second-Lieutenant W.P.M. Brettell, Lieutenant J.M. Carrol, Lieutenant H. Risdon, Second-Lieutenant H.G. Thompson, Second-Lieutenant Rudland, Lieutenant J. Thompson-Hopper, Captain W.H. Hiller. Front row: Captain E. Rasche, Captain M. Wayman, Lieutenant G. Richwood, Major J.W. Hills, Lieutenant-Colonel K.J.W. Leather, Captain and Adjutant P. Spencer, Lieutenant S. Simpkin, Lieutenant-Colonel G.M. Nichol, Captain D.E. Jessop.

hours of being promoted Sergeant, Jones found himself appointed as Company Sergeant Major of A Company. The strength of the battalion increased daily and while men who had been selected to be NCOs were on courses of instruction, the remainder took part in football and cross country running to improve fitness. Some men managed to get cards and letters sent home and Private George Maddison of Birtley wrote to his wife:

> *I have got to this place today, we have been in the train all night till 6 this morning, it is a fine day here but I am going away to Bedale I think. Hoping you and James and Ray are all right, with love to all, George.*

Appointments to various positions in the battalion were made. 20/133 Private Michael Moorin became the Pioneer Corporal and 20/177 H Clark was appointed ORQMS. Every day brought new officers to the battalion: on 3 September Second Lieutenants C E Hopkinson and H Rudland joined for duty and the next day four more subalterns, A Reah, P Spencer, G Richwood and V Neill reported but were immediately despatched on a course of instruction at Bedford. At the same time the Commanding Officer convened a court of inquiry into the absence without leave of 20/4 Private C Fah, a recruit who never returned after enlistment. Private Fah it appears was never caught and his regimental number was reissued to Private C Tatters. The battalion was now strong enough to allow the formation of B Company and officers were appointed as follows:

Second Lieutenants Rudland, Spencer, Dixon and Thompson to A Company and Second Lieutenants Canon, Hopkinson, Niell and Pumfrey to B Company.

The Sunderland Recruiting Committee and several friends of the battalion presented twenty-four silver bugles allowing the formation of a bugle band for the battlion. The Bugle Band led

1 Platoon, 20/Durham LI, in the United Kingdom, 1916. Back row: E. Burton, Reine, Archer, Smith, Price, unidentified, unidentified, Studholme, unidentified. Fourth row: Rogers, W.A. Smurthwaite, Dodsworth, Kennedy, Pickering, R. Longstaff, Taylor, Pickering, Haswell. Third row: unidentified, Wilson, Kennedy, unidentified, Waldren, Cook, Moody, unidentified, unidentified, unidentified. Second row: F. Scott, unidentified, N. Bell, unidentified, J. Smith, Barraclough, Price, M. Oliver, Brewis, Wilson, V. Vains (?). Front row: Lance-Corporal E. Wrightson, Lance-Corporal A. Houston, unidentified, Sergeant Fergeson, Sergeant J.O. Elliot, Second-Lieutenant Rudland, Sergeant G. Barclay, Lance-Corporal J.R. Hopper, unidentified, A. Ayres.

2 Platoon, 20/Durham Light Infantry c.1916. Back row: J.E. O'Halloran, F. Purvis, W. Richmond, unidentified, unidentified, unidentified, Williamson, H. Wayman, unidentified, unidentified. Fourth row: Warren, F. Cowell, Duck, unidentified, unidentified, unidentified, unidentified, unidentified, Lance-Corporal J.S. Crowe, unidentified, Sykes. Third row: Connelly, W. Maughan, P. Keegan, P. Martin, J. Clark, Robson, unidentified, unidentified, unidentified, unidentified, unidentified. Second row: R. Mordey, A. Leadbitter, J. Baines, Hodgson, T. Pearson, Green, unidentified, E. Pounder, unidentified, A. Green, W. Peverley. Front row: W.H. Barkle, unidentified, Sergeant R. Webster, Second-Lieutenant F. Wayman, Corporal P. Richardson, Haswell, R. Lindsay.

20/DLI on its first formal parade on 14 October, when the GOC Northern Command, Major General Lawson, inspected the troops in camp at Wensley. The parade, commanded by Colonel Henry Hatchell, Northumberland Fusiliers, comprised 30 (Reserve) Battalion, Northumberland Fusiliers, 21 (Reserve) Battalion, Durham Light Infantry and 20 (Service) Battalion, Durham Light Infantry. The 'Wearsiders' of 20/DLI now 450 strong, had neither rifles nor equipment and many did not have a complete service dress so those on parade were dressed in clean fatigue uniform, but they were complimented by the GOC who described them as 'smart and steady'.

The catering for the battalion was taken over by the firm of Messers Cooper of Liverpool. The food was described as good and plentiful, with fresh milk, fresh vegetables and eggs being issued twice a week. Initially the meals were taken in large marquees until the weather was too cold and then meals were taken by companies, A in their tents, B and C in the gymnasium and D in the recreation room and the miniature range.

The weather had now turned very wet and in the late autumn the nights were drawing in so permission was received for the battalion to strike camp and move into billets in Barnard Castle. On 20 October an advance party of thirty men under Lieutenant Grubb left Wensley by train to get the billets ready. The next morning the tents were struck and the battalion began their march to Barnard Castle. The first day took them as far as Richmond, where they were billeted in the Regimental Depot of the Yorkshire Regiment, the Green Howards; left behind at Wensley were a rear party under the command of the Quartermaster to clean up and hand over tents and stores.

The next day the march continued and in thick mist they reached Barnard Castle where, just outside the town, they were met by the band of 10/Leicestershire Regiment who were quartered in Deerbolt Camp, who played them into the town. 20/DLI were billeted throughout the town in the following locations: the Witham Hall, the Masonic Hall, 6/DLI Drill Hall, Methodist Sunday School, C of E School, the Council School, Weslyan Sunday School, the Church Army Hall, Weslyan Mission. The Signal Platoon had the good fortune to be billeted in the *Montabello Hotel* and shortly they were issued with signalling equipment as it became available. Also issued to the battalion were a few Lewis guns and 200 drill purpose rifles. A setback occurred at this time when Army Order Number 6 dated 29 October 1915 gave instructions that men required for munitions

Signallers of 20/Durham LI, in the United Kingdom, 1916. Back row: Shields, T.A. Dixon, C. White, J. Campbell, M. Duffy, W.L. Farina, W. Byron, J. Carr, A. Roe, E.G. McClumpha. Fourth row: J. Burn, J. Russell, W. Crosby, W. Hopkins, J. Irwin, G. Catchpole, A. Ayres, W.A. Smurthwaite, D. Goodwin, Wilson. Third row: W. Vickers, H. Bennet, C.D. Harland, Lance-Corporal J.L. Rubin, S. Novinski, T.J. Forster, R.H. Davison, R. Fairer, Hall, W. Davy, Miller. Second row: Lance-Corporal R. Christie, J. Carr, unidentified, Johnson, Teasdale, F. Sharp, L.H. Fearn, R.E. Smith, Green, R. Shillaw, Richards, Corporal E. Edmunds. Front row: S. Asher, Lance-Corporal E. Wrightson, Corporal G. Thubron, Sergeant R. Hooker, Lieutenant G. Richwood, Captain and Adjutant P. Spencer, Lieutenant-Colonel K.J.W. Leather, Major J.W. Hills, Lieutenant A.F. Collins, T. Kinnery, H. Snowden.

work had to be sent home. Up until now 25% of the battalion had been allowed to go home each weekend but on Monday 8 November, nineteen men overstayed their weekend leave: the result was that the following weekend all leave was stopped. The battalion was now strong enough to allow the formation of C and D Companies and on 15 November 20/DLI became part of 123 Brigade of 41st Division which was forming in the Aldershot area; a few days later 123 Brigade Orders were received for the first time. Within a few days Brigadier General A Davidson, commanding 123 Brigade accompanied by his Brigade Major, Captain H C B Kirkpatrick, King's Own Scottish Borderers, visited 20/DLI at Barnard Castle. The highlight of his visit was the Battalion inter-platoon boxing competition. The winner of this competition, Private Shaw, was presented with a silver cigarette case, whilst the runner-up Bugler Hethrington received a silver match box. During the same period 7 Platoon of B Company won the inter-platoon cross-country race.

Sport had played a large part in the training of the battalion, cross country running brought success in Northern Command Competition at Sunderland, where B Company team won easily from a field of 800; 20/439 Private J W Breed from Durham City finishing 13th, and 20/51 Lance Corporal C Eyton from Blaydon on Tyne 14th, closely followed by Private J Mole from Wingate who came 22nd and Private W Wilson was 28th. The football team had several successes: the most notable being against 4/Sherwood Foresters whom they defeated 4-0, the Foresters team had until this match been undefeated. Another incident at the beginning of December was the District

9 Platoon football team, 20/Durham LI, 1916. Standing: Sergeant-Major Henry Clark, unidentified, H.E. Veasey, T. Thompson, Corporal R.S. Falconer. Seated: J. Wilcox, E. Dodds, unidentified, unidentified, C. Anderson. On ground: unidentified, Bryce, J. Wilcox, Robson, Sergeant J. Hedger.

9 Platoon running team, 20/Durham LI, 1916. Standing: unidentified, unidentified, Corporal J. Reed, unidentified, unidentified, W. Buckley. Seated: S. Asher, unidentified, S. Hetherington, Second-Lieutenant A. Reah, Lance-Corporal R. Bennet, T. Winn, R. Lemon. On ground: Lance-Corporal J.M. Carr, unidentified, unidentified, unidentified, unidentified.

C' Company running team, 20/Durham LI, 1916. Standing: unidentified, unidentified, unidentified, J. Wilcox, Robson, J. Wilcox, J. Anderson, J.M. Carr. Seated: E. Dodds, C. Hamilton, S. Hetherington, T. Watson, S. Asher, unidentified, Lieutenant C.E. Hopkinson. On ground: Lance-Corporal R. Bennet, E. Owens, Potts, D. Goodwin, G. Richardson, unidentified.

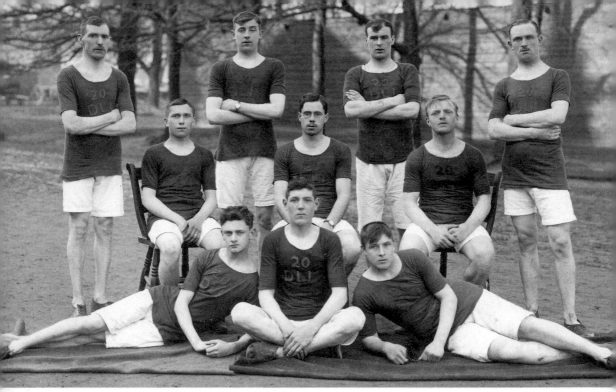

B Company running team, 20/Durham LI, 1916. Standing: A. Nesbett, Sergeant W. Wilson, Corporal W.D. Purvis, J.J. Spooner. Seated: J. Fletcher, Sergeant J. Breed, J. Mole. On ground: Sergeant C.L. Eyton, Wilson, E. Morris.

20/Durham LI football team, 1916. Standing: S. Dawson, F. Blenkinsop, unidentified, Corporal W. McDonald. Seated: J. King, Major J.D. Grubb, unidentified. On ground: Sergeant J.F. Urquahart, Sergeant T. Warlow, Company Sergeant-Major J. Glover, Corporal G. Wilson, E. Morris.

20/Durham LI regimental running team, 1916. Back row: J.P. Mathieson, S. Hetherington, J.M. Hudson, Corporal W.D. Purvis, Corporal T. Cummings, J. Turnbull, J. Wilcox, Taylor. Front row: J. Mole, Lance-Corporal R. Bennet, Sergeant G. Wilson, Lieutenant-Colonel K.J.W. Leather, Sergeant J. Breed, J.I. Spooner, Sergeant C. Leyton, A. Nesbett. On ground: Lance-Corporal J.M. Carr.

Court Martial of 20/585 Private John Wilkinson. The Commanding Officer recorded that 'He should never have been allowed to enlist as he had fifty-four previous convictions against him. He was seldom out of the guard room during his sojourn with the battalion'. On 17 December 1915 he was discharged with ignomy.

The battalion suffered with a number of cases of influenza and a house in the town was taken over as a hospital for the men. An appeal was made to the citizens of Barnard Castle for assistance, which was nobly answered, Miss Beale worked as a nurse until the District Nurse Miss Dickens was able to take over. Food for the sick was cooked by local ladies of Barnard Castle and the local district and it can be said that the battalion owed a debt of gratitude to these kind people and to the skill of the Medical Officer, Lieutenant Francis Heathcote FRCS RAMC; it was owing to his abilities as a doctor that the battalion enjoyed such good health and that only a few came down with the flu. Officers that joined the battalion about this time were Second Lieutenants E Rasche, W A Rodwell, J W Butterfield and D K Dodson along with Captain Myers Wayman. Also posted in on promotion to major, and second in command, was Captain J W Hills.

Major F H S Le Mesurier joined the battalion from 1/Border Regiment.

Captain Miles Wayman, who led A and D Companies to Barnard Castle railway station when the battalion left for Aldershot.

Shortly before Christmas, 3/10966 RQMS Hicks was appointed Regimental Sergeant Major and he began assisting the Barnard Castle War Entertainment Committee with the arrangements for the battalion Christmas party, which took place on 27 December. However, only A and B Companies attended as C and D were on leave, the first named having been granted leave prior to Christmas. The Christmas day meals provided by Messers Cooper Ltd, the battalion caterers, were provided free of charge to the battalion. Breakfast consisted of bacon, sausage, bread, butter and tea. The main meal of the day was a roast turkey dinner with sausages, turnips and roast potatoes, followed by plum pudding and apples and oranges, with free beer for every man. At tea time the meal consisted of bread and butter with fruit cake, mince pies and tea.

So it came to pass that at 5.30 pm on 1 January 1916, the advance party of 20/Durham LI, consisting of a platoon of B Company and the company cooks, under the command of Major Grubb, headed by the bugle band, marched to Barnard Castle railway station and entrained for Aldershot. That night the Warrant Officers' and Sergeants' mess held a farewell dance in the 6/Durham LI Drill Hall, the following morning the battalion paraded for Divine Service in Barnard Castle church and the Reverend F W Bircham preached the sermon and wished the battalion 'God speed'. The rest of the day and all of 3 January was spent cleaning billets and preparing to move. The extremely bad weather made the cleaning up difficult but eventually the job was done to the satisfaction of the Commanding Officer.

On 4 January, 20th (Service) Battalion the Durham Light Infantry (Wearside) was officially taken over by the War Office and later that afternoon two trains arrived at the railway station to convey the battalion to the south. At 1730 hours, A and D Companies paraded under the command of Captain Wayman, then led by the bugle band marched to the station, from where the first train departed at 1825 hours. The buglers marched back to the billets where the remaining two companies as well as the signallers and Regimental Police were parading. This party then marched to the station and entrained and at 1945 hours the second train full of Wearsiders pulled slowly out of Barnard Castle station. Throughout the departure of the battalion the streets were lined with local people all cheering and giving the men a hearty send-off.

The Quartermaster Lieutenant Simpkin, and Lieutenant Gough, attached from the Royal Irish Fusiliers, remained behind with a small rear party to hand in stores and to hand over the billets.

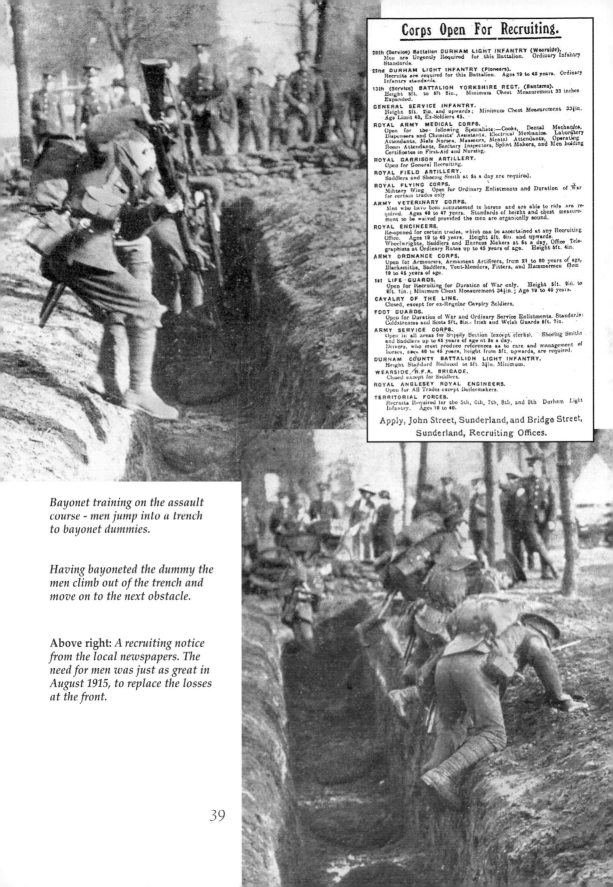

Corps Open For Recruiting.

20th (Service) Battalion DURHAM LIGHT INFANTRY (Wearside).
Men are Urgently Required for this Battalion. Ordinary Infantry Standards.

22nd DURHAM LIGHT INFANTRY (Pioneers).
Recruits are required for this Battalion. Ages 19 to 40 years. Ordinary Infantry standards.

13th (Service) BATTALION YORKSHIRE REGT. (Bantams).
Height 5ft. to 5ft 2in., Minimum Chest Measurement 33 inches Expanded.

GENERAL SERVICE INFANTRY.
Height 5ft. 2in. and upwards; Minimum Chest Measurement 33½in. Age Limit 40, Ex-Soldiers 45.

ROYAL ARMY MEDICAL CORPS.
Open for the following Specialists:—Cooks, Dental Mechanics, Dispensers and Chemists' Assistants, Electrical Mechanics, Laboratory Attendants, Male Nurses, Masseurs, Mental Attendants, Operating Room Attendants, Sanitary Inspectors, Splint Makers, and Men holding Certificates in First-Aid and Nursing.

ROYAL GARRISON ARTILLERY.
Open for General Recruiting.

ROYAL FIELD ARTILLERY.
Saddlers and Shoeing Smith at 5s a day are required.

ROYAL FLYING CORPS.
Military Wing Open for Ordinary Enlistments and Duration of War for certain trades only

ARMY VETERINARY CORPS.
Men who have been accustomed to horses and are able to ride are required. Ages 40 to 47 years. Standards of height and chest measurement to be waived provided the men are organically sound.

ROYAL ENGINEERS.
Re-opened for certain trades, which can be ascertained at any Recruiting Office. Ages 19 to 40 years. Height 5ft. 6in. and upwards.
Wheelwrights, Saddlers and Harness Makers at 5s a day, Office Telegraphists at Ordinary Rates up to 45 years of age. Height 5ft. 4in.

ARMY ORDNANCE CORPS.
Open for Armourers, Armament Artificers, from 21 to 50 years of age, Blacksmiths, Saddlers, Tent-Menders, Fitters, and Hammermen from 19 to 45 years of age.

1st LIFE GUARDS.
Open for Recruiting for Duration of War only. Height 5ft. 9in. to 6ft. 1in.; Minimum Chest Measurement 34½in.; Age 19 to 40 years.

CAVALRY OF THE LINE.
Closed, except for ex-Regular Cavalry Soldiers.

FOOT GUARDS.
Open for Duration of War and Ordinary Service Enlistments. Standards: Coldstreams and Scots 5ft. 9in.. Irish and Welsh Guards 5ft. 7in.

ARMY SERVICE CORPS.
Open in all areas for Supply Section (except clerks). Shoeing Smiths and Saddlers up to 45 years of age at 5s a day.
Drivers, who must produce references as to care and management of horses, ages 40 to 45 years, height from 5ft. upwards, are required.

DURHAM COUNTY BATTALION LIGHT INFANTRY.
Height Standard Reduced to 5ft. 3½in. Minimum.

WEARSIDE R.F.A. BRIGADE.
Closed except for Saddlers.

ROYAL ANGLESEY ROYAL ENGINEERS.
Open for All Trades except Boilermakers.

TERRITORIAL FORCES.
Recruits Required for the 5th, 6th, 7th, 8th, and 9th Durham Light Infantry. Ages 19 to 40.

Apply, John Street, Sunderland, and Bridge Street, Sunderland, Recruiting Offices.

Bayonet training on the assault course - men jump into a trench to bayonet dummies.

Having bayoneted the dummy the men climb out of the trench and move on to the next obstacle.

Above right: *A recruiting notice from the local newspapers. The need for men was just as great in August 1915, to replace the losses at the front.*

Regimental Police of 20/Durham LI, in the United Kingdom, 1916. Standing: J.W. Miller, J. Wilkinson, J. Baines, J. Paxton, W. Emery, R.H. Fair, J.A. Booth. Seated: Lance-Corporal E. Priestley, Captain and Adjutant P. Spencer, Sergeant J.G. Dixon.

The trains halted at Leicester around 0100 hours in the morning, where tea was served to the men before recommencing the journey, which finished at Government sidings in Aldershot at 0630 hours. The battalion detrained and marched to Salamanca Barracks, Aldershot. The barracks were originally designed for a peacetime battalion and owing to the conditions prevailing at the time had to be shared with 23/Middlesex Regiment which meant that the men were crowded into the barrack rooms. The officers had a joint mess with the Middlesex and it was most uncomfortable; however the troops made the best of things, even though the barracks were 'left in an extremely dirty and unsanitary state'.

On arrival in Aldershot word was received that they had four days to re-equip and be ready to move overseas; there was a rush to take in all the new stores, service rifles and Lewis guns were issued and new leather equipment. The transport platoon received new wagons, water carts and harness for the eighty horses that arrived instead of the mules normally issued to infantry battalions. Fortunately, they did not proceed abroad immediately which allowed time for further training. There followed a series of inspections by general officers. The GOC 41st Division Major General S T B Lawford inspected the battalion on 8 January, who was followed by the GOC Aldershot Training Centre, Sir Archibald Hunter.

A small draft of eighty-five NCOs and men arrived from 16/Durham LI and seven days later a further twenty-five arrived from the same unit. B Company began field training in the shape of entrenching at Clay Hill; this was the first opportunity that the battalion had had to engage in digging. As usual the Durham miners amongst the men made short work of it. Two days later, in the gymnasium near Corunna Barracks, Major Campbell from the Aldershot Gymnastic Staff lectured the battalion on bayonet fighting.

As well as drafts of men, Second Lieutenants F Wayman and H Risdon joined the battalion on 10 January. By way of promoting fitness within the division, a football tournament took place. In each battalion a platoon knockout competition took place. In the semi-finals of 20/Durham LI competition, 9 Platoon beat 1 Platoon, 2 goals to 1 and 8 Platoon defeated 14 Platoon, 6 goals to 1. In the final, 8 Platoon prevailed over 9 Platoon and then went on to represent 123 Brigade against 122 Brigade who were represented by a platoon of 11/Queen's Regiment. This match resulted in a resounding 13-nil win for the Wearsiders.

Medical examination of the battalion took place in the third week of January and this resulted in a number of unfit men being weeded out and transferred to the 21st (Reserve) Battalion Durham LI at Hornsea on the Yorkshire coast. As well as Association football, other platoons of 20/Durham LI fought their way through to the finals of various competitions. 16 Platoon of D

20/DLI continued their training at Aldershot, of which no photographs survive. Here men of 18/DLI practice bayonet fighting.

Buglers of 20/Durham LI, 1916. Back row: G. Hill, H.S. Usher, W.F. Hauxby, R. Mordey, Gordon Forbes, T. Dinning, J. Evans, T. Ayre. Second row: J. Richardson, J. Pearson, W. Peverley, A. Green, G.F. Hetherington, F.W. Ede, J. Clarke, T. Johnson, R. Johnson, G.J. Corbett. Front row: W. Wilson, G. Bell, Sergeant-Bugler Davison, Major J.W. Hills, Lieutenant-Colonel K.J.W. Leather, Captain and Adjutant P. Spencer, Company Sergeant-Major Glover, Lance-Corporal W.H. Barkle, A. Leadbitter. On ground: Robinson, T.W. Black, J.W. Reay.

Company represented the battalion at tug-of-war and 12 Platoon, from C Company at cross country running. This last platoon ran so well that they got through to the Aldershot Command finals where they came second to the Reserve Cavalry Brigade. But life was not all sport, route marching commenced with an eight-mile hike via Heath End and Tweezeldown in beautiful weather on 8 February and two days later the Machine Gun Section commenced work on Ash Ranges. On 14 February Company training commenced with a fortnight being allowed. On this day the GOC came round the battalion and watched the men training; he was followed a few days later by Major General, Sir Francis Howard the Inspector of Infantry. One day all the officers were taken away to attend a brigade officers' course, so the battalion went on a route march under the command of the Warrant Officers and NCOs, and had 'a most enjoyable day'.

Medical problems began to emerge in the latter part of February. Private Hannah of C Company fell sick with cerebro-meningitis and became seriously ill. To prevent the infection spreading all the men in his barracks, who were regarded as potential carriers, were isolated. Later in March the same company was struck down with a measles epidemic. But the most unfortunate was 20/894 Private Thomas Bailey, a twenty-year-old resident of Henry Street, Hendon, Sunderland, who died of erysipelas, an acute contagious disease. The battalion held a collection and raised £15 to cover his burial expenses and his remains were taken home to Sunderland for internment in Bishopwearmouth Cemetery.

The weather turned to heavy snow and on 27 February, for the first time since the formation of the battalion, divine service was cancelled. Some lectures were given indoors but by the beginning of March the weather improved slightly so musketry training continued and C and D Companies were able to dig trenches near the Foresters public house, before further heavy snow cancelled all range work for three days. During the lull in training time was found to issue and fit new equipment, but too much time was being lost so the range parties were sent out in the heavy snow.

Out on the ranges one day, a party of Russian journalists who were wearing thick fur coats visited them. The snow was driving into the butts but the shooting of the Durhams was 'not too bad'. One of the Russians insisted on having a shot standing up, from three hundred yards. The men in the butts were tipped off and each shot the Russian fired, the marker went up and indicated a hit, which pleased the Russian. However his rounds were seen to hit the snow well short of the target.

Further parties of unfit men were sent to the reserve battalion, among them a number of 'miniature' men, who presumably were eventually sent to the 'Bantam' battalion. Then on 8 March a party of fifty men arrived from the reserves at Hornsea in an endeavour to keep the battalion up to full strength. Whilst around the same time Captain L Cockburn joined as Officer Commanding C Company and Captain F H Le Mesurier became Officer Commanding D Company; Second Lieutenants, E W Britton, R M Fulljames, F M Fletcher and T W Dormand joined A, B, C and D Companies respectively. Another draft this time from 17/Durham LI was described as 'A particularly fine lot of men'. But fog was hampering the musketry and nearly a weeks' shooting was lost owing to the fog not lifting.

Another sad event took place on 24 March when 20/408 Lance Corporal Matthew English died of meningitis; a resident of Washington Station, who had enlisted in Sunderland, he was taken home to the village of his birth, Hunwick, near Bishop Aukland for burial.

A major victory for the Wearside Battalion took place on 21 March when 8 Platoon defeated 3 Platoon of 23/Middlesex Regiment (2nd Footballers). This last named unit had been recruited by the Right Honourable W Joynson-Hicks MP in London from well-known, professional and

Officers and non-commissioned officers of A Company, 20/Durham LI, 1916. Left to right: Sergeants R. Hooker, Coverdale, W.M. McCorry, and J. Elliot, Company Quartermaster-Sergeant Gore, Second-Lieutenant Rudland, Second-Lieutenant H.G. Thompson, Major J.D. Grubb, Lieutenant F. Wayman, Second-Lieutenant J.W. Butterfield, Second-Lieutenant W.W. Brewer, Sergeants R. Webster, L.A. Floyd, and G. Barclay.

Officers and non-commissioned officers of B Company, 20/Durham LI, 1916. Standing: W. Davey, J. Emery, R. Harris, Sergeant J.E. Walton, Company Sergeant-Major Moralee, Captain D.E. Jessop, Corporal S. Swales, Corporal E.W. Brown, Wilcox, E. Close, Corporal G. Thubron. On ground: C. Chipchase, Lance-Corporal W. Brown, J. Turnbull, G. Brown, J.H. Roberts, E. Morris.

The battalion cooks, Aldershot 1916.

amateur footballers. The report of the game, which took place in ninety minutes of rain and on a quagmire, gives credit to the Middlesex but a very plucky and fit Durham team defeated them:

> *8 Platoon played a magnificent and plucky game. They owed their victory to their pluck and physical fitness. The Middlesex scored in the first five seconds but 8 Platoon equalised after ten minutes. At half time the score was two all. Within a few minutes of the restart 8 Platoon had a man knocked out and were obliged to continue with ten men. In spite of this, Number 8 had the best of the game and put in two more goals, winning the game by 4 goals to 2. They were by far the best all round team. But the Middlesex had one or two good individual players, well known in the football world. Private Morris played a great game.*

The 8 Platoon team was made up of Privates Cummings (Easington Colliery), Stabler (Hetton le Hole), Hudson (Sunderland), Robinson, 20/563 Wilson, L/Cpl McAndrew, 20/562 Wilson (Cassop Colliery), Carter, Cpl Hughes (Murton), Privates Morris and Garthwaite.

Most of this team survived the war: only Privates Cummings and 562 Wilson being killed in action. Training continued and the new drafts commenced their musketry training which had been hampered by the lack of service rifles, only 200 of which had been available to the battalion. On 9 April the battalion paraded at Aldershot for inspection prior to embarkation leave, it goes without saying that there were no absentees from this parade and when the battalion 'fell out' they proceeded on four days' leave.

On 14 April the Sunderland contingent had a hearty send-off from the Mayor and the townsfolk, they were led through the streets to the railway station, by the Regimental Band of 4/Durham LI based at nearby Seaham Harbour. On return to Aldershot only four men were found to be absent. On 17 April the Commanding Officer went out to France and spent a week attached to 6/KOSB of 9th (Scottish) Division, giving him the opportunity to see conditions for himself. Meanwhile the battalion commenced ceremonial drill in preparation for the final inspection of the 41st Division by His Majesty King George the Fifth. The battalion won tremendous praise for their turnout and marching from many quarters, not least the King, who remarked to Lord French riding by his side, 'What battalion is this?' to which Lord French replied,

His majesty King George V accompanied by Lord Kitchener inspected the 41st Division. Of 20/DLI he said, 'They are wonderfully steady.'

'Durham Light Infantry, about 50% miners.' The King then said 'They are wonderfully steady.' That afternoon His Majesty started the eight mile divisional cross country race, which the battalion team won easily with over two hundred points to spare. 20/439 Sergeant John Breed, who lived at Springwell Cottage in Durham City, being the first DLI man home in third place.

The final major act of training at Aldershot was a route march by the whole of the 41st Division. This took place on a very hot 27 April and once again the praises of 20/Durham LI were sung loud in high places. Only sixteen Durham men fell out during the march; 10/Queens had twenty casualties, whilst 11/R West Kents had twenty-three. But some battalions had nearer 200 men knocked out by the hot sun.

The next few days minor training was carried out, a final Church Parade was held, then embarkation tables were brought up to strength and final inspections of the men and the battalion transport took place, as orders were received for the 20th (Service) Battalion the Durham Light Infantry (Wearside) to embark for war service in France.

Lieutenant Colonel K J W Leather with his batman and groom prior to embarkation.

Chapter Three

Foreign Fields

T HE 41ST DIVISION RECEIVED EMBARKATION ORDERS at the end of April 1916 and began moving to embarkation positions on 1 May. That day the Brigadier inspected 20/Durham LI complete with regimental transport on the battalion parade ground at Aldershot and when addressing the men afterwards, praised them for the standard of their turnout. The next two days were spent bringing the battalion stores up to strength and drawing the extra equipment needed for active service. Up to the time of embarkation the battalion had had more than its share of absentees and deserters. There were sixteen recruits who took the shilling then never joined, thirty-seven men who deserted and had not rejoined by the time of embarkation. Eighteen men went absent without leave but rejoined. Two men who enlisted were already deserters, one from the Royal Navy and one from the Argyll and Sutherland Highlanders, both these men were returned to their original units, giving a total of seventy-one deserters and absentees before embarkation.

So it was at 3.35 am on the morning of 4 May the battalion began entraining at the Farnborough sidings in the three trains that would carry the battalion. The last train left at 6.10 am carrying battalion headquarters. There was a long wait in Southampton and the battalion comedian 20/989 Private Telfer, although resident in Heaton, he was born in Sunderland, kept the

Godeswaerwelde Station where 20/Durham LI arrived at the front in 5 May 1916.

49

Lieutenant R D Green and twelve other ranks joined 123 Brigade Light Trench Mortar Battery on 28 May 1916.

men amused throughout the day. There was also singing and dancing which helped to pass the time before the battalion, with a strength of 1,023 all ranks embarked on SS *Arundel*. On what was described as a glorious May evening the troopship made its way down Southampton water with a destroyer escort. Once clear of the coast the order for full speed was given and as the destroyers turned back to England the troopship set a course for Le Havre. The men were crowded on the open deck and it turned quite cold before they reached the French port at 1.00 am. The battalion marched out of the docks and to the rest camp where the night of 4 May was spent.

Breakfast was served early the next day and at 7.50 am the Wearsiders less D Company entrained at the Gare Des Marchandises for the Belgian town of Godeswaerwelde. Here they arrived around midday and after detraining they marched to billets in Strazeele. D Company under the command of Major Le Mesurier caught up by 5 pm. The 41st Division commenced training in the rear area behind the Ypres Salient and on 10 May officers and NCOs from 20/Durham LI went forward into the front line for two days' instruction in trench warfare. The battalion had its first casualty on 11 May when Lance Sergeant J E Morton was slightly wounded. After the return of these parties the battalion moved forward to Noote Boom and from there on 28 May to

20/77 Sergeant J. W. Rawnsley. The battalion's first fatality.

Le Bizet. It was now that 123 Brigade Light Trench Mortar Battery formed and Second Lieutenant R D Green and twelve other ranks were detailed for the new unit. Among a division mainly recruited in the south of England the miners of the Durham Light Infantry were in great demand. The first batch of thirty-one men was attached to the Canadian Tunnelling Company based in Armentières. In Le Bizet billets were taken over from 2/South African Regiment and 20/Durham LI came under orders from the South African Brigade. The next day the Durhams had an introduction to German artillery when the village was heavily shelled. Unfortunately, the Quartermaster lost most of his staff when a shell hit the building used as the battalion stores. Later that day twenty-two officers and 696 men went into the front line, relieving 1/South African Regiment, becoming the first battalion of 41st Division to do so. On 31 May a wiring party was sent out and whilst out in No Man's Land they came under enemy fire. Sadly 20/77 Lance Sergeant John Rawnsley, from the village of Hutton Henry, County Durham, was shot through the head, becoming the Wearsiders' first fatal casualty on active service. At the same time another man was wounded. Lieutenant Thompson-Hopper brought the body of the deceased back to the British lines and then returned for the wounded soldier. On 2 June Lieutenant J H Baker who had been appointed battalion sniping officer was badly wounded and the following day 20/15 Private Tom Lyall of Hendon Docks, Sunderland was killed and another man wounded. So 'daily wastage' began to take its toll of the Wearsiders. On 4 June 23/Middlesex Regiment took over the line and with the relief completed by 1.20 am the Durhams moved back to billets in Armentières. The GOC 41st Division was very impressed by the work of the battalion on their first visit to the trenches: congratulations were received from divisional and brigade headquarters, the brigade commander expressing the hope that all the other battalions of 123 Brigade would endeavour to gain similar praise.

On 10 June the relief of 23/Middlesex Regt took place and the Durhams were holding the line by 11 o'clock that night. Early the next day 21/397 Private John Atkinson from West Hartlepool was killed. A few days later the first draft

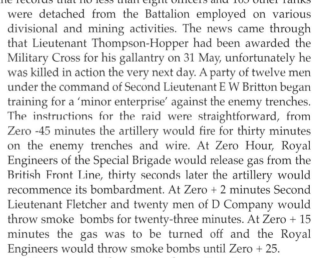

Lieutenant J. Thompson-Hopper was killed in action the day after he was awarded the Military Cross.

of twenty-one other ranks arrived from the Base Depot. Once again the same battalion of the Middlesex Regiment arrived to relieve 20/Durham LI, who returned to the same billets in Armentières. The War Diary for June records that no less than eight officers and 163 other ranks were detached from the Battalion employed on various divisional and mining activities. The news came through that Lieutenant Thompson-Hopper had been awarded the Military Cross for his gallantry on 31 May, unfortunately he was killed in action the very next day. A party of twelve men under the command of Second Lieutenant E W Britton began training for a 'minor enterprise' against the enemy trenches. The instructions for the raid were straightforward, from Zero -45 minutes the artillery would fire for thirty minutes on the enemy trenches and wire. At Zero Hour, Royal Engineers of the Special Brigade would release gas from the British Front Line, thirty seconds later the artillery would recommence its bombardment. At Zero + 2 minutes Second Lieutenant Fletcher and twenty men of D Company would throw smoke bombs for twenty-three minutes. At Zero + 15 minutes the gas was to be turned off and the Royal Engineers would throw smoke bombs until Zero + 25.

After twenty-eight minutes the artillery barrage was to lift and form a barrage on the flanks and behind the trenches

Lieutenant John Hugh Barker, commissioned in December 1915. Although born in Sunderland, when war broke out he was living in Canada and joined the 29th (Vancouver) Battalion of the Canadian Expeditionary Force.

Lieutenant G Richwood, the Battalion Transport Officer, evacuated sick in July 1916.

to be raided, preventing the arrival of German reinforcements.

Second Lieutenant Britton and his party were to cross the parapet and go straight across to the German Front Line, bomb dug-outs and if possible capture one or two prisoners. Support fire was to be from machine guns and infantry on the flanks. That was the plan for the raid: what happened was totally different. In his report to brigade and division Lieutenant Colonel Leather noted that 'practically no damage done to enemy's wire', and this was mostly due to the ammunition, which was 'most unreliable'. The damage to the enemy parapet was very slight although the wind was perfect and the gas and smoke floated well over the enemy lines. As soon as the barrage lifted onto the enemy line there was heavy retaliation within one minute. The British Front Line was heavily shelled with shrapnel and later 4.2 and 5.9 shells and as soon as the British barrage lifted, the German guns shortened their range to cover No Man's Land. Riflemen manned the enemy parapet immediately and at least six machine guns provided covering fire from the flanks. Owing to the uncut wire, which was very thick at this point, it was impossible to carry out the planned raid. Although he considered that it was too light Second Lieutenant Britton volunteered to lead his men over the top and asked permission from Colonel Leather to try against a different spot, this was granted with the strict instruction to return to the British line if the wire was uncut or the German parapet was manned. At the appointed time the raiders quickly went through the British wire and disappeared into the smoke, however they found the enemy parapet was well manned and returned to their own line.

June passed into July and to the south the Battle of the Somme began, but for the time being the 41st Division and 20/Durham LI remained in Flanders. The same pattern of the previous month was repeated, a draft arrived from 41 Infantry Base Depot, small numbers of other ranks were wounded daily and on 2 July Second Lieutenant Wayman was slightly wounded but remained on duty. Once again 23/Middlesex Regiment relieved the battalion, which moved back to the billets in Armentières and then on 7 July to Le Bizet. On 12 July B

20/234 Private Charles Anderson, from Vincent Street, Seaham Harbour killed in action 30 June 1916.

Company left the battalion and moved to the Divisional Lewis Gun School in Bailleul to commence training for a large raid on the enemy lines. On 14 July the battalion again relieved the Middlesex who left one company behind in reserve at Le Touquet Station to replace B Company who were still training. C, D and A companies, in that order formed the garrison for the front line and support line. During this tour the transport officer, Lieutenant G Rishwood, was evacuated sick and Second Lieutenants F C Acklom, H D Munro, J O Richardson and F Wilkin reported for duty from 23 (Reserve) Battalion DLI. During the night of 20/21 July two other ranks became separated and were reported missing whilst on a patrol in No Man's Land. Two day's later during a British barrage these two soldiers crawled into the British Front Line; during this time there had been constant shelling and they had been unable to find their way back. The CO Colonel Leather was wounded and evacuated, command passing to Major Hills.

24386 Private J. W. Mason of Fencehouses killed 21 July 1916.

Also on the same night 20/21 July instructions were received to clear the trenches of infantrymen as M Company Special Brigade Royal Engineers was going to discharge gas towards the enemy lines. Only sentries were left behind with instructions to wear gas helmets throughout the operation. However the conditions proved unfavourable and the operation was cancelled. On 23 July 23/Middlesex Regt took over the line and 20/Durham LI moved back to the billets in Le Bizet.

B Company, still resident in Bailleul, had finished training and their raid was planned for the night of 26/27 July. The object of the raid was to force an entry into the German Front Line and support trenches in the locality of a building known as the 'Red House', to destroy any mine shafts, dugouts and emplacements and if at all possible capture prisoners or machine guns. This was to be done by the employment of five main parties of men:

1 Right Blocking Party	Sergeant Hanlon and eleven other ranks.
2 Left Blocking Party	Sergeant Fletcher and twelve other ranks.
3 Right Assault Party	Second Lieutenant Fulljames and twenty-five other ranks along with three REs.
4 Left Assault Party	Second Lieutenant Britton and twenty-four other ranks with three REs.
5 Covering Party	1st Line three NCOs and twenty-four men.
2nd Line	Captain Jessop and twenty-five other ranks with six machine-gunners.
3rd Line	CSM Walton and twenty other ranks with one RE officer and three Sappers.

A total strength of four officers and 155 other ranks from the

Second Lieutenant E W Britton in command of the assault on the left flank.

Members of the trench raiding party

10834 CSM T Walton commanded the third line.

20/277 Sergeant Thomas Fletcher in charge of the left blocking party.

20/989 Private Robert Telfer, from Heaton, killed during the raid.

20/444 Sergeant Newton Storey from Lanchester fell in the raid.

Second Lieutenant Fulljames led the assault on the right.

20/168 Sergeant John Hanlon from Millfield in Sunderland, brought his men back safely from No Man's Land.

Brothers 20/458 Private George and 20/1006 Robert Reay, born in Langley Moor, both died during the raid.

Wearside Battalion and one officer and nine sappers attached from the Royal Engineers. Wire cutting by the artillery was carried out for 48 hours prior to the operation, with dummy wire-cutting taking place on other possible objectives, in the hope of misleading the enemy. The timetable of events was planned to take place as follows:

One hour before Zero, artillery bombardment on point of attack by heavy artillery, divisional field artillery, trench mortar batteries and Stokes guns. Also at this time the raiders would leave the front line and form up on the tapes laid in No Man's Land. At Zero hour the bombardment would lift from the objective and form a box barrage round the objective. The bombardment of the enemy support trenches would continue. Simultaneously the attackers would commence to advance against the hostile trenches. After ten minutes the shelling of the support trenches would cease allowing the attackers to gain entry to the support trenches if possible. The sappers accompanying the infantry were detailed to carry demolition charges and destroy any mine shafts and deep dug-outs. On the withdrawal being sounded by a bugler, they were to destroy sections of enemy trench under the orders of the raid OC, when it was clear all the infantry had left.

That was the plan, but in a lengthy report Major Hills detailed exactly what happened. The raiders left the trenches as planned and formed up in No Man's Land, but the enemy must have known about the raid, for his artillery opened a heavy fire, most of which was directed against the forming up point. At midnight Captain Jessop led his force to a disused trench just outside the German wire, he halted to reorganise but found that he had very few men with him, his orderly, his tape-layer and three out of four of his signallers had been killed or wounded. He therefore sent Lieutenant Carroll back to collect as many unwounded men as he could, whilst he got in touch with the parties on his right and left. He found Second Lieutenant Fulljames, who reported that he had lost touch with his blocking party commanded by Sergeant Hanlon, and feared that they had become casualties. Second Lieutenant Fulljames reported that his own party had suffered heavily but that he had reorganised. By the time Captain Jessop returned to the centre, Lieutenant Carroll had returned but had only managed to find twelve men. No trace of the left assault party under the command of Second Lieutenant Britton could be found. With the few men available Captain Jessop advanced to the German wire, which he found to be new and uncut. Realising it was useless to continue with so few men he withdrew to the disused trench and reported back to Major Hills at the gap in the British wire. Major Hills ordered a complete withdrawal. He realised that if the British artillery stopped its bombardment the enemy would do likewise, so sent orders for the artillery to cease fire. The enemy shelling stopped as anticipated and the raiders withdrew without further loss, bringing all the wounded and some of the dead back with them.

Lieutenant J M Carroll managed to find twelve unwounded men when sent to find members of the raiding party.

On the left, Second Lieutenant Britton had escaped the enemy fire and having found the wire flat, advanced right to the German trench. Here he found the position occupied and his men had just started to throw bombs at the Germans in the trench when the recall signal was seen. At this point Second Lieutenant Britton withdrew his party and they reached the British lines without

3 Platoon, 20/Durham L I, c.1916. Back row: G.M. Surtees, unidentified, E. Davies, unidentified, Hodgson, Johnson, J. Hannah, unidentified, A. Batley, P. Murphy. Fourth row: unidentified, unidentified, unidentified, J. Hunnam, Hollywood, Ayrson, unidentified, J.W. Middleton, unidentified, unidentified, Turnbull. Third row: unidentified, Robson, (?), Richardson, (?), Taylor, unidentified, unidentified, Adams, Monarch, unidentified, N. Duncan. Second row: F. Sharp, C. White, J. Russell, J. King, J.F. Walshaw, J. Trotter, R.T. Sykes, E. West, Lance-Corporal W. Cherret, T. Brown, J.A. Booth. Front row: unidentified, Lance-Corporal R. Horn, Lance-Corporal G. Brandt, Sergeant L.A. Lloyd, Second-Lieutenant J.W. Butterfield, Company Quartermaster-Sergeant E.T.S. Gore, Sergeant Coverdale, Sergeant R. Hooker, Lance-Corporal G. Foster, Lance-Corporal D. Haswell.

4 Platoon, 20/Durham L I, c.1916. Back row: unidentified, Tate, unidentified, unidentified, unidentified, unidentified, unidentified, unidentified, unidentified, Ambery. Fourth row: unidentified, unidentified, unidentified, Marshall, unidentified, unidentified, unidentified, unidentified, unidentified, unidentified, unidentified. Third row: unidentified, unidentified, unidentified, Skillet, unidentified, J. Gardiner, A. Coyle, E. Brown, Liddell, unidentified, unidentified. Second row: Fallan, unidentified, unidentified, Wood, unidentified, unidentified, T. Johnson, unidentified, R. Goodwin, unidentified, Wood, unidentified, unidentified. Front row: Miller, W. Haines, W. MacDonald, Corporal C. Owsnett, Corporal J.S. Tansey, Second-Lieutenant G. Thompson, Corporal R. Gloyne, Lance-Corporals W. Houston, E. Spalding, and E. Priestley, E.G. McClumpha.

loss. On the right of this party Lieutenant Tandy, Royal Engineers, also found the wire flat and he too had also reached the enemy trench when he was recalled.

The Right Blocking Party under Sergeant Hanlon had a trying time, they had taken up their positions on the tapes in No Man's Land as ordered. Here they were heavily shelled and lost some men. Reacting to the effective enemy fire Sergeant Hanlon moved his party forward, as close to the enemy trench as he could. From this point he could see the British barrage hitting the enemy parapet. Escaping further casualties, at midnight he ordered his men forward to the German wire, which was found to be uncut with new wire mixed in amongst the old. It could be seen that the Germans were manning their parapet and, as he was unable to get in touch with those on his left, Sergeant Hanlon decided to wait. After some time he withdrew; in trying to reach the British line, Sergeant Hanlon and four men, one of whom was slightly wounded, became lost and spent some time looking for a gap in the wire. As dawn was breaking they lay down and slept, then during the day of 27 July, they crawled through the long grass of No Man's Land until they eventually found Gap C. At last by 7.45 pm they reached the British lines bringing all their arms and equipment with them. Later that night Lieutenant Wayman went out with a party of men to search for the bodies of some of the dead

Private Harry Lockey MM was wounded during the raid and was evacuated to England.

whose bodies had been left behind. They managed to find two, who had clearly been killed instantaneously and although a thorough search was made no more were found.

The wounded were of course quickly evacuated and within a few days, 30231 Private Harry Lockey, who was employed as a butcher at the Esh Winning branch of the Annfield Plain Co-op, was writing to his mother, from the Eastern General Hospital in Cambridge. The initial brief letter was usual for the time:

> *Dear Mother,*
>
> *Just a line hoping this finds you well, as it leaves me a good deal better than I have been. I was wounded last Wednesday night and I am now in England. I am just waiting for a few days for the wound cleaning and then I will have the shrapnel taken out. It is a fine place this and we get every attention, we are waited on hand and foot. There is nothing I am in need of Mother except some money. I want a few things such as writing paper and I could buy that here, so I hope you will write by return then I will write and give you a full account of how it all happened. So I will close,*
>
> *Your Loving son*
>
> *Harry*

The second letter was a good deal longer and was the tale of an act of gallantry that brought Harry Lockey the award of the Military Medal.

> *Dear Mother,*
>
> *I received your welcome letter and PO, I am out of all danger now and will tell you how it happened. We had to make a raid on the German Trenches at 11.00 at night, so our big guns were shelling his front lines. We had to go over the top into No Man's Land and wait for an hour. Then*

when our big guns lifted on to his rear trenches we had to make the attack and it was while we were waiting that we got it hot. The Germans were shelling our front lines and were putting sky lights up, then he turned machine guns on us and started shelling us in No Man's Land. That did the trick, one shell burst behind and blew a bayonet off a man's rifle, it went through my boot at the toes and came out at the heel. It did little damage to my foot but I could not pull it out. One chap was mortally wounded and asked to be taken away. It was like a hail storm with shells but I picked him up and managed to get him carried to our lines and was lowering him into the trench when a shell burst behind me and hit me in the back. It knocked me into the air and I fell back into No Man's Land again. With the concussion of the shell I lost the use of my legs. I tried to get away as I knew more shells would drop there, but I could not. Well I had not laid long till another did drop and buried my legs with lumps of soil, I was there for about an hour before I was got out, more than I expected to be alive. I lay in the trench three hours before the stretchers came, our Major stayed with me all the time. The poor chap died that I carried out, he was in an awful mess. Well old Fritz got one on us that time, but we are not down hearted yet. I think there would be about seventy of us wounded and killed together out of 150. It was not long before I got the use of my legs I think I was very lucky and have nothing to grumble about.

Kind regards to all in Wolsingham, Your Loving son
Harry.

As well as Harry Lockey, 27402 Lance Corporal W S Smith and 20/613 Lance Corporal Tom Cummings from West Rainton both received the Military Medal, whilst Second Lieutenant R M Fulljames was awarded the Military Cross for his part in the action.

Congratulations were conveyed to the men for their gallant behaviour under fire from the 41st Divisional Commander, Major General Sidney Lawford, who wrote:

All ranks deserve high praise for the soldierly spirit and gallant conduct which they displayed under severe fire.'

123 Brigade Commander, Brigadier General C S Davidson who wished all ranks to know that the Army Commander expressed his satisfaction with the result and conduct of the enterprise, also endorsed the remarks of the GOC 41st Division.

Three days later on 31 July one of the men who was wounded and missing managed to crawl into the trenches of the battalion who were holding the sector on the left, unfortunately the Battalion War Diary does not record his name. On the night of 1 August the battalion returned to the front line, which was garrisoned until relieved on 9 August by 23/Middlesex Regiment and the Durhams moved back to

20/116 Private T. T. Moses died of wounds in the Casualty Clearing Station at Bailleul, 29 July 1916.

billets in Armentières. With the Somme battle raging to the south it was now the turn of 41st Division to join the battle. Accordingly 20/Durham LI handed over the billets to 13/Durham LI of 68 Brigade, who had just been pulled out of the battle to the south, and began moving back to training area at Mont des Cats. All the detached parties were recalled, twelve other ranks rejoined from 171st Tunnelling Company and twenty-two from 250th Tunnelling Company, then on 17 August a small draft of fifty-nine men joined from 35 Infantry Base Depot. At this time a number of men were returned to England to work on munitions and others, who were found to be under age, were sent to the Base Depot. After completing training, on the evening of 23 August the battalion marched to Bailleul to entrain for the Somme Front.

Chapter Four

The Somme Front

AFTER ENTRAINING on the evening of 23 August the Wearside Battalion travelled through the night to the village of Longpré les Corps Saints where they detrained and marched to Yaucourt Bussus. Whilst billeted in this village two drafts, one of sixty men and the other of eighty men arrived from 35th Infantry Base Depot. Concern had been expressed about the number of young men under the age of nineteen who were serving at the front, a small number of these lads were found to be serving in 20/Durham LI, and although they were now hardened front line soldiers, they were sent to the base for employment as guards at Number 2 Prisoner of War Camp at Ribemont. Several other men were sent home to work on munitions. The battalion concentrated on training for the attack, but this was much hampered by heavy continuous rain.

Whilst the battalion was stationed in this village, on 3 September, six men were reported killed in action: 3/12640 Privates G Armstrong, 3/12313 J Burdess, 30724 H Frater, 28017 W Gillibrand, 30925 J Hunter and 30490 J G Taylor; all six have no known grave and are commemorated on the Thiepval Memorial to the Missing.

20/500 Private W. Richmond, killed in action 11 September 1916.

Was there some explosion or serious accident that blew them all to pieces? Neither the War Diary or the battalion history shed any light on the matter.

On 6 September the battalion transport section paraded and then left by road for the forward area. The following day, training completed, the battalion marched back to Longpré and entrained for the front. On arrival at Mericourt station the battalion detrained and moved on foot to a camp near Becordel, just outside of Albert. The commanding officer, adjutant, the four company commanders and four other officers left the battalion on 8 September and proceeded to the front line to carry out a reconnaissance in preparation for the arrival of the battalion. The next day the battalion moved up 2,000 yards to be closer to the front but at the same time two other ranks were sent back to England for work on munitions. 123 Brigade was now placed in divisional support and 20/Durham LI took over Carlton and Savoy Trenches from 7/King's Liverpool Regiment of 165 Brigade and were behind 11/Queen's Regiment of their own Brigade. These trenches were heavily overcrowded and on 11 September one company moved to York Trench and one company into the Montauban Line. That night two companies went into the front line held by 11/Queen's and went out into No Man's Land for

20/336 Private G. Walshaw, killed in action 12 September 1916.

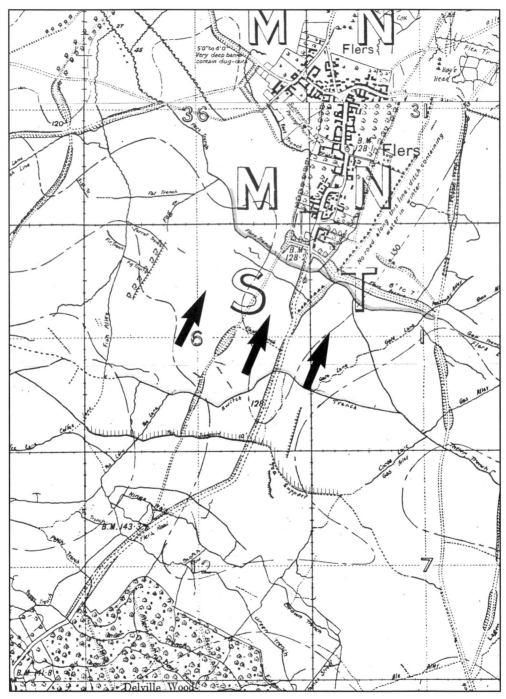

16 September 1916 the battalion moves up to attack German defences at Flers and suffers heavy casualties.

150 yards and started digging a series of posts, about one hundred yards apart. The party then commenced to connect the posts and to dig communication trenches back to the British Front Line. When it was too light to work they withdrew with the exception of C Company which remained to hold the posts, becoming the new British Front Line.

Captain and Adjutant P Spencer in a letter to Colonel Leather stated:

On the Tuesday night previously we had to dig a line of strong points, 150 yards in advance of our front line trench, five in number. The work front line here was from 300 to 400 yards from the Switch (German Trench). McNichol's company [C Company] did it. They took iron rations and water and went out with five Lewis guns to hold the points. They finished the points, but could not get the communication trench done. They were isolated during the day, but as soon as it was dark they started again, connected up the points and finished the communication trench. B Company, Captain Jessop then took over for twenty-four hours.

During this period Lieutenant A F Collins and eight other ranks were wounded and 20/430 Private Clark Green of Shiney Row was reported missing, and later presumed killed.

Orders came that the battalion would relieve 11/Queen's Regiment in the front line, so on the night 12/13 September the Durhams moved forward and the Queen's took over in support. The work started on the new strong points was continued and eventually completed. During the day a number of casualties had occurred, Second Lieutenant J A Struthers was wounded and amongst the other ranks, four were killed, sixteen wounded and three shell-shocked. On the next night 15/Hampshire Regiment came up and relieved the Wearsiders who moved back to Pommiers Redoubt, suffering three men wounded on the way. During 14 September the battalion rested as best they could but not for long, that night they were on their way back to the battle.

Second Lieutenant A F Collins, wounded during the digging of strong points in front of the British Line.

41st Division was positioned in the centre of XV Corps and was now ordered to capture the village of Flers and objectives beyond the village. The British concentrated a number of tanks on this portion of the front, four started from the Longueval-Flers Road and six were to assemble at the northern end of Longueval. Of these original ten machines only seven arrived at the point of departure. Three of the tanks were ditched before arriving at the start point.

The division attacked with two brigades, 124 Brigade on the right and 122 Brigade on the left. 123 Brigade with 20/Durham LI were in reserve. In the right brigade the leading troops moved out into No Man's Land well before Zero Hour and the attack started well. The leading platoons were so keen to close the enemy that many men fell to injuries caused by coming too close to the British barrage. The enemy had suffered so much from the barrage that they had little stomach for a fight and the first objective, the Switch Line, was captured by 7.00 am. The attackers began to

Tanks rearm and refuel behind the lines.

consolidate and then the rear battalions moved through and pressed on and soon after 7.20 am the attack on Flers Trench began. Within half an hour this objective was taken and units of the brigade pressed on to the third objective.

At Zero Hour, on the left, 122 Brigade advanced accompanied by several tanks. The barrage was reported to be excellent and just what the men had been trained to expect. German machine guns and rifles caused casualties among the attacking battalions as they moved forward over the trenches, but within twenty minutes the first objective was taken. Many of the defenders of the second objective, men of 9th Bavarian Infantry Regiment, left their positions without their arms and equipment and the machine guns of the accompanying tanks shot down a number of them as they retreated.

The brigade now had to storm Flers, to take its third objective behind the village. One of the tanks, *D16*, drove forward into the village at around 8.20 am and when the barrage lifted the infantry followed. Firing as it went, *D16* moved up the main street through Flers followed by parties of cheering British infantry. This was spotted by an observer of the Royal Flying Corps and a message eventually arrived at XV Corps HQ timed 8.45 am, 'Tank seen in main street Flers going on with large number of troops following it.'

At midnight on 14 September, 20/Durham LI moved forward to take up positions in the 'Check Line' and on the way forward had six other ranks killed, sixteen wounded, one missing and two shell-shocked. The battalion had hardly time to get settled when the attack commenced at 06.20 am. Orders were then received to move forward into the trenches vacated by the attacking battalions. Writing to Colonel Leather, the Adjutant, Captain P Spencer said of this day:

Second Lieutenant Harold Risdon was originally a company quarter master sergeant who was numbered /1 in his battalion of the London Regiment, another of the officer casualties.

21/235 Private A. J. Peart, from Darlington, killed in action 15 September 1916.

Early on Friday morning the row started. How many guns were firing it would be impossible to say, but the staff said never before had such an amount of stuff been thrown at the Hun position. We got orders to move to York Trench, and almost immediately further orders to go to our old front line. Hills sent me ahead to choose the best route, and I have never been so astonished in my life. At 6.00 a.m. it was not always safe to move about along the top of Curllon and Savoy Trenches, in fact Collins was hit whilst doing so. When I got to the top of the rise, all No Man's Land, the Switch Trench etc, were covered with troops, transport for the artillery, limbers, batteries taking up new positions etc. Never was such a change in one place. On its side lay a disabled tank, another in the distance flew the "out of action" red flag. But all around, all over, everywhere were men, horses, guns.

The battalion had been in this position throughout the day and as the day progressed the number of casualties had increased. Second Lieutenant F C Arkless was wounded and missing, and among the men, one had been killed, thirty-five wounded, two were missing and six shell-shocked. At some time during the day the battalion was ordered to move forward into the Flers defences and remain there in reserve. This move was made through an extremely heavy enemy barrage and the battalion suffered a large number of casualties. Seven officers were wounded: Captain and adjutant P Spencer, Captains D E Jessop and H Risdon, Second Lieutenants T M Fletcher, W Mitchell, C E Hopkinson and F Wayman, the last two named were only slightly wounded and remained on duty. But among the men six were killed, nineteen wounded, one wounded and missing, and five missing. Considering they had done no fighting a heavy toll indeed, but it was not over yet.

The Adjutant continued his letter to Colonel Leather:

I got a hole knocked in my right thigh by

Captain D E Jessop, wounded at Flers 15 September 1916.

Second Lieutenant Thomas May Fletcher, also wounded.

The Battalion Adjutant, Captain Percival Spencer, had served in France with a service battalion as a sergeant before being commissioned, he too was among the wounded.

a piece of H.E. when about three hundred yards north of Flers on Saturday last. I am most anxious about Hills. He was as usual a perfect lion, and led the advance with the first Company. It was a great battle, and our men were perfect. They had five days with practically no sleep and very little food or water, yet behaved like veterans advancing through a hellish barrage stoically.

Throughout the afternoon of 17 September the enemy subjected the British Lines to heavy shelling, using both H.E. and tear gas, and it was a thankful battalion that welcomed the 7/King's Liverpool Regiment, in pouring rain, to take over at midnight. When the relief was complete, the battalion commenced its move to the Montauban line. During the day and on the way out a further two men were killed, nineteen wounded, one wounded and missing and five reported missing. The War Diary records that they arrived at the Montauban Line at 5.00 am and from there moved to a camp near Becordel.

After resting for a while Major Hills wrote to Colonel Leather,

We have been through it, are out now, but shall go back again. We have not suffered so heavily as some. Everyone did splendidly. Many officers are wounded, none killed, though Arkless is missing. Spencer, Jessop, Risdon, Fletcher, Collins, Struthers and Mitchell are all wounded. Regimental Sergeant Major Clark severely wounded [he died], *Company Sergeant Majors Walton and Seago wounded and Sergeant Dent. I have made Jones RSM, Noton CSM of C Company, Hutchinson B Company, King D Company. [The last three*

New Zealand infantrymen in the line near Flers.

5 Platoon, 20/Durham L I, c.1916. Back row: unidentified, unidentified, unidentified, unidentified, unidentified, unidentified, unidentified, R. Swales, unidentified, unidentified. Third row: unidentified, unidentified, unidentified, Armstrong, unidentified, Taylor, unidentified, unidentified, unidentified, unidentified, unidentified. Second row: Wilcox, Sergeant M. Storey, unidentified, unidentified, unidentified, unidentified, J.W. Hayes, Corporal M.S. Holdsworth, unidentified, G. Coleby, unidentified, H. Dowson, C. Chipchase. Front row: G. Hill, W.D. Purvis, Sergeant R. Coldwell, Corporal J. Jackson, Sergeant G.W. Hutchinson, Lieutenant J.M. Carroll, J.A. Armstrong, Corporal G. Wilson, J. Gray, M. Duffy.

6 Platoon, 20/Durham L I, c.1916. Back row: E. Close, unidentified, Iveson, unidentified, S. Dawson, unidentified, T. Dobinson, F. Blenkinsop, unidentified, unidentified. Third row: unidentified, unidentified, J. Mole, R. Telfer, C.E. Tate (?), J. Burniston (?), T.T. Moses, unidentified, R.S. Robinson, T.H. Hutton, F.W. Ede. Second row: W.F. Hauxby, Lance-Corporal Lee, T.F. Golightly, Stokel (?), unidentified, A. Calvert, C.E. Tate (?) or J. Burniston (?), T.W. Adamson, J. Fletcher, E. Emery, unidentified, unidentified, Gordon Forbes. Front row: Lance-Corporal J. Humble, Lance-Corporal J. Gregson, unidentified, Corporal Lindsay, Sergeant J.W. Carr, Captain D.F. Jessop, Company Sergeant-Major Moralee, Corporal T. Snowden, Corporal W. Mountford, Lance-Corporal R. Davidson.

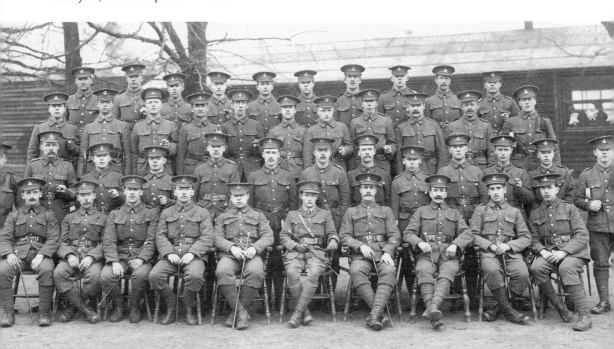

named would all be killed in action before the end of the war.] *Young Wayman, Adjutant; Hiller to command B Company; Brown to D Company. My fighting strength is still 600, so you will see that we have not lost so many men as the number of officer casualties would indicate. The Division scored a thundering success.*

After resting where possible, the time spent at Becordel was spent training for the attack. However the conditions in the 'Camp' can scarcely have encouraged the men.

Major Hills, in another letter to Colonel Leather on 23 September, recorded the true state of the bivouac:

Major Hills wrote to the colonel about the conditions in the trenches.

Here we are still behind the line, we have been here unexpectedly long. The Battalion will certainly get some honours. What, I don't know. McNichol and Scott have gone in for immediate reward. We had the worst time we ever had when we were relieved. All the afternoon we were shelled with 5.9 and tear shells, and at midnight we had a very difficult relief, expecting a counter-attack every minute. My orders were to march to a spot four miles from the front line, when our cookers would meet us with breakfast, and then march four miles to our bivouac. At 10.00 p.m. it began to rain hard; relief was complete at 2.00 a.m. and the companies marched off. We had an awful march down: pouring rain, pitch dark, slippery ground and barraged on and off and on the whole way. Our bivouac consisted of tents for the officers and tarpaulins stretched over liquid mud for the men. I just fell on my sleeping bag and slept for seventeen hours. The place dries up quickly and the men are happy again.

Whilst out training one man was accidentally wounded and then on 27 September, the battalion began moving forward again. On 28 September the battalion relieved 8/King's Liverpool Regiment in reserve trenches and came under command of 21st Division. Carrying parties for the front line came under fire, having five men killed and around a dozen wounded. The next day the Wearsiders were ordered to relieve 11/Queen's Regiment in the front line. Two companies went forward at 2.30 pm and must have been seen by enemy observers, who quickly called down a heavy and accurate barrage on the two companies of Durhams moving forward; D

20/776 CSM Fred Seago served during the Boer War and then became a policeman, on re-enlistment he was quickly promoted. Major Hills reported his wounding to Colonel Leather. When he returned to the front he was posted to 19/Durham LI.

66

20/253 Private Fred Purvis, from Willington, County Durham, killed in action 16 September 1916.

20/33 Private Albert Barratclough from Hendon, Sunderland, killed in action 16 September 1916.

20/153 Private William Purvis, from Sunderland, killed in action 17 September 1916.

20/177 Regimental Sergeant Major Henry Clark, died 19 September 1916

Company suffered a number of fatal casualties from this fire as they made their way into the front line. The two remaining companies withdrew and after darkness had fallen at 7.30 pm came forward again and completed the relief of the Queen's in Support and Reserve. As soon as things settled down working parties were sent up to the front line to assist the garrison to deepen and strengthen the position, which had been dug the previous night in front of Grid Support and the old German Trench. During the day four men were killed, thirty-one wounded and three missing. Of the officers Lieutenant C E Hopkinson and Lieutenant Colonel J W Hills MP were wounded. Two weeks earlier a report had reached Durham City that the then Major J W Hills MP had been killed in action. The Major's brother, Colonel Hills, Director of Durham University Observatory, had come north to attend a meeting in Newcastle and, at the invitation of Dr Robinson of Durham University, had called in at Durham on his way back to London. After his departure for Durham a telegram arrived at Newcastle announcing the death of Lieutenant C H Hills. The telegram reached a third party, who not knowing the Colonel had two sons and a brother at the front, assumed it was his brother. This news was then telephoned to the Colonel. In Durham the bell was tolled in the cathedral as a mark of respect. However matters were put right when the Colonel returned to London. He went to the War Office to make enquiries about his brother only to learn that the dead officer was his youngest son, serving with the Manchester Regiment.

On the afternoon of 1 October the brigades on either side of 20/Durham LI were ordered to advance to straighten the line. To assist this operation the battalion sent out three patrols of one NCO and seven men, behind a barrage. Their orders were to find out if the enemy trench in front was occupied or not. If it was, the patrols were to dig in, not closer than 200 yards to the enemy trench. In spite of heavy machine-gun and rifle fire, the patrols went forward and finding the trench occupied dug in as ordered some 200 yards from it. They then held these posts for seven hours until relieved when 8/Royal Fusiliers took over the line from 20/Durham LI, who made

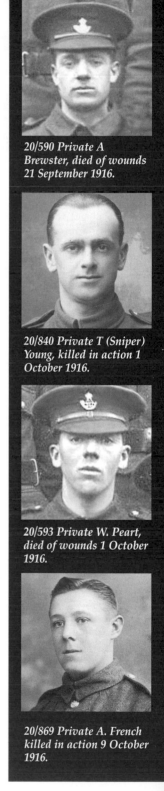

20/590 Private A Brewster, died of wounds 21 September 1916.

20/840 Private T (Sniper) Young, killed in action 1 October 1916.

20/593 Private W. Peart, died of wounds 1 October 1916.

20/869 Private A. French killed in action 9 October 1916.

Second Lieutenant J A Struthers listed as wounded in the Second-in-Command's letter.

their way back to Pommiers Redoubt near Montauban. The patrols were under the command of Second Lieutenant Ronald Fulljames MC, who was awarded a Bar to his MC for his work that day.

The battalion rested at Pommiers Redoubt and Major P W North 5/Royal Berkshire Regiment joined to assume command, his servant Private James Harris, an Irishman, from Dublin, accompanied him. Private Harris was transferred to 20/Durham LI and unusually was given the number 20/1068, the last number allotted in the original battalion sequence. On the afternoon of 3 October the battalion moved to a camp near Mametz Wood, where they remained for the next few days resting and training.

The next orders came on 7 October, when the battalion was ordered to proceed to Savoy trench in Divisional Reserve. The other two brigades of the Division were advancing, so in the afternoon the battalion was called upon to move closer. They moved up to Switch Trench about 800 yards behind Flers where they spent the night. The following afternoon they were ordered into the front line, to take over from troops of 124 Brigade. The previous day's objective had not been taken and 124 Brigade had dug in about 200 yards from the original front line. This relief was carried out successfully and a quiet night followed with no casualties. The next day was quiet

Infantrymen and some of the crew shelter near a knocked out tank.

German prisoners are escorted back across No Man's Land.

without much shelling. The shelling that took place caused a few casualties, two killed, five wounded and one missing. The next night under heavy machine-gun and rifle fire the battalion sent out wiring parties and the whole of the front line was wired, before they were relieved by 2/Bedfordshire Regiment and moved back to the camp in Mametz Wood. On the way out Second Lieutenant J W Butterfield was wounded, along with twelve men. They rested for two days at Mametz Wood before orders were received to move back to Dernancourt. On 15 October the GOC 41st Division, Major General S T B Lawford, who presented medal ribbons to those who had earned gallantry awards, inspected the battalion. Military Medals were awarded to Private Champion, Corporal Abernethy and Lance Sergeants Dazley and Winter. Unfortunately Privates Hardy and Anderson who also had won the medal had since been killed in action.

On 17 October, 20th (Service) Battalion the Durham Light Infantry (Wearside) began marching away from the Somme, they entrained at Dernancourt at 2.00 pm and travelled via Amiens and Longpré to Oisemont where they arrived on 18 October 1916, and marched to billets in Citerne, where they were met by the Transport Section

Lieutenant C E Hopkinson, another of the casualties at Flers.

20/Durham LI, Transport Section 1916. Back row: J. Johnson, J.M. Suddes, W. Elliot, N. Snaith, H. Lewis, Tallantire, unidentified, Potts, N. Crozier, A. Nadier, unidentified. Second row: E. Howard, J.D. Drummond, Stephenson, T. Bradley, R.J. Birk, A.T. Thompson, J. Thompson, W. Provo, W.T. Beadle, Lance-Corporal R. Hodgson, W. Longstaff, Lance-Corporal W. Weightman, H. Ferry. Front row: Wood, C.A. Mordey, J.W. Middleton, Sergeant S.J. Dinsmore, Lieutenant G. Richwood, Captain and Adjutant P. Spencer, Corporal T. Robinson, J. Steedman, J.G. Shaw, R. Lemon, F. Lemon. On ground: A. Nesbett, J. Hambery.

who had travelled by road.

After the battalion had left the Somme Front they received the following from Headquarters Fourth Army:

> *41st Division.*
>
> *I desire to place on record my appreciation of the work done by the 41st Division during the Battle of the Somme and to congratulate all ranks on the brilliant manner in which they captured the village of Flers on September 15th. To assault three lines of strongly defended trench systems, and to capture the village of Flers as well, in one rush was a feat of arms of which every officer, non-commissioned officer and man may feel proud.*
>
> *It was a very fine performance and I offer my best thanks for the gallantry and endurance displayed by all ranks.*
>
> *The work of the Divisional artillery in supporting the Infantry attacks and in establishing the barrages deserves high praise, and I trust that at some future time it may be my good fortune to have this fine Division again in the Fourth Army.*
>
> *Sgnd H RAWLINSON*
> *General*
> *27 October 1916*
> *Commanding Fourth Army.*

Since arriving in the battle area on 23 August the battalion had suffered ninety-eight fatal casualties and over 200 wounded. These are relatively light compared to some units fighting on the Somme, but still hard to replace and the reinforcements came from many regiments and all over the British Isles.

Chapter Five

After the Somme

THE 20th BATTALION LEFT THE SOMME on 18 October and, having rested two days at Citerne, the men marched to Pont Remy where they entrained for Godeswaersvelde. Arriving at 5pm they were quartered on the outskirts of the town. The next day a party of officers went forward to reconnoitre the trenches in the Dickebusch sector, while the remainder of the battalion spent the day resting. On the morning of 22 October the Wearsiders moved by route march to a camp at Renninghelst and went under canvas for the night. The relief of 49/Australian Battalion was carried out the next day in broad daylight without casualties. The trenches were described as fairly good but the front line was very wet and required continual draining. The original support line was not held, the old reserve line being pressed into service as a support trench because of its better condition. The German Artillery was very quiet at this time, the adjutant Second Lieutenant F Wayman recording in the War Diary, 'We are never shelled', and on

Motorised and horse-drawn ransport moves toward the Ypres Salient.

Second Lieutenant J H Butterfield had served as a private in the Northumberland Fusiliers prior to being commissioned into 20/Durham LI.

20/521 Private James Ringer of Trimdon, killed in action 20 October 1916.

25 October, 'Another quiet day, no artillery fire on either side. Last night we wired a good deal on our front'. But the peace was not to last long. British generals started to stir things up and the next day the British artillery was 'fairly active'. The Germans were quick to reply and they put several *minenwerfers* over onto the British Line. This caused the deaths of Privates James Ringer, from Trimdon Foundry and Eber Shaw, a reinforcement from Leicester, as well as wounding another three men, before British counter bombadment caused the enemy to cease fire. Several officers from 12/East Surrey Regiment came up to the line during the day to reconnoitre the trenches in readiness for taking over. The weather turned and there were frequent showers of rain over the next two days, which made the trenches quite muddy. Captain F C Chatt rejoined the battalion and two new officers reported with him, Second Lieutenants A T Browne and H K Walton. On 29 October after being relieved the battalion marched to Quebec Camp at Reninghelst. Once again the relief had taken place in broad daylight with only one man wounded on the way out. Quebec Camp was really muddy and most of the land round about was under water. This brought warnings from division and brigade about trench foot. The next couple of days were spent cleaning up and preparing for an inspection by the Army Commander. On the morning of 1 November the planned inspection took place, the battalion paraded with the rest of 123 Brigade and General Sir H Plumer GCMG KCB commanding Second Army took the salute. That afternoon training commenced, rifle practice, bombing and bayonet drill being the order of the day. The quartermaster department was kept busy with the issue of new gas respirators to all ranks; this was much lighter than its predecessor and was supposed to be more effective against enemy gas. The next day the whole battalion paraded and marched to the Divisional Gas School for instruction in the use of the new respirators. Afterwards the musketry and bombing training continued.

It was now time to return to the trenches and on 3 November, once again in broad daylight, the relief of 12/East Surrey Regiment took place in the trenches that

A German machine-gun crew either firing at aircraft or in a supporting fire role.

were held on the previous tour. The front line trench was described as dirty and under water. The following day the morning was quiet, but in the afternoon the British Artillery commenced a very heavy bombardment on the enemy trenches and unusually there was little retaliation from the German gunners. As winter was drawing in the ground became worse and drainage became one of the most pressing problems facing the battalion. Another worry at this time was the wind direction, for over a week it had been blowing from the north-east, which had kept the gas alert at dangerous. The next day was again quiet, five men were wounded, one of whom, Private Thomas Wandless of Esh Winning, died from his wounds. The weather turned wet and the trenches began to collapse and several dug-outs became unsafe, owing to the trenches being flooded. There was little artillery activity over the next couple of days and at 10.30 am, on 9 November 12/East Surrey Regiment again took over the front line, 20/Durham LI moving back to the rear area into Ontario Camp. The next week was quite busy, a miniature range had been constructed and musketry and Lewis gun drill was carried out. There was an inspection by the GOC 123 Brigade, who presented the ribbons of the MC to Second Lieutenant R M Fulljames and the MM to 20/502 Sergeant Edward Winter, of Sunderland. The next few days were spent providing working parties and then further training took place before the front line was taken over in front of Dickebusch. Again the relief was in daylight and the battalion War Diary records the amazement that the enemy, who must have been able to observe the handover, didn't shell the

7 Platoon, 20/Durham L I, c.1916. Back row: unidentified, Smith, Lance-Corporal Matheson, unidentified, W.T. Beadle, unidentified, J. Hopper, unidentified, J. Sheaville. Third row: B. Little, Scott, Matheson, unidentified, J. Bell, R. O'Brien, E. Bell, J.H. Roberts, unidentified, S. Thomas. Second row: Corporal J. Breed, W. Gibbon, R. Ramage, Kennedy, Robson, G. Reay, R. Reay, J. Ross, unidentified, R. Harris, Lance-Corporal R.R. Wilson, Corporal R. Hodgson. Front row: A. Roe, W. Crosby, Corporal T. Urwin, Sergeant A.E. Miller, Company Sergeant-Major J.E. Walton, Lieutenant Rasche, Company Quartermaster-Sergeant Gibson, Watson, W. Davy, Lance-Corporal E. Wrightson. On ground: R. Johnson.

troops. 'The communication trenches are so open that one's head & shoulders show over the sides and as the enemy hold the high ground they must see almost every movement.'

At this time the men were issued with leather jerkins, which were lined with cloth, these were waterproof and very warm and comfortable. The weather had turned very cold so to the front line soldier these items of clothing were a godsend. Another improvement was the issue of two extra Lewis guns, bringing the battalion total to ten, the extra firepower being a very welcome addition. On 18 November snow fell which made movement in the line very tricky, especially for those engaged on working parties, as all the duckboards became wet and slippery. Later the snow turned to rain, and the already muddy trenches began to fill with thick sticky mud. For the next few days all available men were put to work trying to shore up the crumbling trenches, thankfully the enemy artillery was silent and the work was unmolested. Although there were several men wounded, there were only two fatalities during November, both Sunderland men: 20/633 Private John Adey was accidentally killed on 19 November and 20/936 Private Robert Waiter was killed three days later.

23 November saw 12/East Surrey Regiment take over the line once more and the Wearsiders moved back to the hutted Ontario Camp near Reninghelst. Here the next day was spent scraping the mud off uniforms and equipment and the following day training commenced. For some unlucky men working parties were the order of the day, transporting rations, ammunition, barbed wire, bombs and all the other items required in the front line. The battalion War Diary every

month supplies a return of all the men with the battalion; it is interesting to see how a battalion was dispersed and its fighting strength whittled away.

20th Battalion Durham Light Infantry Strength State 18-11-16:

	Officers	Other Ranks
In Trenches	16	513
Remaining Behind	-	28
Transport & QM Stores	1	66
Attd to Div HQ	1	4
Attd to Bde HQ	2	15
Hospital	4	45
Absent without leave	-	1
Absent with leave	3	6
Attd to M.G. Coy	-	9
Detention	-	2
Attd to A.S.C.	-	2
' ' 250th Tunnelling Coy	-	10
' ' 1st Canadian Tunnelling Coy	-	9
' ' 12th Canadian Tunnelling Coy	-	9
' ' R.E.	-	4
' ' 233rd Field Coy	2	25
' ' 123rd T.M. Battery	-	5
Pigeon Personnel	-	6
On Command	-	10
Salvage Coy	-	2
2nd Army H Qrs	-	7
Traffic Control	-	1
Divisional Guard	-	12
Brigade School	-	32
Trench Warfare School	-	5
Total	**29**	**828**

Typical tented camp in the rear area of the Ypres Salient.

8 Platoon, 20/Durham L I, c.1916. Back row: J. Garthwaite, N. Morcombe, G. Stabler, P. Todd, unidentified, W. Elliot, unidentified, R.W. Wigham. Fourth row: Lance-Corporal W. Brown, J.M. Hudson, A. Brewster, W. Peart, unidentified, Robinson, G. Hayes, M. McCullagh, G. Wilson, G. Wilson, T. Walker. Third row: Turnbull, unidentified, unidentified, Hudson, unidentified, Rowell, unidentified, Atkinson, Sergeant T. Cummins, unidentified, unidentified, Cleminson. Second row: R.H. Davison, A.T. Thompson, C. Tate, W. Todd, J. Reed, E. Morris, J. Ringer, G. Brown, Gilam (?), E. Rickaby, J.W. Alderson, R. Henderson, Powell, H. Morris, T.J. Foster. Front row: Wilson, Lance-Corporal Cresswell, Corporal E.W. Brown, Sergeant T. Fletcher, Sergeant Hudson, Captain A. Pumphrey, Sergeant J. McElvogue, H. McAndrew, E. Oglethorpe, H.S. Usher.

Carrying party with containers of hot food for men in the trenches.

Second Lieutenant W P M Brettell.

Second Lieutenant J E Dixon.

Second Lieutenant H H Brewer.

Captain E Rasche.

Infantry move up to the front in the Ypres Salient during the bitter winter of 1916/17.

An interesting addition to the return for the following week was that two men were shown as being at 'Base Prison', but whether as guards or prisoners is not recorded, most likely the latter. With these as average strength returns it can be seen that only 55% of officers and 61% of other ranks were actually in the line. The coal miners of the Durhams were much sought after by the Tunnelling Companies and those attached would be supplemented by large working parties when there was a specific requirement.

The end of the month saw the battalion back in the same trenches, as before the relief carried out in daylight without casualties. There was thick fog lying about and the British artillery commenced firing on hostile emplacements, on 29 November the enemy didn't reply to this fire, but on the following day all their trench mortars and artillery carried out a heavy barrage of the British lines, fortunately the Durhams suffered no casualties.

December started with an encounter in No Man's Land, an early morning patrol came across a German patrol and threw bombs and fired on them, before withdrawing to the British line. That day two new officers, Second Lieutenants L W Shepherdson and G Frisby, reported for duty from 10/Entrenching Battalion. The same routine relief and move to Ontario Camp took place on 3 December and on arrival the battalion was employed finding working parties for the front, with a little time spent training before going back to the line again. This pattern continued throughout the month until on 15 December a Church Parade was held in the morning and in the afternoon the battalion 'did nothing at all save rest'. The camp and parade ground were very muddy and after the battalion had cleaned up and everyone had bathed, they started practising ceremonial drill. All the battalion's horses were inspected by the GOC 41st Division, he then went on to inspect the camp and watch the companies at training. On the morning of 21 December, after all the hard work the battalion formed up with the rest of 123 Brigade along the Reninghelst–Ouderdom road and were inspected by the Commander in Chief of the BEF Sir Douglas Haig, who afterwards congratulated the battalion on its turnout and steadiness on parade. Three new officers arrived from 3/Durham LI, Second Lieutenants N W H Cartwright, N Southwell and W O M Stephenson, just in time to join the battalion as it spent Christmas in the front line. The same trenches, which were very quiet, were taken over from the East Surreys.

Patrolling No Man's Land was given priority and valuable

Second Lieutenant W A Rodwell.

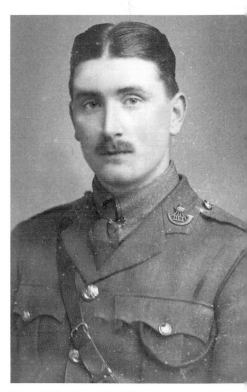

Second Lieutenant H G Thompson.

Infantry enjoy their Christmas dinner in close proximity to a comrade's grave.

information about the enemy wire was gained. Christmas Day opened with a fair amount of trench mortar activity, which resulted in one man being evacuated wounded. On Boxing Day, which was quiet, Second Lieutenant Browne from A Company led a patrol out into No Man's Land inspecting the enemy wire and gathering information.

Over the next day or so little of interest happened, British trench mortars continued to bombard the enemy trenches with only sporadic return fire from the enemy.

29 December saw the East Surreys take over the line and the Wearsiders moved back to Ontario Camp, where cleaning up and inspections took place under company arrangements. During the morning of New Year's Eve a church parade took place, afterwards all the officers and 150 men of the battalion attended a demonstration at the Brigade Trench Mortar School. During the demonstration there was an accident with one of the Stokes guns, which resulted in a number of casualties. In the afternoon the men had their Christmas dinner, this had been provided for them out of a fund set up by the Mayor and City of Sunderland. After dinner the men were given the rest of the day as a holiday and were free to do what they wished. So ended 1916 for the Wearside Battalion: they had fought hard but there was still a lot more fighting to do in 1917.

Chapter Six

1917 – January to June

WE LEFT THE WEARSIDE BATTALION at the end of 1916 in Ontario Camp in the Ypres Salient. New Year's Day 1917 saw 20/Durham LI training and where possible the men had a bath. B Company went out to a nearby hill and practised bombing, rifle shooting and operating the Lewis gun. C Company went to an area known as Micmac and practised bombing up a trench line with dummy bombs. A Company however were put to work building a new bombing range near to Ontario Camp. The following day the whole battalion were employed on RE working parties, one man, 42552 Private Albert Percival a reinforcement from Grimsby, was wounded and sadly died of these wounds later in the day. On 3 January a daylight relief of 12/East Surrey Regiment took place, with only one man wounded during the change over. This tour in the line was marked with the activity of the enemy artillery and trench mortars, who kept destroying the British Front Line and the communication trenches. Each night was spent repairing the damage and working parties of a hundred men came up to assist. On 6 January, the British artillery bombarded the German trenches and wire between 1430 and 1500

British officers peer towards the German line through the front line barbed wire.

20/22 Private Tansey from Southwick died of wounds 17 January 1917, aged 20.

hours. The Germans replied in kind and again knocked in the British Front Line, which again required the assistance of a 100-man working party. A Company were in reserve at a location known as Sunderland Farm, which was shelled by the enemy without loss or damage to the company. That night Second Lieutenant W O M Stephenson led a patrol out into No Man's Land and gained some useful knowledge about the enemy wiring parties. At some stage during the day 20/902 Private William Richardson from Sunderland was killed in action. Once again at the end of the tour of duty the 12/East Surrey Regiment relieved the battalion. The day was very wet and with a strong wind blowing, by the time Ontario Camp was reached the battalion was soaked to the skin. A similar training programme was carried out and on 9 January the Army Commander, Sir Herbert Plumer visited the battalion at training: work carried on as usual as he went round the camp.

Four new officers joined the battalion during this period of rest, Second Lieutenants B Wilkinson, W R Brooke, R Jennings and P L Dobinson were posted in from the 5th Training Reserve Battalion, originally a unit of the Leicestershire Regiment; along with them 180 other ranks arrived from the 35th Infantry Base Depot, they should have been on their way to 19/Durham LI. No sooner had they arrived, than the battalion was ordered back into the trenches. The draft however was left behind to practise respirator drill; and on 17 January came up and took over Sunderland Farm from D Company 23/Middlesex Regiment, who had been lent to 20/Durham LI until the draft was fully trained.

One of the men that arrived with the draft from 3/Durham LI in South Shields was a Spennymoor man, 38950 Private George Thompson, a nineteen-year-old trainee school master. Having spent time training in England this was his first time at the front:

Right: 20/1068 Private J Harris, an Irishman from Dublin, joined the battalion with Colonel North from the Royal Berkshire Regiment. He lost both legs and was employed by Colonel North after the war.

Below: The Card of Honour describing how Private Harris won the Military Medal.

To Pte. J. Harris.
20ᵗʰ Battⁿ D.L.I

I wish to place on record my appreciation of your devotion to duty on the night of Jan 22ⁿᵈ near WHITE CHATEAU. You remained all night, during heavy shelling, in an open trench from which troops had been cleared on account of shell fire, in order to call your Commanding Officer whose servant you were at 3. A.M.

Sydney Lawford

Major General.
Comdg 41st Division

NOTE. — It does not follow that your name will be submitted to higher authority.

82

'We went up from Etaples by cattle truck to Reninghelst in Belgium, the camp we arrived at was Machine-Gun Section 20/Durham LI, 1916. Back row: Johnson, J.W. Garham, J.W. Alderson, N. Morecombe, W.J. McPhee, R. Henderson, T. Dodsworth, unidentified, T.H.S. Mathieson, J.P. Mathieson, unidentified. Second row: J. Oliver, J. Hannah, J.G. Skillet, G. Stabler, Fowler, Sergeant W. Wilson, A. Barraclough, J. Harrison, unidentified, G. Turner, G.W. Moody, unidentified. Front row: T.T. Caulfield, J. Gray, Lance-Corporal E. Spalding, Lance-Corporal C.L. Eyton, Lieutenant J. Thompson-Hopper, Major J.W. Hills, Captain and Adjutant P. Spencer, Second-Lieutenant W.A. Rodwell, Lance-Corporal J.T. Hardy, Lance-Corporal R. Horn, J. Humble. On ground: A. Coyle.

The rest camp for 20/Durham LI (they were in camp when we marched in) I was assigned to Number 10 Platoon, C Company. The camp was hutted and quite warm, each hut had a big stove in the middle of it. The battalion was out of the line at the time; each sector was held by two battalions, one in the trenches and one in the rest camp. The next day the battalion went up into the trenches, but we newcomers were left behind for another day. We were then taken up on our own. There would be over fifty of us – I realised it was going to be a tough job, but then we were not bothered by lice yet. We marched up to Ouderdom and turned right and when we reached a crossroads we broke up into tens and did the next mile or so in small groups. In front of us was a small ridge with trees along it and we took a footpath over the fields behind a wood to a ruined brewery, "The Brasserie" as it was called and just behind the brewery the communication trench began. This led to a small copse where the real trenches started: a place called "Shelley Lane".

In the early hours of that morning Second Lieutenant G T Browne had taken a patrol out into No Man's Land, to see if the enemy were alert after their wire had been cut by an earlier patrol. The enemy were in fact wide awake and threw a number of bombs at the Wearside patrol, with the result that Second Lieutenant Browne and 20/22 Private Joseph Tansey were wounded. The unfortunate Private Tansey died of his wounds later in the day. The weather was very cold and snow fell throughout the day and remained on the ground. The cold weather did not stop the German gunners though and Battalion Headquarters and Sunderland Farm were bombarded twice, the latter building being hit six times. The men of the draft had managed to get out before the shells struck the house. The front line also received the attention of the enemy artillery and one dug-out was completely blown in, killing 20/75 Private David Pickering from Sunderland and 45782 Private Charles Spence a Durham man, whilst the other three men in the dug-out escaped with wounds.

On 21 January the battalion was relieved again, this time in darkness owing to the snow that still lay on the ground. Yet again they marched back to Ontario Camp, where training took place at the Brigade Trench Warfare School, with instruction at the Rifle Grenade Range and also in bayonet fighting. The next day the whole battalion paraded for work under the RE and then back to training this time in open warfare at Micmac Camp: here the army commander, Sir Herbert Plumer, came round and inspected the battalion at training. The divisional commander was also expected to inspect C Company but did not arrive. Musketry was not neglected either and Chippewa Range was allotted to 20/Durham LI on 27 January and all ranks fired the fifteen rounds a minute practice. The following day it was back into the line, the same sector as before taking over from 12/East Surrey Regiment in broad daylight.

LCpl Ernie Wrightson from D'Arcy Street in Sunderland, after recovering from his wounds he was transferred to the South Lancashire Regiment.

Private George Thompson described his first visit to the front line in this way:

The communication trench was six feet deep and zig-zagged so that if a shell fell in one part of the trench shrapnel couldn't fly along and affect another part of the trench. They were fitted with duckboards but very often the water underneath rose over the duckboards, which it wasn't intended to. With frost and snow it was bitterly cold on that first visit and it was a sort of a nightmare, that part of it I remember most of all. All was quiet that night and in the front line, the parapet was higher than the back, the parados. The trench was deeper than six feet, that's why you had to have the fire step, to stand on and look over and shoot. The trenches were very carefully made, they dug a deep ditch and put in what were called 'A Frames' a letter A made of wood turned upside down went in the trench and the duckboard went over the cross bar of the A. Between the soil and the boards they put wire meshing to hold back the soil, the Germans by the way used cane work for this purpose; then of course there was a very wide parapet of sandbags, tightly packed, filled with soil. There were some dug-outs but mostly steel shelters on ground level, like a beehive shape with sandbags piled on top of them. There was a dug-out for Company Headquarters, and of course there was a special dug-out for the CO and Battalion Headquarters and the signallers.

That night, two patrols left the Front Line, one under Second Lieutenant Jennings and the other led by Second Lieutenant Bainbridge. The snow still lay on the ground and owing to this fact both patrols were spotted by the Germans before they reached the enemy wire. Over the next three days the enemy artillery shelled the battalion, A Company had one man killed and six wounded, whilst two others were killed and one more wounded.

Having arrived at the front line George Thompson described the cold conditions and the clothing he wore to try to combat them.

The first night I spent in the trenches in the bitterly cold frosty weather, I half fainted, that's the only time it was as bad as that. An officer was passing at the time and he gave me a drink of something, I don't know what it was, it was some sort of spirit or other, whether it was whisky or not I don't know. I was alright after that. The frost was well into the ground at that time, the ground was as hard as iron at the rest camp and up the line. I had on a vest and of course a khaki army shirt, above that a woollen cardigan, then over that my tunic and then my overcoat and on top of all that I wore a goatskin with the hair outside. Some had sheepskin but mine was goat. You couldn't keep your feet warm. You see the cold spread upward through the legs. To get "Trench Feet" was an offence; if you rubbed your feet with whale oil you couldn't get trench feet. But whale oil made your feet cold. "Trench feet" was caused by wet feet, feet soaked and softened with water and whale oil helped keep the water out.

Sergeant R Longstaff from Middlesbrough, killed in action 14 February 1917.

In the first few days of February the battalion worked hard keeping the trenches clear, then the cycle was repeated, 12/East Surrey Regiment came back in and took over the line and 20/Durham LI went back to Ontario Camp once more. A slight variation in training took place when a route march in fighting order (small pack and equipment) took place, and advancing in artillery formation for open warfare was practised. After the normal seven-day period the cycle continued with 20/Durham LI taking over from 12/East Surrey Regiment once more. On the way in this time three men were wounded, however, this was a very quiet tour in the line, only one fatality, 20/553 Private Robert Longstaff of Middlesbrough who was killed on 14 February, and a total of four wounded. Also at this time Captain W D Hiller was struck off the battalion strength having been evacuated to England sick.

By 17 February it was time to go out again and the battalion marched back to Ontario Camp once again, here Second Lieutenants R M Upton and W P McGibbon joined from 4/Durham LI at Seaham Harbour. A church parade was held on 18 February prior to which the commanding officer inspected the battalion, after which the whole day was spent cleaning up and resting. Apart from fight training, time was also found to allow the buglers time to train together and the next time the battalion went into the line the buglers remained behind to practise. The weather had turned very wet and the mud of the salient was everywhere as the battalion made their way back towards the front line. This time the trenches were found to be in a terrible condition, the thaw meant the trenches were falling to bits.

On 24 February, the 10/Royal West Surrey Regiment of 122 Brigade raided the enemy trenches, the whole battalion going over at 1700 hours in daylight. 20/Durham LI assisted, by sending up white rockets from 1650 until 1705 hours. This brought heavy retaliation on the Durhams' trenches, the enemy assuming that they were also going to be involved in the raid. The Front Line had however been cleared, but was badly blown in as were two communication trenches, casualties were considered light with only four killed and five wounded. Among the dead was Sergeant Winter MM who had led a six-man patrol into No Man's Land at 2315 hours to try to locate an enemy working party. Having located a strong enemy working party the patrol returned

10 Platoon, 20/Durham L I, c.1916. Third row: soldiers Angel, fourth right, and H. Moon, third right. Second row: soldiers Paddy Smith, second left, Fair, fourth left, and McDonald, fifth left. Front row: Bugler J. Reay, second left, Sergeant Foulkes, fourth left, Company Sergeant-Major Jones, fifth left, and Second-Lieutenant Struthers, centre.

9 Platoon, 20/Durham L I, c.1916. Front row: G. Catchpole, Hall, Lance-Corporal J.W. Rawnsley, Sergeant R.S. Falconer, Lieutenant C. Hopkinson, Sergeant Hird, Lance-Corporal W. Raine, unidentified, J. Richards.

A transport section stop at a rest station on the way back from the line, having spent most of the hours of darkness taking rations up to the men at the front.

to the British lines and brought down artillery fire on the German working party. Later, the patrol went out again to attempt to discover the extent of the enemy's losses. They encountered a German patrol and a fight ensued. Sergeant Winter was seen to bayonet one of the enemy soldiers, before retiring to his party mortally wounded himself. Unfortunately, Sergeant Winter died and a private soldier was also killed and one more wounded. The bodies of the dead were brought in with the wounded man by the rest of the patrol. The next day the whole battalion was employed repairing the damage caused by the enemy gunners. Sporadic shelling occurred throughout the day and altogether nine men were wounded, with 33177 Private David Young dying from his wounds the following day.

Early next morning, having arranged a code with the artillery, a patrol went out to try to locate another enemy fatigue detail thought to be in No Man's Land. The enemy working party was located in their own trench system and the code word signalled back to the gunners. Immediately a barrage came down on the German party. From the British Front Line, white Very lights were sent up and rapid fire opened from Lewis guns and rifles at the enemy who could plainly be seen. Later 12/East Surrey Regiment arrived to take their turn once more.

Back at Ontario Camp after his first spell in the trenches George Thompson found he had some new friends, who he vividly remembered:

> The biggest problem was lice and I suffered from them myself both times I was in France. I suffered from impetigo sores that came from rubbing, as far as I know you got a sore on your leg and it turned septic, that came from lice. The lice themselves used to irritate, the irritation was tremendous and on a hot day, dear me they were terrible. Another thing about them, when we were in our full equipment on the march, we had shoulder straps and ammunition pouches on our chests. Well that imposed a pressure that the lice didn't like and they all gathered in the V of the neck where there was no pressure. People used to send things from home, "Keating's Powder" and such like, not that they were very

effective. The most effective way was to take your tunic off, light a candle and run the flame of the candle up the seams of the jacket, they were alive with lice and kill them that way, you couldn't get rid of them altogether though, they aren't all gone in any case. One day I was sitting on the step of the hut at Reninghelst, busy with running the candle flame up the seam of my tunic when the Medical Officer went past saying, "That's right lad, get at it." I remember that distinctly.

Out at rest this time a boxing competition was organised, as was an inter-company football competition. In the first round A Company beat B Company 2-1, no result is given for the C Company-D Company tie, but in the final A Company emerged winners, beating D Company 8 goals to 2. There was also a battalion church parade. Those of the Church of England and the Non Conformists held their service in the YMCA hut, whilst Holy Mass for the Roman Catholics was held in the local parish church at Reninghelst. The battalion also made good use of the baths in the same village, but by 5 March it was time to give the East Surreys a rest and the battalion was back in the line again, that night it snowed but when daylight came a thaw set in, it was very misty during the day which gave very poor visibility. In the sector held by the Durhams things were described as 'quiet' but a mile or so to the south the Germans raided the trenches held by the 16th (Irish) Division, this fact kept those in the line on the alert. As the tour of duty came to an end Second Lieutenant W O M Stephenson was slightly wounded as the battalion was being relieved. Baths, training, working parties, boxing and football all featured in this period of rest, the officers beating the sergeants 5-1 but only managing to draw against the corporals, 1-1.

During the next spell in the line the Germans shelled Battalion Headquarters on a number of occasions, each time no casualties occurred, but on 18 March the signals dugout received a direct hit and was wrecked. Sunderland Farm was also hit by several shells and set on fire. However the battalion had a prearranged scheme and the building had been evacuated so again no casualties occurred. After being relieved once more and moving back to Ontario Camp the news came through that Second Lieutenant L W Andrews was posted to the 22/Durham LI (Pioneers). On 24 March heavy firing was heard along the front line and having gone out to rest and spend the day training on the ranges at 1940 hours the battalion 'stood to' expecting to be called back into the line, however the order was cancelled shortly afterwards and they 'stood down', for the expected attack had not materialised.

The main event of this period of rest was a parade at Chippewa Camp when the Divisional Commander, Major General S T B Lawford, presented medal ribbons to those officers and other ranks who had carried outs of acts of gallant conduct to earn their awards. The next day four junior officers, Second Lieutenants J G Pacy, G M Little, F Brunt and J A Ballantyne reported for duty. The next few days, the normal round of training carried on, but on 29 March the weather was so wet that the battalion remained in camp preparing for the next tour in the line.

Having moved back into the line the battalion came under strong enemy artillery activity daily. Each day one man was killed and a few wounded, on 1 April 20/987 Private Ernest Pounder was killed, next day 20/529 Private Malcolm McCulloch and on 3 April 28337 Private Joshua Gailes was killed when the communication trench 'Queen Victoria Street' was badly knocked about by enemy retaliation to British medium trench mortars. The next day it was the turn of the Front Line and at night Crater Lane was badly hit, Second Lieutenant J A Ballantyne having been with the battalion less than a week was evacuated wounded. Arriving at Ontario Camp once more the battalion paraded for medical inspection and five officers and 239 other

20/987 Private E Pounder, a 19-year-old Sunderland man killed in action 1 April 1917.

89

An infantry transport section loading barbed wire pickets onto mules for carrying to the lines.

ranks were inoculated. The next day the battalion marched to the Steenvoorde area and billeted for the night. The next day the march continued to Nordpeene and another overnight billet. A third day of route marching took the battalion to Eperlecques and into new billets. It was noted with some pride that 20/Durham LI and 23/Middlesex Regiment were the only battalions that did not have a single man fall out on this three days of marching.

20/575 Lance Corporal R. Henderson from Pittington, killed in action, 26 May 1917, aged 24.

That evening a lecture for all officers and NCOs of 123 Brigade was held at Houlle. The Brigade Commander, Brigadier General C W E Gordon spoke to the assembly and informed them that the Brigade would soon launch an attack upon the Damstrasse. Three battalions would be in the line: 23/Middlesex Regiment on the right, 10/R West Kent Regiment in the centre, and 11/Queen's Royal West Surrey Regiment on the left.

These battalions were supported by A, B and D Companies of 20/Durham LI respectively. C Company 20/Durham LI was to be split up to provide mopping up parties for each battalion. Training began in earnest, but was hampered by bad weather; on a number of days the battalion returned to billets early owing to the cold, the wind and the snow. A new practice was tried out on the range: firing the rifle and operating the Lewis gun from the hip. It proved successful. By 13 April the battalion was practising wave attacks on a definite objective. The divisional commander came and watched each company in turn go through their paces. In the evening, after returning to billets, the commanding officer lectured all officers, and then the platoon commanders in turn lectured their platoons. On Sunday voluntary services were held in the morning and later A Company football team defeated an RAMC Company by two goals to nil. The same day Second Lieutenants W D Clark and W H Kipps reported their arrival from 3/Durham LI, both being posted to A Company. By 16 April the manoeuvres were being carried out with the other three battalions and digging in and being held up by a strongpoint was practised. However the weather worsened and training was cancelled, the men being lectured instead. The commanding officer instituted a new method of sending in reports during an attack: each officer made a number of traces of the brigade front from the main map at battalion headquarters. On these maps they simply marked their own location and that of the enemy and also any troops to the left and right. This method proved successful and saved a large amount of writing. On 21 April an exact replica of the attack was practised, watched by the Army Corps commander General Morland.

On 23 April it was time to leave the training area and with 20/Durham LI in the vanguard 123 Brigade began moving back towards the front line. The first day's march, fourteen miles, took them to billets in Waemers Cappel, again not one man of the battalion fell out. The next day the village of Steenvoorde was reached, followed on the third day by the battalion reaching Reninghelst, here A and B Companies returned to Ontario Camp and C and D Companies were housed for a few days in huts at Micmac Camp.

The period in training was recalled many years later by George Thompson, who had by now been on a Lewis Gun Course and was part of the Lewis Gun Section of 10 Platoon, C Company.

About the middle of March, as far as I remember, we marched from Reninghelst to a village quite near St Omer. In the village we slept in barns and during the day we were taken out for battle training in the fields. They had laid out big coloured tapes, Blue, Red and Yellow. These three colours represented the Front, Support and Reserve lines of the Germans. Day after day we launched attacks on these three lines. We just lined up further back and went forward as we were ordered to go forward. The idea was to seize all these three lines, we just went on over and over, advancing over these three lines in a long straight line with the men five yards apart or something like that. We were there about three weeks. There was a rifle range quite near and we did some shooting too. We went back to a camp near Reninghelst and then we were put to work digging gun pits and camouflaging them with branches and green netting.

On 26 April the brigade commander came and inspected the battalion's boots and afterwards the time was spent fitting and adjusting gas helmets and box respirators. Having had a few weeks out of the line the battalion must have had a bit of a shock, when on 28 and 29 April, they were on working parties for the Royal Engineers and Royal Field Artillery and the enemy began shelling the new dump at Ouderdom and the new railway east of Reninghelst. This shelling continued, at intervals throughout the night, then on 2 May at about 2200 hours the gas alarm was sounded and immediately the whole battalion stood to, until orders were received that everything was alright and they were stood down. At 0120 hours the fire alarm sounded and the commanding officer's hut and the Battalion Orderly Room were found to be on fire and eventually burnt to the ground, despite valiant efforts by men of the battalion. All the battalion papers and official documents were lost and most of the CO's personal kit was burnt. As the huts had been tarred, the flames resisted all efforts to put the fire out.

The next day 20/Durham LI relieved 21/King's Royal Rifle Corps in reserve, A and B Companies moved into Micmac Camp and C and D Companies marched to billets in Dickebusch.

Preparations for the Battle of Messines: left, mining operations; above, the barrage; below, results of a bombardment – German dead; below, front-line area on Messines Ridge.

The battalion now provided working parties and although the enemy artillery were actively shelling the reserve area, the only casualties were Second Lieutenant G M Little, and one other rank both wounded. On the night of 6 May the enemy artillery had a bit of luck and landed two direct hits on D Company officers' dug-out in Dickebusch; although no officers were hurt, four men were wounded. All night long the enemy heavily shelled the back area and in Dickebusch the men of C and D Companies had to lie out in the open fields to avoid becoming casualties. The shelling carried on into 7 May, so in an effort to stop the enemy shelling the back areas, at 0855 hours every gun in Second Army opened rapid fire for five minutes on the enemy communication trenches. The enemy retaliated at 2200 hours, so orders were given to repeat the barrage at 2300 hours and to repeat it at 2315 hours. This was successful and for the remainder of the night the enemy was quiet.

The next few days were spent providing working parties until on 12 May the battalion relieved 23/Middlesex Regiment in the line, the handover being complete by 1715 hours. That night a few shells were dropped on the Brasserie but the British heavy guns replied, firing on a position known as North Redoubt. A small draft of eighteen trained men reported to the battalion during the day with further drafts of fifty-two and forty-six men arriving on 13 and 14 of May respectively. The British Artillery now began cutting the enemy barbed wire and shelling his front line and at the same time the British trench mortar batteries joined in, by 16 May it was reported that practically all the enemy barbed wire had been destroyed on the battalion front. The next night 20/Durham LI carried out a silent raid on the German trenches opposite their position and were fortunate enough to bring in a prisoner. The raid was repeated the following night, but this time the enemy were ready and waiting for them. The raiders had two men wounded and were forced to retire back to their own lines.

On 20 May Second Lieutenants W G Penrice and A G Roden arrived from South Shields, where they had served with 3/Durham LI. Relieved by 12/East Surrey Regiment the Durhams moved back to Micmac and became the reserve battalion once more. Working parties once again were the order of the day and where possible training was carried out. Meanwhile all officers and NCOs visited Reninghelst, where a model of the trenches about to be attacked had been constructed. For the next week or so the battalion provided working parties, although each night there were one or two wounded only two men died of wounds.

On 30 May an attempt was made to raid the enemy lines near North Redoubt. It was a bright moonlit night with hardly a breath of wind, hardly the best conditions for raiding. It was arranged that a party of signallers would be in No Man's Land with a telephone. When the raiders reached the enemy wire, the signallers would pass a message to the artillery. This would bring a barrage down on the enemy front and support lines. The plan worked perfectly, the barrage fell in all the right places and on time, but the enemy had gone, no wounded had been left behind and all dugouts and posts had been cleared. The raiders however suffered two casualties, both slightly wounded.

The next day was spent on working parties until on 1 June relief, in the shape of 26/Royal Fusiliers arrived. By 1500 hours 20/Durham LI were well on their way to Woodcote Camp, they did, however, have three men wounded on the way out. The next few days at Woodcote were taken up with inspections, bathing and being fitted out with changes of clothing. On 4 June the news came through that the adjutant, Captain F Wayman had been awarded the Military Cross in the King's Birthday Honours list, probably for his work at Flers the previous year. The same day the GOC 41st Division came and spoke to the assembled battalion at the conclusion of which, the battalion gave him three resounding cheers.

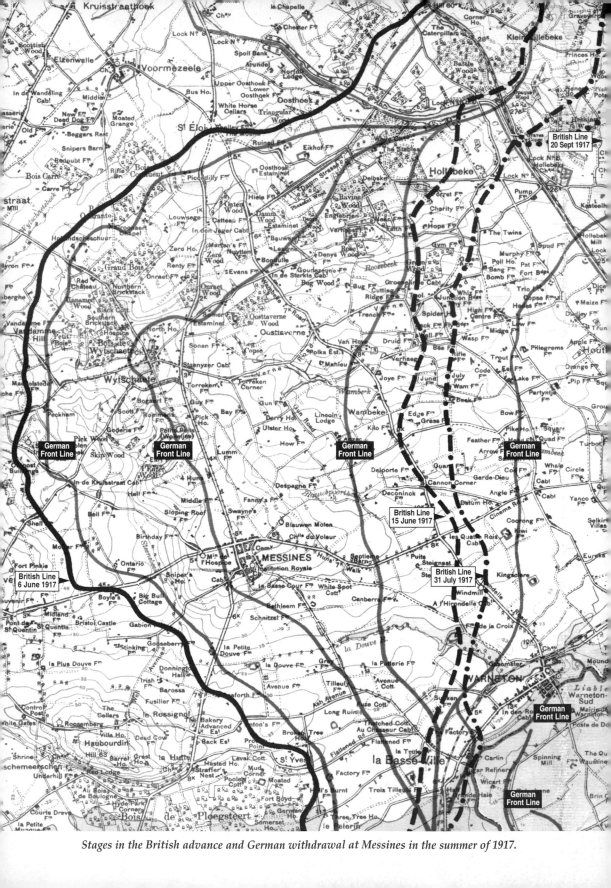

Stages in the British advance and German withdrawal at Messines in the summer of 1917.

Infantry waiting to go over the top, 6 June 1917.

Artist's impression of the attack at Messines.

5 June 1917 was a holiday for 20/Durham LI, inter-company sports were held, all platoons and companies being well represented in all the events and at the end a prize-giving took place.

Now all was ready for the start of the battle that was planned to push the enemy out of Flanders, the whole series of battles would eventually be known as the Third Battle of Ypres, but the one that was about to take place would be known as the Battle of Messines. Ever since the New Year of 1916 tunnelling companies of the Royal Engineers had been working underground all along the eastern edge of the Ypres Salient digging tunnels and constructing mines. Although mines had been exploded on the Somme the previous July, this time the attack had been planned on a grand scale, although twenty-one mines had been dug, no less than nineteen mines would explode simultaneously at Zero Hour. Many of the working parties, which the men of 20/Durham LI had been employed on, were for the tunnelling companies. The regiments of the north country, their ranks filled with miners from the Northumberland, Durham and Yorkshire coal fields were always in demand. Many of them preferred the work underground, as they felt they were back at home in a northern coal mine. The shafts in the salient had to be driven deeper than normal to get below the high water table of Flanders, and then down deeper to try to avoid detection by the enemy. One of these was Bus House Sap, where 20/Durham LI manned a pumping station to keep the mine clear of water. It was recalled by Private George Thompson:

> We took turns at pumping water out, there was a hand pump with a lever on it and you just stood beside it and pumped up and down. This pumped the water out of the sap and over the parados into the land behind the trench. There were three of us on the job and we relieved each other. We did about twenty-four hours on the job and then we were relieved.

Now after eighteen months the chambers had been excavated and filled with ammonal and packed tightly with sandbags to ensure as much of the blast as possible would go upwards from deep under the German Front Line positions.

It was now the time for all the hard work to pay off: all along the front, from Ploegsteert Wood in the south, to Hill 60 in the north, the men of the assaulting divisions began to move into position. During the day, in 41st Division area, the enemy had shelled Ridge Wood and Scottish Wood but had no effect on 20/Durham LI, who were lying resting nearby. At midnight the battalion moved off by companies at 5 minute intervals to the assembly area, where mine tape had been laid out for the battalion to form up on. By 0200 hours the battalion was in position as had been practised, three companies in support to the three leading the battalion and the fourth company deployed in half platoons, to act as 'moppers-up' across the brigade front.

Then at 0310 hours on 7 June 1917 nineteen mines exploded and at Zero hour + three minutes the battalion began to advance. They moved forward to their objective without stopping to the enemy front line and then staying closed up they pushed on to the support line. There were only a few casualties, owing to the fact that the troops had stayed close up behind the British barrage, the enemy counter barrage fell behind the battalion. The trenches were littered with enemy dead, mostly killed by the British Artillery and the 'moppers-up' soon cleared the trenches of any survivors. The rest of the battalion pushed forward and soon they had dug a good strong line of trenches, including strong points. In this position special attention was paid to the traverses, these were made as large as fourteen feet across, as enfilade fire was expected from the left flank, or further north in the salient. The fact that the new line had been pushed so far forward was a bonus for the Wearsiders. The enemy continually shelled their old positions thus doing little damage to the new line. Machine gun posts were chosen well forward of the new line, these posts had excellent fields of fire and good cover and all hands worked hard to get them dug in; as soon as the moppers-up finished their task, they joined the diggers as no time was to be lost or wasted and in particular souvenir hunting was not allowed, as a counter-attack was expected at any time. Having gone so far into the enemy line the battalion morale was very high and

Lieutenant W. G. Penrice joined the battalion at the end of May. He was killed in action 7 June 1917.

Captain A. S. Davidson, 20/Durham LI.

An artist's impression of the fighting at Messines 7 June 1917.

20/576 Private J. W. Alderson from Hetton le Hole, missing 7 June 1917.

20/379 Private R Angel from West Hartlepool, missing 7 June 1917

20/859 Signaller J Burn, a Darlington man, died of wounds 8 June 1917.

20/312 Private M Duffy from Fencehouses, died of wounds 8 June 1917.

that of the enemy shaken to breaking point, as one captured officer is reported to have said, 'We are done! The English are too good for us.' Casualties had been 'light' among the officers, only Second Lieutenants Upton and Penrice had been killed, and Second Lieutenant Kipps wounded. But among the rank and file, eighty had been killed eighty-five wounded, seven missing and two gassed.

George Thompson had got through unscathed and years later recalled the events leading up to and during the battle.

On 5 June we left that area and went to a village called Meteren, only about a mile and a half or a couple of miles away. On the following day we were told it was a day off duty, that was on the sixth of June, and they organised inter-company football matches. The biggest surprise of all was instead of bully beef stew, which we had eaten for months on end we got rabbit stew, it was quite a change! Then some of the old soldiers who had been at the Somme were very uncomfortable with this sort of cheering you up for the battle which was to come, for that was the idea. We younger ones knew it was unusual but were quite ready to accept what was to happen, was going to happen and that's what we were preparing for.

Just after tea there was a Church of England Communion Service in a barn, I'm C of E so I went, there would only be about a dozen or so of us there. The padre had his chalice on an upturned barrel with a candle, I remember that distinctly. I was pleased I went and this of course added to what was about to happen. Just as it was dusk we set off, back again, once again into the old area. We crossed by overland route to Voormezeele and waited there for an hour or two in a trench and then we moved to St Eloi. Then we lined up, long lines in front of the Messines Ridge. The front was very uneasy, there was regular gunfire and the sky was lurid red with the flashes from the guns and shells, like a nightmare really. After we lined up I don't know how long we stood with our bayonets fixed and so on with a Second Lieutenant in front of us, when there was a terrific explosion which shook the ground that we stood on. A cylinder of yellow and red flame shot mighty high up into the air, I don't know how high, but a terrific height. This was our Bus House sap going up underneath Whysheate village which the Germans had turned into a fortress. Then the guns started a terrific barrage, continuous thundering, thundering, thundering and over our heads we could hear the hissing of our machine-gun bullets. Our machine-gunners were plastering the enemy ridge with machine-gun bullets. Then the whistle blew and we went forward.

It was light enough to see by then and the opposition was NIL, absolutely NIL. I was in the third wave, the first and second waves just kept going ahead of us, they weren't stopped by anything, there were one or two dead bodies about, German and English but not many. Our objective was this sunken road which we reached, it had been quite a fortress but our guns had hammered it to pieces. The concrete emplacements were all smashed in, the road and the banks were chewed up. We planted our Lewis gun in a shell hole on the edge of the sunken road and that was our position for the time being. As night fell we were ordered forward against an expected counter-

Former German positions being consolidated by British infantry.

attack, but it didn't materialise. The next day was not a day of fighting but of burying the dead bodies. We put them in a shell hole then covered them over with soil and stuck the rifle in the ground upside down, so that some time later the real burial party could take them away and bury them properly somewhere.

There was this very nice looking German lad laid dead on the edge of our shell hole where we had the Lewis gun. A very nice looking young fellow, with a fair moustache. I remember I was very sorry for him lying there, still he was there nearly all day. Messines was a success, the most successful of any, the only thing was it was only a 1,000 yard advance. You know all those years of preparation of mines and that sort of thing, just for a short distance. We were relieved after about four days and went back to where our old front line had been.

The work of consolidating the position carried on, unwounded enemy prisoners were used to assist with the removal of the wounded and for fetching water. Wiring commenced and soon a strong line of barbed wire was in place to protect the new line. Another task that was carried out was that of salvage, any type of equipment was rescued and dumps formed, this was then transported to the rear for repair or refurbishment prior to being put back into service. The next few days were marked by the enemy using all calibres of artillery to shell the British positions. On 10 June at around 2230 hours a red light was sent up, this was the signal that the enemy were counter-attacking and the British artillery and machine guns immediately opened a terrific fire. The enemy artillery joined in and before long a German SOS rocket was seen, evidently the Germans in their front line thought an attack was coming also. Throughout the night both sides kept up sporadic firing, although little damage was done to the trenches held by 20/Durham LI. At 1800 hours on 11 June A and B Companies were relieved and moved back to the R Line near the Bois Confluent, where they spent a quiet night. Exactly twenty-four hours later they were joined by C and D Companies. The next few days were spent training and although 20/Durham LI were earmarked to support an attack by 122 Brigade, they were not required and returned to the bivouacs in R Lines. Training was carried out under company arrangements, with a special musketry class for NCOs. A new sector was to be taken over, so each company commander went forward during the evening of 18 June to reconnoitre the new sector, whilst Second Lieutenant Shepherdson with Battalion Headquarters went up and established a new headquarters in the line. At 0300 hours on 19 June, one officer per company and one NCO per platoon went up and took over the new line of trenches to be held by the battalion. They remained in the line all day until dusk, when assisted by guides of 12/East Surrey Regiment they brought the battalion up and took over the sector of Optic Trench to its junction with Oblique Row. In the early hours of 22 June two Germans presumably lost were seen standing in front of the wood in front of the battalion strongpoint. Several rifles opened fire upon them and one was seen to stagger into the wood, closely followed by his companion. During the following day Major G McNicholl DSO was wounded along with seventeen other ranks. That night 10/Royal West Kent Regiment came into the line and took over, 20/Durham LI went into support, the companies remaining in the old German Front Line. Three companies were relieved and immediately moved back each using a different route which hastened the march back, thus avoiding casualties had the enemy got wind of the relief taking place. The next three days were spent in support at the Spoil Bank, no work, save carrying rations and water into the front line, took place. Although there was a steady trickle of casualties as each day one man was killed and several wounded. On 27 June the battalion took over from 10/Royal West Kent Regiment in the front line. C Company, 20/Durham LI took over the left front and D Company the right front, with A Company in support and B Company in the old British Front Line. During the night all companies garrisoned the trenches, but during the day the garrison was reduced to four Lewis gun teams per Company. Each Lewis gun team had four bombers attached to it. The weather had turned wet and the ground became very bad for movement and the trenches were now becoming extremely muddy.

20/572 Private Norman Morcambe, another man from Hutton le Hole, he was killed in action 26 June 1917.

So after a few days in the line, on the night of 30 June, with heavy rain falling, which turned to a continuous drizzle, the men of 23/London Regiment, part of the 47th London Division, arrived and took over the front line from 20/Durham LI.

Chapter Seven

1917 – July to December

AT 0300 HOURS ON 1 JULY, 20/Durham LI left the line and marched back to Murrunbidgee Camp, where on arrival breakfast was served, after which the whole battalion got their heads down and slept. At 1500 hours dinner was served and then the battalion paraded at 1730 hours. Off they set again and marched to Mont des Cats, where they arrived at 2230 hours. The next day was spent re-equipping and sorting out the platoons, as this was going on Second Lieutenant E Smith arrived with a draft of 234 other ranks from the Infantry Base Depot. Nearly all of them had been out with the BEF before and brought a useful level of experience with them. The training that was to be carried out now was in preparation for the forthcoming attack that would open the series of battles that would become known as the Battle of Passchendaele. 41st Division would be the left hand division of SECOND Army, and under the command of Lieutenant General Sir Thomas Morland's X Corps. To their left were II Corps of FIFTH Army, who would suffer during the first days of the battle.

A Sunderland man, 20/387 Private A Coyle, wounded in 1916 he was transferred to the Manchester Regiment and killed in action 30 July 1917.

Over the next week the battalion carried out every possible type of training: map reading, Lewis gun, bombing, close order drill and a lot of time was spent on the range improving the battalion's musketry. The nearest baths were over four miles away and each company went in turn, no doubt de-lousing in the process. On 6 July another draft arrived, this time 115 men from 2/7/Durham LI.

On the afternoon of 9 July ceremonial drill was practised in preparation for an inspection by the GOC, and then again the following morning. Finally the day came and at 0900 hours on 11 July the battalion formed up *en masse* for inspection and presentation of medal ribbons, to those who had won gallantry awards, by the General Officer Commanding 41st Division, Major General S T B Lawford. The general expressed his satisfaction at what he had seen and urged the old soldiers of the battalion to tell the new drafts what an excellent fighting record and name the battalion had made for itself. Four days later the brigadier inspected all the new men who had arrived since 7 June; this was followed in the afternoon by a brigade sporting competition in which the battalion was most successful. The same evening they carried out a practice in forming up in waves, on taped lines, in the dark. A number of useful lessons were learned which would benefit the battalion later. The whole brigade took part in a practice attack the next night, forming up at 1800 hours: the previous day's experience paid off and the brigadier was quite happy with what he saw.

On 19 July all officers and NCOs were taken to Reninghelst, where a large model of the ground over which the battalion was to attack had been made. The plan of attack was explained to all present and they were able to familiarise themselves with the key positions. While this was going on the regimental medical officer organised a stretcher-bearing competition, which proved a great success. There was another brigade parade on 20 July, followed afterwards by a brigade drill competition, every platoon in the brigade taking part. For 20/Durham LI, Number 6 Platoon of B Company came in a very creditable third place. Further practice attacks were carried out, but bad luck hit 123 Brigade even before they went back up the line. The brigade commander, Brigadier General C W E Gordon, late Black Watch and his brigade major, Captain G F Pragnell an officer on the General List, had gone forward to carry out a reconnaissance of the ground over which the brigade was to attack. As they came near a position known as the Bluff, the party came under enemy shellfire and both officers were killed and were buried at Reninghelst the following day.

The brigade started moving up; the first move for 20/Durham LI was to Wood Camp, which they left at 1400 on 25 July heading for the front line. At Ridge Wood a halt was called and the battalion was provided with tea. Then it was onwards once more into the line via Spoil Bank and Ravine Wood. C Company took over a line of advanced posts with D Company in support in the ravine in Fusilier Wood. B Company held the Caterpillar with A Company in support in Ravine Wood. Battalion headquarters was close to B Company in the Caterpillar and the leading companies were placed under command of Captain A Pumphrey, who had his headquarters in the ravine. On the way in four men were wounded. The news came in that the expected attack had been indefinitely postponed, so it was decided that the companies would rotate through the various posts, in order to familiarise everyone with the positions. However the German artillery was becoming a real nuisance and each day the casualty lists were growing longer. On 28 July the battalion lost Second Lieutenant A R Willis and five men killed, thirty-two wounded, eight gassed

German gun emplacement smashed by British artillery near Zonnebeke, 23 September 1917.

and one man missing, probably blown to smithereens. A Company, owing to the enemy shelling, withdrew into Caterpillar Wood leaving only the Lewis gun teams to hold the strongpoints in the ravine in Fusilier Wood. The next day the companies moved round again and again lots of casualties, forty-two wounded and thirty-six gassed. Word came through that the attack would now take place at 0350 hours on 31 July, so that evening, Captain Pumphrey reported back to Battalion Headquarters and Second Lieutenant Shepherdson went out to where string had been laid as a marker and replaced it with the white tape, on which the assaulting waves were to line up. The battalion moved off to the assembly area on the evening of 30 June and on the way in ran into a heavy enemy barrage which caused a number of casualties.

Second Lieutenant W R Brooke 'on his way to the assembly area he led his men with great skill in pitch darkness and under shellfire, keeping them on the move forward at a time when delay would have been serious. Later he displayed great courage, coolness and good leadership during the attack and afterwards when consolidating the position' was how his Military Cross citation described his gallantry.

Before Zero Hour the battalion had moved into position and were lined up on the tapes and ready to go. On the right D Company, under the command of Second Lieutenant Fletcher, were in touch with 10/Royal West Kent Regiment on the right, and formed up with two platoons in the leading wave and the third platoon behind, half as a carrying party and half for mopping up. Behind them in two waves came B Company, led by Captain Fulljames. On the left in the same wave formation, under the command of Captain Hand was C Company, with their left flank

Captain F. Wayman, the battalion adjutant, was killed instantly when a shell hit the Battalion Headquarters dug-out on 31 July 1917.

resting on the Klein Zillebeke road; this was the left flank of X Corps and SECOND Army, and the next troops to the north were from 24th Division of FIFTH Army. Behind C Company was A Company also in two waves, with Second Lieutenant Britton in command. At Zero Hour the leading waves were to assault the enemy-held Imperfect Trench, known as the Red Line. The second wave was to follow the leading wave and mop up any enemy left in the Red Line and then push on and, supported by the third and fourth waves, assault the enemy second line. Once this line was taken the third and fourth waves, or what was left of them were to pass through and under the cover of a covering barrage dig a new line to be known as the Green Line some 400 yards further forward and sited for observation. Behind that a Blue Line would be dug, which was to be a support line. The divisional Royal Engineers were to support the battalion and assist with the consolidation of the Red Line, but while 20/Durham LI were there the Engineers did not turn up.

At 0350 hours then, the whistles blew and some sources state that the battalion buglers sounded 'The Charge', as the battalion went 'over the top', the enemy opened fire with their heavy machine guns and down came the enemy barrage in answer to their infantry's SOS rockets. In the teeth of this hail of fire, taking casualties as they went, the leading waves of 20/Durham LI ejected the Germans from Imperfect Trench. What the officers and men of the attacking British battalions did not know was that the enemy had built lots of concealed concrete pill boxes, which the British barrage had failed to destroy, all these positions provided covering fire for other posts each with interlocking arcs of fire.

Having taken Imperfect Trench, the battalion pressed on to the Blue Line, but were unable to get any further forward, so they started to dig in. The enemy snipers and machine-gunners were causing a lot of casualties, and on the right flank the enemy held their ground. However, on the left the attack was reasonably successful.

Second Lieutenant W C Brown, in the words of his Military Cross citation:

...led his company boldly and skillfully to their objective, carrying other troops with him. After reaching the objective under heavy shellfire he at once reorganized not only his own men but men of other regiments.

Another platoon commander led his men with great skill and gallantry and was awarded the same medal; Second Lieutenant Bernard Wilkinson led his company to their objective with great ability. Having reached it he at once cleared the enemy dug-outs, organised his prisoners, dug a well-sited trench and mounted a machine gun he had captured, as part of the defence.

But now it started to rain, the start of the wettest European autumn for many years.

The battalion was roughly located along the Blue Line, but officer casualties were mounting, Second Lieutenants Fletcher and Clark were both wounded. Second Lieutenant Russell had sprained his ankle on the way in to the assembly area and took no further part in the action. But some men of C Company led by Captain M Hand pushed too far forward and were cut off and never heard from again. Also with C Company was Private George Thompson, who recorded:

We knew something was pending, we knew Messines was only a beginning, but it was 30 July, the night before that we knew anything was happening. The night before the battle we occupied some trenches further back from the front, we lined up there and the rum ration came round, three or four times if you wanted it. Towards morning, still in the dark we moved off towards the front and lined up again on the tape in the dark, one thing we didn't expect to meet when we attacked was the concrete pill boxes, this was the first time they had been encountered. The Germans built these concrete emplacements with a machine-gun slot in the front of them.

A British sentry silhouetted against the ruins of the Cloth Hall in Ypres, September 1917.

Captain Fulljames was wounded and Second Lieutenant Britton killed both near the Blue Line and among the men the casualties were very heavy. Tragedy now hit the Wearsiders, an enemy shell hit the battalion headquarters dug-out, the adjutant, Captain F Wayman, was killed instantly and the commanding officer, Lieutenant Colonel North, was slightly wounded. Word was sent to the rear and Lieutenant Cox was ordered up to take over as Adjutant, but before he reached battalion Headquarters he was wounded by shrapnel. The next officer chosen was Second Lieutenant Walton who was killed shortly afterwards.

20/637 Private N. Rowell, from Seaham, killed in action 31 July 1917.

At this point the enemy mounted a counter-attack on the right. The CO, even though he was wounded, collected an assortment of battalion headquarters personnel, batmen, cooks, signallers, storemen and clerks and fifteen men of B Company. Armed with a Lewis gun, the CO himself led the counter-attack and was again wounded. Command of the battalion fell to Captain Pumphrey, who as soon as he could sent Second Lieutenant Shepherdson back to the rear to bring up two companies of 21/King's Royal Rifle Corps from support positions. Meanwhile the forward positions were involved in bitter hand to hand fighting; each enemy position was taken with the bomb and the bayonet. However the German Artillery now put down a massive barrage that covered all the original assembly area, No Man's Land and the area of the enemy line captured. Through this storm of shells Second Lieutenant Shepherdson brought up the KRRC companies who were placed between B Company and the remains of C and D Companies. On the right flank, contact was made with 10/Royal West Kent Regiment which had established a visual signalling station which was in communication with the artillery in the rear. By this method Captain Pumphrey was able to call down SOS fire on the battalion's right flank. With those men available firing rapid rifle fire and the Lewis gunners joining in and along with the assistance of a Vickers gun of 123/Machine Gun Company, which the crew had managed to get up, yet another enemy counter-attack was broken up.

By nightfall the front had grown reasonably quiet, but small enemy parties continually tried to penetrate the forward positions. Battalion casualties had been very heavy, among the officers there were three killed, five wounded and one missing, presumed dead. Among the men the initial figures showed eighteen killed, 153 wounded and seventy-three missing, a total of 244, however when the battalion got out of the line and revised the figures there were no less than 431 casualties.

One of those whose sojourn with the battalion ended at this time was Private George Thompson, who in later years said:

> *After the artillery bombardment we went forward in the usual way, I was in the fourth wave, we were well back but everybody got into trouble that morning, the first, second, third waves, all the lot of us because of the concrete pill boxes' machine-gun fire. There wasn't much artillery fire. These pill boxes were so built that one covered the other. If you were busy attacking one, you came under fire from another one, they all covered each other. The only way to clear them, which some of our men used was to creep up underneath the machine-gun slot and put a Mills bomb through the slot. One bomb was sufficient as a rule to*

Another officer killed in action on 31 July 1917 was Lieutenant J. A. Ballantyne.

A German OP made of strong reinforced concrete. These turned the German line into a fortress which the British had to take by storm.

Bombers attacking a pillbox: this photograph was probably posed on a training area and was made into a stereoview card.

clear the inside of them.

I hadn't gone much further forward before I was hit; I saw the blood running down my hand and so on. It was painful of course and that is as much as I know of the battle. In a shell hole a friend bandaged the wound and I went back, I had been wounded in the hand by shrapnel. I was walking wounded and walked back to a Red Cross dug-out; they had a look at the wound and said they thought the hand was fractured. I walked back from there with some wounded men, all walking wounded, to Ouderdom. At Ouderdom there was a Casualty Clearing Station, a CCS to us soldiers, there was an ambulance, well it wasn't an ambulance but a lorry, that picked us up and took us back to a base hospital in Etaples. I was so pleased to get a Blighty wounded.'

After the action the gallantry awards came in: as well as those already mentioned the Commanding Officer, Lieutenant Colonel North received a well-deserved bar to his DSO:

For conspicuous gallantry and devotion to duty. He led his men to the attack with utter disregard of danger under heavy fire and the dash with which his battalion went forward in the attack and secured a considerable number of prisoners was largely due to his fine personal example. He was shortly afterwards severely wounded in the chest and back.

Among the other ranks fourteen Military Medals were awarded but a couple of these were for actions at Messines in June.

On 1 August the Germans again launched a counter-attack which was dispersed by artillery and rifle fire, then that night the remainder of 21/KRRC came up and relieved the Wearsiders, who marched off to reform in Bluff Tunnels, while resting there a sudden enemy barrage took a further toll on the battalion and a further three men were killed and twenty-two wounded. With the CO evacuated wounded, Major R C Smith 1/Durham, LI who up till now had been Second in Command of 11/Queen's Royal West Surrey

being HQ, A, B C and D Companies in that order. Marching with fifty yards between each platoon, at each crossroads or complicated track junction, Headquarter Company dropped off two guides, who had orders to ensure the rest of the battalion took the correct route, which was the track north of Voormezeele, and thence on a new plank road known as Towsey's Walk. On arrival the battalion was accommodated in trenches in the wood.

The next day 20 September was to be the opening of the next stage in the Third Battle of Ypres, known as the Battle of the Menin Road, 41st Division had now come under the command of I ANZAC Corps, commanded by Lieutenant General Sir William Birdwood. Zero Hour was set for 0540 and 123 Brigade were in support to 122 and 124 Brigades, who were both attacking on a two and a half battalion front. The Army Commander had left little to chance and he had ensured there was plenty of artillery support for the attacking battalions. The leading troops of 41st Division went over and met some opposition from enemy machine guns in pill boxes, at 0940 hours orders came for 20/Durham LI to move forward into the British Front Line between Shrewsbury Forest and Bodmin Copse, then at 1145 hours further orders came in for a company to be sent to the divisional right flank and assist 124 Brigade to take its second objective, known as the Blue Line. Accordingly the CO sent D Company on this task.

21884 Private Peter Wilson from Nelson Street, Thornley Colliery, he had been wounded in 1916 serving with 13/Durham LI and when he returned to the front he was posted to 20/Durham LI. He would be wounded again with the latter battalion.

Ten minutes later further orders arrived, that 20/Durham LI would move up into the first objective, the Red Line and dig in there and be ready for an enemy counter-attack. It took until 1400 hours to get up to the Red Line and when they arrived, a runner came in with orders to push on to the Blue Line and join up between 122 and 124 Brigades.

124 Brigade had failed to cross the Bassevillebeek and were held up so 20/Durham LI pushed on and reached the Blue Line about 1500 hours. A couple of hours later orders came in that the battalion would attack and take the third objective, the Green Line, which was on the forward slope of Tower Hamlets Ridge. However these orders were received too late, so the battalion dug in on the backward slope of Tower Hamlets Ridge, beyond the Bassevillebeek. Unfortunately the right flank was 'in the air' owing to the failure of 124 Brigade to get over the beck. But D Company returned at around 1800 hours and dug in. The enemy had been shelling all day although the casualties in the battalion had been light, Second Lieutenant R T Charlton was killed and four other officers wounded, whilst among the men, 44301 Private William Carden, a Londoner and 23434 Private Thomas Robinson from Gateshead, were the only two fatal casualties, with a further six wounded.

Having spent the night in this position, preparations were made to continue the attack on the

20/441 Private Patrick Smith from Brandon won the Military Medal at Tower Hamlets in September 1917. He had fraudulently enlisted into the Gordon Highlanders under the name John Hughes in 1914. He had then deserted and re-enlisted into 20/DLI. On 11 December 1917 he was tried by Field General Courts Martial for striking a superior officer and sentenced to 28 days' field punishment. Later promoted to lance corporal he was reported missing in March 1918, but had been taken prisoner during the German attacks on the Somme.

Green Line next morning. At 0700 hours the expected order came in, in conjunction with 10/Royal West Kent Regiment on the left, each battalion attacking on two half-company fronts. The barrage would come down at 0900 hours and then at 0908 hours the attack would commence. That was the plan; at 0900 hours the barrage consisted of a few shells sent over at intervals. The leading troops went over and advanced some 200 yards to a point where they were compelled to dig in, having suffered heavy casualties. The enemy relied on his rifle and machine-gun fire to hold the position, hardly any shellfire falling on the British troops. In the afternoon at 1500 hours the enemy launched a counter-attack over the Tower Hamlets Ridge, the British inflicted heavy casualties among the Germans who came over at this time and drove the survivors back with rifle and Lewis gun fire. An hour later the enemy put a box barrage around 20/Durham LI's forward position and attempted another counter-attack, a British counter barrage and fire from the infantry put paid to this attack also. Casualties during the day were Captain A Pumphrey DSO and Second Lieutenant N W Cartwright, killed in action, and six other officers wounded, one of whom Second Lieutenant Bambrough would die from his wounds four days later. Among the soldiers thirty-three were dead and 188 wounded. Over the next day the enemy was fairly quiet; both sides had some intermittent shelling, but the casualties in 20/Durham LI were mounting. A further six men were killed and fourteen wounded, along with twenty-one missing. At 0100 hours on 23 September 13/Royal Sussex Regiment arrived and relieved 20/Durham LI, who started on their way back to Micmac Camp, on the way out Second Lieutenant W P McGibbon and six men were killed by shellfire and a further ten men were simply listed as missing. They didn't stay long in Micmac Camp, only long enough to rest and then at 1400 hours they marched to the railway sidings at Hubertshoen and entrained for Caestre. On arrival at Caestre the battalion detrained, then marched to St Sylvestre-Cappel where the battalion went into billets. Here they were joined by a draft from the base depot, among them Hubert Hodnett, originally in the North Staffordshire Regiment, who kept a small diary of his time with the battalion, who wrote:

> We proceed up to the line to join 20/Durham Light Infantry, 123 Brigade 41st Division. Detrain at Caestre, near Hazebrooke and march two kilometres to where we are to be billeted at an old farmhouse. I am put into Number 5 Platoon B Company.

The normal round of cleaning equipment and parades, inspections and reorganisation took place. Meanwhile the Battalion Transport Platoon was proceeding by route march to Wormund, stayed overnight there and continued on to Teteghem the next day.

A convoy of motor buses arrived at St Sylvestre-Cappel on the morning of 26 September and 20/Durham LI was transported to Teteghem, arriving at around 1300 hours, having been transferred from SECOND Army to FOURTH Army. In the late afternoon the battalion transport rejoined the battalion. They were now in the rear area of the defences on the Belgian coast. On 27 September the battalion moved nearer to the line and relieved 2/7/Lancashire Fusiliers in the Sanitorium Sector of the Zuydcoote Sub Sector. Over the next three days the men were given every afternoon off, a lot of time was spent bathing in the sea, on the last day of the month there was a Church Parade in the morning and then the rest of the day was observed as a holiday, the

Casualties at the Battle of the Menin Road Ridge: Top, *Major G. McNicholl DSO, died of wounds 20 September 1917;* centre left, *Lieutenant N. W. H. Cartwright,* right, *Captain A. Pumphrey,* bottom left, *20/578 CSM F. King,* centre, *20/193 Sergeant R. Gloyne all killed in action 21 September 1917; bottom right, 20/724 Private R. France died of wounds 23 September 1917.*

men being free to do as they wished.

The first days of October followed the same pattern, light company training in the morning and bathing in the afternoon. The weather turned wet on 4 October and all training was confined to billets. Preparations were made to go back into the line and two days later they had taken over from 1/7/Manchester Regiment in the left sub sector of the divisional front. That night a corporal and three men were out on patrol on the sea shore and came under attack from *minenwerfers*, fired at some distance, however they were able to avoid being hit and returned safely. Later at 2200 hours the enemy welcomed them back to the front with a heavy artillery barrage mainly landing around the Headquarters of B Company, who suffered four casualties.

The weather became very wild and windy with a certain amount of rain, every night the same four-man patrol went out but there was little to report, the shelling continued by day and only on 10 October, when there was enemy sniper activity was there anything to report. Fortunately the sniper missed his target. The relief by 23/Middlesex Regiment was completed by midnight on 11 October and the battalion

The memorial to the two brothers in the church at Anyhoe, Banbury, Oxfordshire.

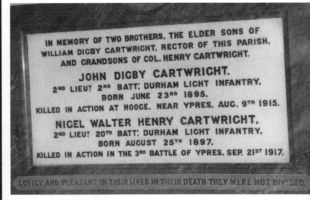

IN MEMORY OF TWO BROTHERS, THE ELDER SONS OF WILLIAM DIGBY CARTWRIGHT, RECTOR OF THIS PARISH, AND GRANDSONS OF COL. HENRY CARTWRIGHT.

JOHN DIGBY CARTWRIGHT.
2ND LIEUT 2ND BATT: DURHAM LIGHT INFANTRY,
BORN JUNE 23RD 1895.
KILLED IN ACTION AT HOOGE, NEAR YPRES. AUG. 9TH 1915.

NIGEL WALTER HENRY CARTWRIGHT,
2ND LIEUT 20TH BATT: DURHAM LIGHT INFANTRY,
BORN AUGUST 25TH 1897.
KILLED IN ACTION IN THE 3RD BATTLE OF YPRES. SEP. 21ST 1917.

LOVELY AND PLEASANT IN THEIR LIVES IN THEIR DEATH THEY WERE NOT DIVIDED.

less A Company, who were not relieved, moved back to Middlesex Camp. Then after a few days they moved further back to Bray Dunes where training in open warfare took place, another feature of the training at this time was that of crossing canals on rafts and boats, having first to make the raft or boat. Over the next two weeks all the various types of training took place and on 23 October they went out to practise canal crossing, but it was so wet that all training was cancelled. A number of junior officers joined during this time spent on the coast. On 29 October the 41st division was told to prepare to move and consequently kit inspections were stepped up and all equipment brought up to scratch.

Crisis on the Italian Front

On the Italian Front the Austrian and German armies had launched a major offensive at the end of October, by 2 November the Austrian 55th Division had forced a crossing of the Tagliamento and the German 12th Division rushed a footbridge at Pinzano and at the same time they forded the river a little further south. The Italian Second Army was routed and according to the Germans, simply disappeared. By 3 November the situation was critical and the Third and Fourth Italian Armies withdrew to the Piave. France and Britain now agreed a plan to aid the Italians. From the British there was to be an initial deployment of an Army Corps and XIV Corps Headquarters, under command of Lieutenant General the Earl of Cavan was selected. Under his command would be two divisions, the 23rd Division who had just come out of the line at Passchendaele and 41st Division who at that time were on the Belgian coast. The 23rd Division began entraining on 6 November, followed by 41st Division on 12 November. However it soon became clear that more troops were needed and 7th Division, 48th Division and 5th Divisions were ordered to move in turn. The French sent two Army Corps, XII [French] Corps consisting of 23rd and 24th [French] Divisions and XXXI [French] Corps with 46th, 47th, 64th and 65th [French] Divisions.

20/37 Private Frank Scott, killed in action 28 September 1917 on the Belgian coast.

Private Hubert Hodnett served with the North Staffordshire Regiment and was posted to 20/Durham LI in France. He kept a small diary from the time of his arrival until he was wounded in March 1918.

Meanwhile 20/Durham LI entrained in two trains at Loon Plage for Italy on 14 November, carrying ten days' rations, the journey was a tonic for the men after the mud of the Ypres Salient, just to be able to relax away from the sound of continuous shelling was such a welcome change. The train took them to Abbeville and on to Amiens, east to Paris and then south to Marseilles. The blue of the Mediterranean and the bright sunlight of the French Riviera brought cheer to everyone on board. At each station they passed through gifts were poured onto the officers and men and when they crossed the Italian Frontier they received a rapturous welcome. When the second train

11 Platoon, 20/Durham LI, in the United Kingdom 1916. Back row: Bugler Hetherington, third left. Third row: soldier T. Lushby, second left. Second row: soldier Paxton, left. First row: named soldiers are Company Sergeant-Major King, Sergeant Dawson.

12 Platoon, 20/Durham LI, in the United Kingdom, 1916. Front row: unidentified, unidentified, unidentified, unidentified, Sergeant Veitch, Captain Risdon, Sergeant Thompson, Sergeant Vasey (?), Lance-Corporal Carr, unidentified, unidentified, unidentified.

A British infantry working party arrive at the scene of their labours on the Italian Front early 1918.

carrying members of 20/Durham LI arrived in Genoa, they were given a public reception by the Mayor of the city. The train took them as far as Isola della Scala, where they detrained on 19 and 20 November and from there it was 'Shanks's Pony', by forced march to Camposampiero where they arrived nine days later on 28 November.

Hubert Hodnett recorded the journey:

> *Entrain at a station outside Dunkirk at 1800 hours, weather still very miserable; now know that we are on our way to Italy. We pass through Amiens, Paris and Lyons; we have beautiful weather and we see some very fine sights. Next day we pass through Marseilles and on to Toulon where we have a very enthusiastic reception from the population. We then travel along the Riviera, very hot down this part, passing through Nice, Cannes and Monte Carlo. We cross the frontier into Italian territory where we see the most beautiful scenery, passing through Savona, Turin, Milan and*

Vincenza. We arrive at Cesca and detrain after a six day journey. March from Cesca (or Cerea?) to proceed to the line. Pass through Padua and finally reach Giavera on November 27 having marched a distance of 110 miles in six days so that we feel rather "fed up". We are now about four miles behind the line at the foot of the Montello Ridge.

The next day they relieved Italian Infantry on the Piave. C Company relieved Number 8 Company, of the 54th Regiment, D Company relieved Number 4 Company, of the 53rd Regiment and B Company relieved Number 7 Company, of the 54th Regiment. The two Regiments relieved formed the Umbrian Brigade of the 1st Italian Division. The sector now held was along the right bank of the Piave above Nervesa. There were scarcely any trenches and an observation line was established along the river bank, but the main trench line was some way back on higher ground. There was going to be a lot of digging and the Durham miners would soon be needed. They had scarcely been in position for twenty-four hours when the commanding officer went out on a reconnaissance of the new area, the Austrians sent over a few stray shells and the CO was badly wounded and died from his wounds. Command of the battalion now passed to Major A V A Gayer DSO 23/Middlesex Regiment, who was soon promoted to lieutenant colonel.

The battalion proceeds up the line, rather difficult journey as there are many hills to get up. Anyhow, we get there and relieve the Italians on the River Piave. At this time the great Austrian offensive has come to a standstill. The Austrians do not disturb us much while going up, being unaware of the presence of any British troops on that front at the time. C Company goes on outpost duty along the river bank while our company are in support in a big cave in the rocks. We stay there

British positions on the Piave.

for four days, during which time things are pretty quiet; we just have a few whiz bangs over occasionally. We then relieve C Company on outpost duty. Very intense cold prevails at this time. The CO, Colonel Smith is killed by shell fire; we have about six other casualties altogether, so that we had a rather quiet time on the whole. The battalion is relieved by the Royal Fusiliers of 124 Brigade and we march back to billets at Selva. Very heavy snowstorms and intense cold prevail. Being our first rest since landing in Italy I have a good look round and see many interesting things. Most of the refugees having left with the approach of the Austrians, the places are rather quiet, but many are returning again as the Austrians had now been definitely held up on the last range of mountains.

Captain Harold Goodley. Originally with 9/Durham LI, he served in France and Italy with 20/Durham LI.

This was how Hubert Hodnett recorded the battalion's first time in the line and moving back into rest on the Italian Front.

On 6 December they were withdrawn into support positions and went into billets in Selva. Here training was carried out. The billets were recalled by Captain Harold Goodley, from Gateshead, many years later:

When we were billeted in a village the troops spent most of their off duty time in the cow sheds with the families. Cow byres were very roomy with ample space behind the stalls for all sorts of purposes. Wives and mothers usually had one corner where they gossiped, knitted and did their mending. The men had another corner where they smoked, drank vino or coffee and played cards, while the children had the middle of the floor for their games and toys. The troops found a corner for housey-housey, letter writing, kit polishing and sometimes there were social evenings when soldiers and villagers had music and dancing. Often there was a peasant with his own musical instrument and there was always a DLI fellow who was an expert with his mouth organ. The heat from the bodies of the nearby cows provided a superior form of central heating which was very acceptable in a land where coal was rarely seen.

Just as in France the battalion out of the line in reserve was called upon to provide carrying and working parties. With the trenches in poor condition a new line had to be dug. Captain Harold Goodley commanded one such party one night just before Christmas 1917.

Digging trenches, machine-gun posts and dug-outs were the night time occupations which kept everyone happy and busy. As the only North Country unit in the division the Durham pit lads were in popular demand. They were often called upon for trench digging when they were in reserve positions. On one occasion I was in charge of a working party of 100 men, when I reported to the Royal Engineers officer in charge of the defences he asked, "Who are you?" "Durhams," I said. "Jolly good," he replied. "Last night we had the ..shires, and they didn't finish the job." He showed me over the line marked out with broad white tapes. The task was to dig 100 yards of trench: each man was to dig a yard length, a yard width and a yard deep. My Sergeant got the men round him.

[In a broad Durham accent] *He told them, "Noo lads, ivry man hes te dig a yerd lang, a yerd wide and a yerd doon. An when yer dun yer cen gan yem."*

The ground was as hard as iron, the top four inches was frozen. In two

20/513 Private G Hayes from Houghton le Spring, having won the Military Medal on the Italian Front was KiA 23/3/18.

British, French and Italian troops examine captured enemy machine guns.

hours the job was done and the inspecting officer was not to be found – he must have gone for his supper. At last I found him. "What, done already?" he said. I took him along the new trench which he examined very carefully. He was very pleased with it and added, "I am going to give you some more." "No jolly fear," said I. "A bargain is a bargain. Fall in chaps, we're going home." We sang all the way back to our billets.

Private Hubert Hodnett wrote his version in his diary:

We proceed up to the line again to a place four miles to the left of the previous sector and relieve the KRRC and are billeted in a house in the reserve line for eight days. We go to the front line, trench digging each night. One night, the enemy having discovered our game gives us a hearty reception in the way of opening fire on us with one of his batteries from the other side of the river. Anyhow, we escape with no casualties.

In front of the battalion position lay the River Piave, in winter it was a raging torrent and in places

British troops enjoy a drink of wine outside their billet in an Italian village.

over a mile wide, the British needed information about the far bank, what lay there and what the enemy positions were. To this end patrols were sent forward with orders to attempt to cross, owing to the power of the swift running current no one could get across. But one young officer, Second Lieutenant Philip Davies, Border Regiment attached 20/Durham LI, showed great devotion to duty in trying. He led his patrol down to the river in an attempt to cross and ascertain the depth and if possible to reconnoitre the far bank. He made two attempts and was in the water for over two hours and was repeatedly swept off his feet, yet he didn't give up trying until overcome by the cold.

They relieved 23/Middlesex Regiment in the line at Christmas and stayed there until the end of the year.

'This being Christmas Eve, we go up to the front line and relieve the REs,' wrote Hubert Hodnett, however, the last word for 1917 is from Captain Harold Goodley:

> On Christmas Day we were in the front line. We slept in the dug-outs during the day and worked and kept watch during the hours of darkness. It was a very easy life; a few patrols to the water's edge: it was rather a novelty to hear a shell burst or see an enemy aircraft.

So here we leave the Wearsiders, but we will hear from them again soon.

Chapter Eight

1918 – The German Onslaught

AFTER SPENDING A COLD NEW YEAR'S DAY on Front Line duty, on 2 January after seventeen days in the line, 20/Durham LI were relieved by the Queen's Regiment and moved back to Giavera. The village was under observation from Austrian Artillery Observers high in the mountains and the battalion has only been there a couple of days when they were heavily shelled. The shelling went on for over six hours and there were a large number of casualties, but only two fatalities, 205155 Private William Carter, from Gilesgate in Durham City, and 35701 Private Alexander Robson, a South Shields man. The shelling was so bad that they were forced to move out of the village until it stopped. On 9 January, they were back into the front line, a few miles to the left of the sector previously held and although the Austrian artillery was very busy there were only a few casualties. By 17 January the Royal Warwickshire Regiment of 7th

British troops on the move in Italy.

An infantry battalion from a second line division marches through the ruined village of Hermies.

German infantry await orders to move forward.

Division took over and they again marched back to Giavera where they spent one night, before moving back a further ten miles to a village near Volpago, where another night was spent. Then on 19 January another ten mile trudge took them to Castelfranco and a small village named Valla. Two very quiet weeks were spent training before being ordered to Possagno to commence digging a reserve line. Ten days were spent on this work before moving back to Altivole, where more of the usual training took place for Lewis-gunners, signallers, stretcher-bearers which included musketry and kit inspections. On 19 February, 123 Brigade were ordered up into the reserve positions at Montebelluna, 20/Durham LI taking over from the West Yorkshires of 69 Brigade. The battalion was due to go up into the line but all of a sudden the orders were changed. As Hubert Hodnett recalled in his diary:

> We are to proceed to the front line tonight, but just before we are to move an order comes through to pack up and we are all under orders for an unknown destination, which we presume to be the east, but we are all disappointed, as will be seen later on. We march back to Montebelluna and stay there about a week, still not knowing where we are going.
>
> The Division starts on the move again and we march further back about 14 miles to the town of Camposampiero, where we stay nine days anxiously awaiting the next move.

With the Germans expected to attack at any time on the Western Front, the decision had been taken to withdraw two of the British divisions from the Italian Front. One of those selected was the 41st Division, whose battalions soon started entraining at Italian stations to be transported back to France. 20/Durham LI spent the time at Camposampiero training and waiting their turn for a train.

On the morning of 2 March the commanding officer inspected the battalion which was drawn up in full marching order. A party of three officers and a hundred men went to the railway station to act as loading party. At 1630 hours C and D Companies along with half of Headquarters and half of the transport platoon entrained in the 'luxurious' cattle trucks of the continental railways to begin their four day journey. A and B Companies, along with the remainder of the battalion, had to wait until 0830 hours the next morning, before following by a later train.

Hubert Hodnett remembered the journey back to France:

> At last we get definite orders and entrain at Camposampiero station for the (beautiful) land of France. We come back practically the same way as going. We reach a certain place, from where we can see the Alps in Switzerland and Austria, meanwhile passing some more wonderful scenery. We arrive at Marseilles early morning after four days in the train (or rather cattle truck). Here, we turn north again, passing through Lyons, Paris and Amiens. 19 March, tonight, at about 2330 hours we reach our destination and find ourselves down the Somme way, detraining at Doullens. We march to Ivergny, about twelve miles south of Arras, where we get a much needed rest. Here I find a record mail waiting for me, which consists of fourteen letters, several papers and postcards and best of all a parcel, which I soon do justice to.

Half of the battalion, having arrived at Ivergny on 7 March, rested and then began cleaning up. It was two days later before the other half of the battalion finally caught up. They were allowed to rest until midday and then they too started cleaning up. Some sport, mainly football, was organised in the afternoon.

Captain Harold Goodley recalled the arrival of 20/Durham LI back in France:

> France again! What a change from the almost delightful war conditions on the Piave River in Italy. Life was very easy there, my battalion only suffered the loss of three or four killed and six wounded in four months' warfare. Doullens is a dull spot to detrain at, after such a feast of scenery

The crew of a 21cm mortar in action during the German offensive.

A tented British stores depot has been overrun. The stores and litter left lying about indicate the panic that had set in among the retreating British troops.

obtained free of all cost, by way of a ride along the Italian and French Riviera coasts. [We are] now in hard training to prepare for the coming great enemy offensive. Brigades have been reduced from four battalions to three; we are feeling the shortage of manpower.

10 March was a day of rest apart from Divine Service, the Roman Catholics paraded at 1030 hours for a Mass conducted by the RC padre, whilst those of the Church of England and Non Conformist faiths had their services at 1100 hours, and afterwards the day was free. Nearby was a training area in the Lucheux Forest, this was used for training the battalion in the attack. A Company acted as enemy and they practised withdrawing. As Captain Goodley recorded as in every other division the brigades were reduced to three battalions. In 41st Division this was done in 122 Brigade by the disbandment of 11/QOR West Kent Regiment. In 123 Brigade the reduction was done by transferring 20/Durham LI to 124 Brigade. This latter brigade disbanded two battalions, 32/Royal Fusiliers and 21/King's Royal Rifle Corps and then being brought back up to three battalions, by 20/Durham LI. The battalion marched out of 123 Brigade area and as they approached Warluzel where 124 Brigade were quartered they were met by the bands of 26/Royal Fusiliers and 10/Queen's Regiment who played them into their new brigade. Here the battalion was joined by Second Lieutenant F W Paley DCM, MM, from 21/KRRC and Lieutenant and QM A Higham 32/Royal Fusiliers. On joining 124 Brigade the battalion was placed at two hours' notice to move and during a tactical exercise the next day, at 1330 hours, word was received that they had to be at the start point at 1555 hours. To reach the start point in time meant that they would have to move off at 1420 hours. The battalion had to leave the training area, collect all necessary equipment and then they paraded in full fighting order, every man with an extra fifty rounds of ammunition and carrying the next day's rations and were ready to go at 1425 hours, just five minutes late. As they were about to move off

20/965 Private Thomas Hepple of Sunderland, killed in action 24 March 1918.

they were told it was a practice and they marched to the brigade starting point and then into a field where they were given a lecture on PT and bayonet fighting. They were also inspected by their new brigade commander, Brigadier General W F Clemson DSO, who expressed his satisfaction with the turnout of the battalion and in particular the transport.

Captain Harold Goodley didn't seem impressed by this when he wrote:

Rumours are wildly confusing. Speedy mobilisation at fictitious railheads is a frequent form of "Joke". The remarks of the troops on these occasions can scarcely be called mild. There is not much fun in having to leave your dinner, pack up all your belongings and assemble at Sus-St-Leger Church two miles distance. To return to cold stew after two hours loitering in the rain is hardly conducive to amiability.

In the early hours of the following morning, from the east came the sound of artillery fire, gradually getting louder as the morning progressed. It was 21 March and the long expected German Offensive had begun. The B Echelon and battalion transport proceeded to Saulty Station where they entrained for Albert, from where they moved to Henencourt. The rifle companies and battalion headquarters moved off at 1320 hours to the same station and same destination. The train travelled through the afternoon and on arrival at Albert the railway transport officer greeted the battalion officers with new orders, they were to remain on the train and travel right up to the front line at Achiet-le-Grand.

This journey was recalled by both Captain Harold Goodley and Private Hubert Hodnett, the officer's account first:

The secret is out; the distant cannonade betokens the commencement of the Great Battle. Rumour travels about. Now the Guards have been wiped out – now we hear they haven't, but are holding on at Arras. By 2 p.m. the real move begins and we march to Saulty to entrain. "A precautionary move to Albert," was the Staff explanation. So officers went in their best clothes, revolvers and warring equipment went in the baggage. At Albert, a worried RTO ordered us to remain in the train and proceed to Achiet-le-Grand, "if the line is still intact", he added. The engine made hard work of the climb, the drivers groped carefully in the dark – some odd shells sailed safely over. We detrained safely at our destination. There were feverish conferences of higher officers, whilst the troops watched the long trail of westward bound traffic coming from Bapaume. Huge guns, transport wagons, ambulances and smaller vehicles crawled slowly past, all eager to flee from the advancing enemy. Wounded tried desperately to find walking room on the crowded roads. Every conceivable kind of unit seemed to be packing up to join the westward stream, only we infantrymen, now sorting out our fighting kit, seemed to be preparing to go east.

But Hubert Hodnett, as with most other ranks was more worried about rations and the lack of a good meal:

At 0900 hours we entrain at Saulty Station, travelling south, passing through Amiens and Albert, finally detraining at Achiet-le-Grand at midnight. During the day the place has been practically reduced to ruins by the enemy's bombardment. We have had a sixty-mile journey in the train and having had nothing to eat since 0900 hours begin to feel a bit hungry, though we are to go longer than that without food soon. Anyhow, we march to huts about four miles behind the line and get a couple of hours' sleep. At 0600 hours we equip ourselves in battle order and after having a drop

British dead lie in a hastily dug trench. Weapons and equipment are scattered everywhere. Note the Lewis gun.

Having retreated for days some remnants of British infantry dig in, in the rain.

of soup only are rushed up the line in order to stem the German advance, he having advanced about ten miles in this sector since yesterday morning.

Having detrained at Achiet-le-Grand the battalion marched to a deserted hutted camp at Favreuil where they got a few hours' sleep. At 1030 hours orders were received to move up and hold a reserve line behind Vaulx-Vraucourt. This move was made in Artillery Formation and when they reached the trenches, being Durhams, they started to dig. At 1700 hours numbers of men from the division who are holding the front, start to fall back through the battalion position. The night passes quietly and a number of patrols are sent out, to try to locate the enemy and gain some information.

During the day there had been three men killed and fifteen wounded.

Captain Harold Goodley again:

'"Now we're for it", was the unanimous feeling amongst our fellows. We threaded our way single file through the traffic. Two hours' sleep in a deserted hutment camp, a snatch of breakfast, and at daybreak we marched to Vaulx. We relieved the ragged remains of N Division, who had gallantly resisted the onslaught for twenty-four hours.

But Hubert Hodnett was one of those selected to go out into No Man's Land looking for the enemy.

I have the "wind up" very much, but of course I'm far from being the only one. We appear to have suffered heavy casualties, for many wounded are making their way back to the dressing station. This is the first time I have experienced anything like this, having had rather a quiet time up to now. Well after much difficulty in dodging shells, etc., we take up a position in the third line trenches, about three miles from Bapaume, being at the foot of the ridge, a very unpleasant position for us. The day is now very hot and we are eagerly looking forward to having some rations come up, but we are to have none that day. During the afternoon Scottish troops are forced, in the face of superior numbers of the enemy, to retire from the front line positions and take up position half a mile in the rear of us; we now being the front line. Consequently we have to be on the alert. At 1500 hours we can see them (the Germans) coming over the ridge in front of us in droves, so that our artillery gives them a very hearty welcome, which I fancy would send no small number of them to their last resting place. By 1600 hours he is within a mile of us. I am included in a patrol which is sent out to find out if Jerry is in the village of Behagnies which is about three quarters of a mile from our trench. We get about 200 yards towards it when we very quickly find out that he is in the village, as he opens fire on us with machine guns. Being on the open road we have to lie flat. Anyhow, we push on a little further, but are forced to retire back to the trench again, it being impossible to get through his machine-gun fire. We suffered no casualties and afterwards the night passes rather quietly and we dig what cover we can in readiness for the attack, which we know he is sure to continue next morning.

In a thick mist early next morning, the enemy launched an attack against the two companies on the right. The companies held their ground and the Germans, although they get close up to the British wire, were driven back leaving a lot of dead and wounded in front of the battalion positions. Captain J H Iveson, Officer Commanding B Company, is killed at this time, along with Second Lieutenant R Kay and eighteen men, other casualties are one officer, Second Lieutenant W Turnbull, along with sixty men wounded and five are missing. The attacks go on throughout the day, often under the cover of an artillery barrage, but each one is successfully driven off. A major problem is the supply of ammunition, indeed in this action 20/Durham LI fired over half a million rounds of .303 rifle ammunition. Every officer of the battalion had armed himself with a rifle and fired as hard as any private that day.

In fact Hubert Hodnett recalled 23 March in his diary in these words:

At 0500 hours Jerry launches his attack under cover of a heavy mist and without any bombardment. With heavy rifle fire we hold him up for a time but by 0900 hours he reaches our wire. Captain Iveson rallies the company for a counter-attack, but unfortunately he is killed by a hand grenade, part of which enters his head, so we decide to stay in the trench. At 1100 hours the enemy, failing to break through us, eventually retires, after us having inflicted very heavy casualties on him. But he doesn't mean to let us rest for long, as a few minutes afterwards he sends us a good supply of hand grenades over, which cause us several casualties, and afterwards sends gas over. After this he remains quiet until 1400 hours when he puts up a barrage on our trenches for two hours. This is where I have my nearest escape, after the barrage has been on for about an hour and a half, when a shell drops immediately behind me in the trench, but as fate decreed, one of our chaps who is dashing past at the time gets the whole of it for himself and here I see one of the worst sights of all, for when I look round I see hardly anything left of him but the bottom part of his legs, so that his life meant the saving of mine. When the barrage lifts at 1600 hours to our great surprise, what is left of us, for we have had to pay the toll in life, there were only five of us left in our platoon, which was thirty-one strong when we came up the line, and about thirty in the company altogether, the rest having been killed or wounded. After this he keeps rather quiet to our great relief and we manage to get a few rations up, the first for two days. At 1900 hours he starts to get busy again and we discover one or two of his patrols near our wire and open heavy rifle fire upon them. Anyhow, later on he quietens down again. At midnight we are relieved from this trench by A Company, and proceed to take over trenches about half a mile to the right. It had been a bit quieter here and had escaped the barrage which we had had. We get settled down there, but are unable to get any sleep as we have to keep on the alert all the while and only a few of us being left, we are unable to relieve each other on sentry duty. This is Saturday night and we have had no sleep since Thursday morning so that we all feel just about "fed up".

The night of 23/24 March passed fairly quietly; 20/Durham LI sent out a number of patrols in an effort to keep the enemy away from the wire. As dawn broke, the enemy started shelling the battalion position once more. In the rear, Major General Lawford, commanding 41st Division was making contingency plans in case a withdrawal had to be made, these plans were issued to the brigade commanders who in their turn made their plans.

At battalion headquarters, 20/Durham LI, word was received that the division on the right had fallen back, however the battalion, in spite of a heavy barrage that fell on them at 1700 hours, held on in what was known as the Green Line astride the Bapaume–Vaulx-Vraucourt road until 1900 hours. This was recalled by Captain Harold Goodley:

20/965 Private T Hepple of Sunderland was killed in action 24 March 1918.

2203624 Private W B Teasdale from Ryton on Tyne died of wounds 29 March 1918.

20/531 Lance Sergeant E Spalding, a Sunderland man died of wounds 30 March 1918.

20/501 Private F Sharp born in Bishop Auckland, died of wounds 1 April 1918.

20/235 Corporal S Dawson, a Washington man, died of wounds 2 April 1918.

Last night's circle of lights and gun flashes was very discomforting. We seem to be at the apex of a sharp salient – the line falls back more particularly on our right. Still we are holding on, not an inch of ground lost. One Company has fired a million rounds of SAA and still wanted more ammunition. Our field artillery is wonderful firing in the open meadowland over open sights. At 1400 hours there was a feverish conference at Brigade Headquarters. Orders for a retirement had been given. Within two hours it had begun. What a sight! They came back in parade ground fashion – each company covered by the fire of another. At 1700 hours a runner reported to Brigade that the Germans were only 250 yards away and were being held by our men. The Brigadier and his staff went quickly and calmly to their new quarters. By evening a new line had been dug behind a wood. But the enemy gave us no rest, he was nearly behind us again on the right.

The orders to withdraw were given that both 122 and 124 Brigades should fall back and hold a line from Avesnes to east of Sapignies and units began to move. However in the confusion they did not fall back far enough, but held a line some distance in front of the intended line. Unfortunately this left a gap between the right of 124 Brigade and left of 19th Division. With a lack of available infantry Major General Lawford ordered the commander, Royal Engineers, Lieutenant Colonel E N Stockley to take the three Field Companies, Royal Engineers and fill the gap.

During 24 March the casualties had been Second Lieutenant A Brown, wounded and two other ranks killed, thirty-three wounded and fifteen missing.

Hubert Hodnett wrote at length about this day also:

The weather continues to be very hot. About 1600 hours he attacks again and, before overwhelming numbers of the enemy, our troops are forced to fall back on our right flank, and at 1700 hours we commence to retire from our trenches voluntarily to prevent being outflanked. His aeroplanes are very busy over our heads as we retire, being very low down. After we have made an orderly retirement of about two miles we get news that the FIFTH Army on our right (we being in THIRD Army) has retired back much further. At this point the battalion is nearly outflanked, the enemy being within 200 yards of us on the right. We are about to give up all hopes when D Company stand firm and hold him up while we retire further back, but by saving the rest of the battalion from capture they lose many prisoners themselves. We retire a further two miles and dig ourselves in, but are only there for about thirty minutes when we have to retire again, as they are advancing rapidly on the right flank. We now pass through the village of Sapignies, but to our surprise we find that Jerry is already there, and he opens fire on us with machine guns, so that we have to scatter the best way we can. After reorganising again, we dig in again. We have now come back about five miles altogether since 1800 hours and it is now midnight, and we are ready for him next morning.

The morning of 25 March began in much the same way as that of 24 March, German patrols pushed forward probing for gaps in the line and trying to

13 Platoon, 20/Durham LI, 1916. Back row: Hanshaw, R.W. Williamson, Hepple, G. Long, F. Armstrong, J. Purnell, S. Lewis, unidentified, T. Barnes, R.W. Yeoman, J. Copeland. Fourth row: Charlton, Lazzeri, J.G. Ashcroft, W. Bryan, Lowery, unidentified, unidentified, unidentified, unidentified, unidentified, unidentified. Third row: G. Pickering, Johnson, S. Lawrence, Corporal Wilson, Kipling, R. Brown, unidentified, R. Dixon(?), J. Finlay, R. Dixon (?), R. France, T. Elias, H. Chapman, A. Hartley, J. Scott. Second row: Teasdale, unidentified, Armaford, R. Slater, Bates (?), Fairless, Gibson, Thompson, Sanderson, unidentified, unidentified, unidentified, unidentified, K. Bevin. Front row: Bugler Pearson, Lance-Corporals Curd, Middlemass, and Briggs, Sergeant Seago, Captain Rasche, Sergeant Sheriff, Corporal Goway, Corporal Wood, Campbell.

14 Platoon, 20/Durham LI, in the United Kingdom, 1916.

find a way round the flanks of units in the line. As the day passed the fighting grew in intensity as there seemed a chance that the enemy would break through and force a break between V and IV Corps, and as night came on the fighting died down. On the battalion front at 0800 hours the enemy attacked Sapignies from the left and got into the village. This left the left flank of the battalion 'in the air' and they were forced to withdraw to the ridge along the Bihucourt–Sapignies road where they dug in. As they went back the battalion kept up a rapid fire on the Germans in Sapignies. At 1315 hours the enemy forced his way into, and captured the village of Bihucourt and as this threatened the left flank of 20/Durham LI, this forced the remnants of the battalion to withdraw to a line on the reverse slope of the ridge north-west of the Bihucourt–Sapignies road.

In the afternoon, as they went further back they passed through a battalion of the Lancashire Fusiliers of 42nd Division, and they took support positions behind them.

> *At 0900 hours Fritz gets on the go again. This is to be the last day of the retreat, for which I am not at all sorry. We repulse his attacks for about three hours, during most of which time I am one of a party engaged in fetching ammunition up to our trench while he is shelling the road heavily all the while. At 1300 hours we are forced to retire again towards Achiet-le-Grand, and all of us being in rather a state of confusion I somehow or other get lost from my battalion and therefore join myself onto the LFs. After having come back about another two miles, having left Fritz some way behind us, we take things rather easily, for he has made us run for over a mile and just as his artillery is quietening down again a stray whiz-bang came over, a small fragment of which hits me in the left shoulder, as I happened to turn round at the time, but concussion from the shell knocked me flat. A*

Trenches at Gommecourt. After refitting the battalion moved into the line on 26 March 1918 and held a sector that had originally been occupied by the Germans in 1916.

20/485 Corporal James Hannah of Washington MM, killed in action 25 March 1918.

chap who is walking with me has half his head blown away by a piece of the same shell, while another is seriously wounded in the leg, so that I escape very luckily. I am wounded just by Achiet-le-Grand station, which, it will be remembered, is the place where we got off the train four days ago. Anyhow I make my way down to the dressing station which is a journey of about six miles.

Wrote Hubert Hodnett about his last day in the battle.

The next move was to Gommecourt village where the battalion reorganised and counted the cost of the last few days Captain B Wilkinson MC had been wounded as had Second Lieutenant T Duddy, whilst Lieutenant H Munro was missing, presumed killed the previous day. Among the men eight were killed, forty-eight wounded and twenty missing. Early the next morning they moved into a sector of the old front line held by the Germans on 1 July 1916, south of Gommecourt Wood. The battalion held this line throughout the day, which was described as quiet but they had lost Second Lieutenants A O Parsons and J Carmichael, both of whom died of wounds; in the ranks four were dead, twenty-four wounded and twenty-four missing.

On 27 March, at 0100 hours an order was received that the battalion would withdraw to Bienvillers-au-Bois, where they arrived at 0500 hours, they rested where possible and then began re-equipping. They remained in the village for the night and at 0730 hours the

20/817 Private W H Egglestone from the tiny village of Daddry Shield in Weardale, killed in action 20 May 1918.

following morning were ordered to move back up to a line east of Gommecourt in support to the 42nd (East Lancashire) Division. That night a number of patrols were active trying to get in touch with the troops in front and to find out where the British units were round Rosignol Wood. These positions were held for two days until it moved up and relieved a battalion of the Lancashire Fusiliers, in the line in front of Bucquoy. The two days until the end of the month passed quietly enough but there was a lot of activity by the enemy artillery, this caused a steadily rising casualty list with

20/678 Bugler C A Morde from Sunderland, killed i action 11 May 1918.

Second Lieutenants C J Ruffle and J Black wounded and eight other ranks killed and thirty four wounded.

On 1 April the battalion spent a quieter day than they had of late and at 2300 hours 1/7/Lancashire Fusiliers came up and relieved them. After being relieved 20/Durham LI made their way to Bienvillers and rested for the night, the following day embussing for Halloy at 0700 hours, where on arrival they began the usual clean-up session after a spell in the line. But they weren't allowed to stay long, the next morning at 0830 hours they tramped to Mondicourt and there were met by buses and transported to Bonnieres. The battalion transport, less four cookers and a water cart formed up on the Haloy–Lucheux Road with the head of the column just south of the L'Esperance crossroads at 0930 hours. At that time, under the command of the brigade transport officer, it commenced to march to Bonnieres. When the men arrived they waited at the village church until guides came from the battalion and showed them where the billets were. So as to be able to feed the battalion when the cookers arrived, the cooks worked and cooked as the cookers went along the road.

In Bonnieres the day was spent reorganising the companies and then at 1520 hours the battalion entrained at Frevent Station to be taken north into Belgium, to Hopoutre sidings, where they arrived at 2130 hours; waiting for the battalion was a convoy of buses and they quickly transferred onto them from the train and were carried to the Steenvorde area. Here a large draft of 448 men arrived to replace those casualties of the March fighting, among them a few of the slightly wounded returning from hospital. They spent two days absorbing the draft and reorganising the companies and then on 7 April they marched to Vlamertinghe and found

A weary Tommy rests near the make-shift sign identifying the outskirts of Ypres. Taken 27 April 1918.

accommodation in one of the many hutted camps in the area. The next morning a move was made to Branhoek Station and they proceeded to St Jean where after detraining they relieved 1/Border Regiment in reserve, being accommodated in one of the camps in the area. Four days were spent training and the officers carried out a reconnaissance of the routes to the front line. Then suddenly on the night of 12 April the order came in to move up behind the front line and dig in. This was carried out and the digging of a series of strongpoints was commenced. The front line was reduced to a number of outposts and was not strongly held. All the next day the work continued and when the positions were dug, the battalion commenced to wire them in. When this was completed a composite company of two platoons from A Company and two from C Company were left in this position and the battalion moved to a position further back and commenced digging another new line of trenches, which would become the new support and reserve trenches.

The work carried on throughout 15 April with each company working for four hours, then at night the two platoons of A Company in the outpost line were relieved by the remaining two platoons of C Company, thus the whole of C Company was in the outpost line. In the early morning of 16 April the whole of the old outpost line was withdrawn, leaving C Company as the new front line. Late that afternoon the Germans, having discovered that the positions had been vacated, were seen advancing towards them but they stopped about 1000 yards from the new line. Two days were spent working without hindrance from the enemy, but, on 19 April in the early morning the Germans launched an attack on Hill 35 which caused a few casualties. At noon two platoons of 20/Durham LI counter-attacked and gained the objective, but were driven off by a German unit superior in numbers. This attack left two officers and thirteen other ranks missing and eleven other ranks wounded. But twelve officers arrived from the base to bring the battalion up to strength. The positions were held until 26 April, and although the enemy shelled the lines regularly it did not interfere with the work going on. That night the outpost line was withdrawn and 20/Durham LI were relieved by fresh troops in the newly made front line. After being relieved they made their way to Dead End at Ypres and occupied a newly dug line, which was to become the new front line. The enemy having discovered the withdrawal began a heavy shelling but this was replied to by the British guns, which silenced the enemy but not before the battalion had lost three men, among them 20/613, Sergeant Tom Cummings MM of West Rainton.

1 May passed quietly and that night they worked on a new outpost line in the rear of the position now held, in case of a further withdrawal being ordered. The following night 15/Hampshire Regiment came up and 20/Durham LI moved back to Vlamertinghe where they and the rest of 124 Brigade became divisional reserve. Even this far back a new line was being constructed and the Durhams were soon put to work with pick and shovel. Nine days were spent digging, specialists were trained and apart from a break on Sunday 5 May, for Divine Service, the work continued without let-up. The work was supervised by the Royal Engineers, until on the night of 12

Second Lieutenant Frederick Yedwell, killed in action 18 May 1918.

May, when 20/Durham LI relieved three companies of 1/King's Shropshire LI and one company of 1/West Yorkshire Regiment, in the line. Night patrols were now very active and on the night 14 May a patrol of 20/Durham LI captured a soldier of the 458th Infantry Regiment. Raised in 7th Corps District in Westpahlia, with young boys of the 1918 class, and returning wounded, this regiment was part of the 236th Infantry Division. Having been employed during the Somme offensive the previous month they had arrived on the Passchendaele front on 6 April, about the same time as 41st Division.

During the day men were rested as much as possible but at night working parties improved the trenches and patrols were very active. On 19 May 10/Queen's Regiment relieved the battalion who moved further back; A Company to the Dolls House Line, D Company manned the Canal Switch, whilst C and B Companies were in the Goldfish Château area. In these support positions the battalion provided working parties even though the weather had turned wet and dull. On 27 May the enemy made an attack and 20/Durham LI were stood to and occupied an assembly position between 1030 and 1830 hours when they returned to Brake Camp. As the weather improved the battalion spent the days training under Company Commanders and the Battalion specialists paraded under their respective officers. Each day until the end of the month was spent in the same way.

On 3 June the battalion marched out of Brake Camp and marched to the light railway and were carried to Proven, transferring to the broad gauge railway they were carried to Watten, from there they went by route march to Lederzeele. A few days were spent cleaning up and resting and then on 8 June they moved to Bonningues-les-Ardeux by route march. Over the next two weeks or so every aspect of training was carried out, on 22 June, in the morning the battalion was inspected by the commanding officer and then in the afternoon by the brigade commander. On 25 June the march back to the line began with a move back to Lederzeele and then onwards the next day to Ouderzeele. A few days' rest followed and reconnoitring parties went up to the Boeschepe Line. On 29 June the battalion moved to Abeele and advanced parties went up into the trenches near Kemmel. The next night, 20/Durham LI relieved 102 Regiment d'Infantry of the French Army in the vicinity of Kemmel. Here we will leave them for the time being.

Chapter Nine

July – November 1918 – It's all over now

THE BEGINNING OF JULY saw 20/Durham LI holding the line at Kemmel, where every night there was plenty of work to do carrying up stores and provisions, also patrols were out prowling about No Man's Land trying to identify the enemy. With a large number of young soldiers in the drafts that had joined the battalion, where possible they were taken and given further training out of enemy observation. They were relieved on 5 July by 26/Royal Fusiliers but two days later they were back in the line again, with the same carrying and working parties to provide. In the Kemmel district the water was contaminated and every drop had to be carried up from the rear. On 10 July they were relieved again, this time by 10/Queen's Royal West Surrey Regiment and moved back to billets in Brigade Reserve. All through the month they rotated from reserve, to holding the front and back into reserve, but the most trying thing was, that every night working parties had to be provided so there was little rest for anyone.

On 2 August 20/Durham LI and 1/108 US Infantry Regiment joined together and formed two battalions. A battalion consisted of A and B Companies 20/Durham LI and A and B Companies 1/108 USIR, whilst B Battalion was formed from C and D Companies 20/Durham LI and C and D Companies 1/108 USIR. A Battalion relieved 106 US Infantry Regiment in the Front Line and

American 'Dough Boys' move up to the training area by train from disembarkation ports.

American troops training in France under direction of the British Army.

B Battalion relieved 26/Royal Fusiliers in Support. During the next few days the Durhams instructed the Americans in all aspects of trench warfare, until on 7 August the two battalions separated and reformed in their original battalions, 20/Durham LI taking over the support line. On 10 August they moved back to Reninghelst in reserve, where they carried out some training. They were then put to work on the Scherpenburg–Dickebusch Lake Line. Every day for the next two weeks, two companies were working and two training. Even when they took over the Front Line on 23 August, from 26/Royal Fusiliers, one company was sent back to work on the defence line.

On 30 August the Germans began withdrawing on the Kemmel front and 41st Division started pushing out patrols to maintain touch with the enemy. 20/Durham LI were in support and did not come back into the line until 2 September, when they relieved 1/105 USIR in the Dickebusch sector. During the relief Lieutenant G H Johnson and two NCOs were wounded.

On the night of 4 September, 20/Durham LI attacked the enemy front line, the objective being to reach the Wytschaete-Voormezeele road. There was no time for reconnaissance and the orders were issued late in the day. There was to be no preliminary bombardment and as the two leading companies formed up for the attack, the enemy fired a very heavy shrapnel and machine-gun barrage. In the advance that followed the right hand company drifted too far south and although they fought their way in and took the first objective, their flanks were 'in the air'. The enemy was able to bring machine guns up and bring enfilade fire onto their left flank. By this time all of the officers and the majority of the NCOs had become casualties. The Germans now launched a counter-attack, and 245420 Sergeant H Ebbs, took command of the survivors of the company, moving about among the men and organising them against counter-attack. Owing to heavy casualties he was eventually obliged to withdraw a short distance across the railway. They now needed help badly and Second Lieutenant Frederick Wood, with about forty men, of two platoons of the support company rushed forward. Collecting stragglers he organised his men in forward isolated posts, moving amongst them under heavy fire and encouraging them to hold on until almost surrounded. Despite heavy casualties he stood fast until ordered to retire. While all this was happening on the right, on the left flank, Captain Norman Wilson Turnbull gained his first objective in twenty minutes in the face of heavy machine-gun fire. However the enemy counter-attacked down a trench, using bombs and he was forced to retire. Fortunately the support company pushed up reinforcements and he was able to form a defensive flank, which saved a larger withdrawal.

Casualties were heavy. Second Lieutenants E Russell and J S Wills were killed, Captain W R Eppstein died of wounds and Second Lieutenant P T Conrath was wounded and missing. The Commanding Officer, Lieutenant Colonel A V A Gayer DSO was gassed, with four other subalterns T H Bassett, C G Lavell, A MacLaren and F Brunt all wounded. Among the men no less than twenty-three had been killed, almost all of the young reinforcements with less than one year's service. Of the original twentieth battalion men, still with the battalion, three were among the dead, 20/689 Sergeant William Willis and 20/981 Lance Corporal Thomas Jeffery, both came from Fencehouses, County Durham, whilst the third, 20/796 Private William Wardle, was a Sunderland man.

The battalion was relieved by 26/Royal Fusiliers and moved into Brigade Support, where they began refitting and re-organising, platoons were re-formed and the men cleaned their equipment and themselves. Major C Pannall MC now assumed command of 20/Durham LI, and it was then that more training started. The weather, however, turned showery and on some days training was cancelled. Working parties were called upon to work on the Vierstraat switch line, where they

Number 15 Platoon and below number 16 Platoon 20/Durham LI, 1916. Sadly no names are recorded for these two platoons.

came under heavy shelling, nightly; on 11 September one working party had three killed, and nine wounded, almost all of whom died the following day from their wounds.

At 0600 hours on 15 September the battalion entrained at Wippenhoek sidings and was carried by broad gauge railway to Lumbres, where they switched to a narrow gauge railway and were taken to the training area at Bonnigues where they were accommodated in billets. Over the next ten days musketry and all forms of infantry training were carried out with attention being paid to the battalion in the attack.

On two nights the brigade commander gathered together all battalion commanders, adjutants and company commanders and discussed forthcoming operations. By 27 September the training was over and at 0730 hours they once again marched to the narrow gauge railway at Bonnigues and were transported to Lumbres where they changed onto the broad gauge track for transportation to Reninghelst. They detrained in pouring rain and marched to billets in Brandhoek, where the battalion was complete by 2145 hours. The following day, in heavy rain, the battalion moved forward to an assembly area near White Château and from there to forming-up positions near Hill 60. 124 Brigade attacked and A B and C Companies of 20/Durham LI acted as a flank guard along the banks of the Ypres–Commines canal. They advanced as far as Kortewilde with only a few casualties and with Second Lieutenant Lax evacuated, gassed. On 29 September D Company continued the flank guard and continued the attack as far as the village of Houthem where they mopped up the village and took thirty prisoners with ten machine guns. Unfortunately, Captain A T Browne was killed in action and Second Lieutenant Parker wounded. Although among the men only one, a Pelton man, 22133 Sergeant James Thompson, who the previous year had been awarded the Military Medal and then a Bar to the same medal, was killed. Three were wounded and one was missing. The last day of the month saw the battalion still in support to the attacking battalions. In heavy rain the companies struggled forward, A B and D Companies behind 26/Royal Fusiliers and C Company behind 10/Queens Royal West Surrey Regiment. There were only four casualties, all wounded during the day and later C Company moved up on the right of 10/Queen's Royal West Surrey Regiment and occupied a position near Hospital Farm.

On 1 October, owing to the fact that 124 Brigade had got ahead of the troops on either flank, they stood fast on the Werwcq–Commines line and 20/Durham LI remained in support. The next day the other brigades of 41st Division continued the advance against the Gheluwe switch, which 19/Durham LI had already tried to take. 20/Durham LI did not see any action that day, although they did come under enemy shellfire, which wounded Lieutenants Atkinson and Blair and caused four casualties among the men. On the evening of 3 October at 1830 hours the battalion moved forward and relieved 1/KOSB of 29th Division at Gheluwe; the relief was complete by 0200 hours, but there had been a number of casualties, five men were wounded and one, 82042 Private Eric Lea, from Manchester was killed. The position was held throughout 4 October and then at 2245 hours on 5 October they handed over to a battalion of the Queen's from 34th Division.

The next day was spent in support positions and even here they came under shellfire and lost another man killed and six wounded. But on the afternoon of 7 October they were relieved by 23/Middlesex Regiment and moved back to Hell Fire Corner where they bivouacked and waited to entrain. On 8 October they entrained and were transported back to the Abeele area and moved into a hutted camp. The other ranks were set to cleaning up and resting on the first day, whilst the commanding officer, adjutant and company commanders went to brigade headquarters and attended a conference to plan the next attack.

The next three days were spent training and on the afternoon of 11 October the Brigade Gas

British artillery cover the advance.

NCO inspected all respirators in the battalion. In wet weather on 12 October the battalion practised the attack. This took place between Abeele and Poperinghe on ground similar to that which they would be going over in a couple of days' time. The next day, at 1100 hours, the battalion entrained at Remy Sidings and were carried forward on the light railway to Stirling Castle and bivouacked in the region of Glencorse Tunnels. At 0800 hours an advance party had left the battalion by motor lorry and had been taken up to the assembly area, where they laid out tapes for the battalion to form up on ready to go over. At 2300 hours, in wet weather, the remainder of the battalion left Glencorse Tunnels and marched up to the assembly area and got into position ready for an attack at dawn.

Just before Zero Hour a ground mist started to rise and this soon was a thick fog, when at Zero - three minutes a terrific barrage was let loose on the enemy positions. At Zero Hour, which was at 0535 hours the attacking battalions of 124 Brigade went forward but it was impossible to keep in touch with men on either flank. The advance was maintained by small parties advancing on their own. The acting battalion commander Major, Acting Lieutenant Colonel Charlie Pannall MC was awarded the Distinguished Service Order for the part he played in the attack, keeping his men together, he displayed great gallantry, and fine leadership which greatly contributed to the success of the battalion under his command. He directed the attack on the first line personally through dense fog and towards the end of the day placed his men in position on the final objective exposing him self throughout to heavy shell and machine-gun fire.

By 1100 hours the mist had cleared and with D Company on the right of C Company in the front line the attack was pressed home and the final objective carried with little resistance. Several machine guns, nine field guns, and three howitzers were captured. Against this there was the loss of Lieutenant J Foster, who died of wounds and Captain Brant, Lieutenant Goodley MC and Second Lieutenant W J Scott all wounded, with six men killed and sixty-five wounded. The next day patrols were pushed forward to the River Lys and Second Lieutenant F B Davison took out patrols and gained valuable information. Despite heavy machine-gun fire, he pushed forward with patrols, and eventually established a line of posts on the River Lys. But later that day relief arrived in the shape of 2/Loyal North Lancashire Regiment, who took over and allowed 20/Durham LI to go back to Moorseele in Brigade Reserve. Although they were able to clean their equipment and rest as much as possible the battalion was unable to find bathing facilities for the men. Platoons were reorganised and PT and drill were carried out. On 19 October the Company Commanders went forward to the River Lys and reconnoitred footbridges and crossings over the river, meanwhile the battalion marched forward and moved into billets near Marionetteberg.

On the morning of 21 October at 0500 hours the battalion moved forward to the start line for the attack which would drive the enemy across the Scheldt at Bossuyt. 124 Brigade had 10/Queen's Royal West Surrey Regiment on the left, 20/Durham LI on the right and 26/Royal Fusiliers in support. 20/Durham LI had D Company on the right, C Company on the left, with B Company as right support and A Company as left support. On the right 35th Division were attacking also. The battalion also had a section of 18-pounder guns, two Stokes mortars and two Vickers guns allocated for the attack; they were also allotted a section of Royal Engineers who were to assist in the crossing of the Courtrai–Bossuyt canal, which ran obliquely across the brigade front. At 0730 hours in wet showery weather the advance began and the battalion moved forward,

Germans are winkled out of their pillboxes and (below) a prisoner is searched before being sent to the rear.

British gunners familiarise themselves with a captured German gun that they will soon turn against its former owners.

although they had to pause to allow 10/Queen's Royal West Surrey Regiment to cross the canal. They then pressed on and cleared the village of Knockerhoek with little resistance. However they soon ran into the enemy main line of resistance, from where they came under heavy machine-gun fire and some shellfire from the German artillery. But these caused only a few casualties and in spite of this the battalion fought its way forward for over 6,000 yards. The section of guns attached from the Royal Field Artillery played an extremely useful part and were used with great success, as were the Vickers guns which aided the forward movement. Most of the casualties occurred after the men had dug in, when a German trench mortar opened fire on D Company. The battalion came under heavy fire from the left flank which was exposed and they were forced to form a defensive flank. That night the line was consolidated and touch was made with 26/Royal Fusiliers who had come up between the two leading battalions to close the gap. Casualties amounted to Second Lieutenant J W Armstrong, killed in action, and Second Lieutenants J Wood and S W Warwick wounded, with two other ranks killed and forty-five wounded. Patrols were pushed out to try to locate enemy positions for the artillery to bombard. On 23 October the battalion was relieved by 1/7/Cheshire Regiment and moved back to billets and became the Brigade Support Battalion. The next day was spent resting and reorganising and then that night advance parties moved up the assembly area to lay out tapes for the battalion to jump off from the following morning. At 0300 hours the battalion moved up to the assembly positions and dug in until Zero Hour. The Brigade had been ordered to take Avelghem and to do this 20/Durham LI were to attack on the left, 26 Royal Fusiliers on the right and 10/Queen's Royal West Surrey Regiment were in support. 20/Durham LI adopted a similar formation to the last attack, but this time B Company was on the left front, A Company on the right front, with D Company as left support and C Company as right support. The attack did not start until 0900 hours and as they advanced the leading companies experienced very heavy fighting, the enemy were holding every farm with machine guns, which fired until the last possible moment, until they were almost surrounded, before the crews escaped. This made the advance very slow and the left flank became

A British soldier inspects a captured German ammunition dump.

This orphaned Belgian boy was adopted and fed and clothed by the battalion.

exposed and the leading companies suffered a number of casualties and had to be replaced by the support companies. Although several machine guns were taken there were few prisoners as many posts had to be taken at the bayonet point, owing to the severe resistance put up by the German troops opposite. The attack was pressed forward and the line Driesch–Bosche was reached where they dug in and consolidated, but later that night the line was pushed further forward. Two officers, Second Lieutenants W Hebron and D Lax were killed during the day, along with twenty-two other ranks, whilst among the wounded were Captain B E Wilkinson MC, and Second Lieutenants J Appleton, F Wood MC and A Donnelly and 111 men.

The next morning information was gathered from local civilians that the enemy were withdrawing and the attack was continued. Patrols were sent forward and reached Avelghem, the village was reported clear of the enemy by 1000 hours. Later they fought their way into the northern outskirts of Rugge, but were unable to take the village completely before being relieved. 10/Queen's R W Surrey Regiment relieved the battalion and they moved back to billets in the southern outskirts of Courtrai. Here they were rejoined by the battalion details, those men left out of battle to form a nucleus on which to reform the battalion, if the battalion had heavy casualties. Weapons and equipment were cleaned and platoons were reorganised. Although the town had not been too badly damaged, very few shops were open, there was however a cinema, which had been captured intact from the Germans and it was open for business on 30 October less than ten days after the enemy had left the town.

They rested in Courtrai until 1 November when they moved by route march to Krote, where dinner was served and the battalion then took over the front line. During the break for dinner Lieutenant Colonel A V A Gayer arrived back with the battalion and took over command from Lieutenant Colonel C Pannal. On arrival in the line D Company relieved one company of the 17/Lancashire Fusiliers in the left front sector. A Company went into support at Haelendries and relieved a company of 18/Lancashire Fusiliers, whilst B Company took over the right front sector and C Company the centre front sector, where they relieved two companies of 19/Durham LI along the Scheldt near Tenhove and Kerhove. During the relief 20/Durham LI had five men wounded. The front was actively patrolled but the enemy artillery paid a lot of attention to the battalion forward sector causing a number of casualties. On 3 November the last original enlistment, 20/617 Lance Corporal Andrew Price from Sunderland was killed along with 93086 Private Thomas Bramhill, a Yorkshireman who had originally served with the York and Lancaster Regiment. Two Lewis gun posts were established by a patrol of B Company on the enemy side of the river, but as the enemy

British troops enter the newly liberated French town of Lille, there were similar scenes in Belgium where 20/Durham LI were fighting.

were attacking them, they were withdrawn back to the British held bank. The enemy artillery was also shelling the countryside with tear and gas shells.

On 4 November, 11/Queen's Royal West Surrey Regiment relieved 20/Durham LI, who marched back to the Vichte area and took over billets; on the way out they suffered one man killed and two wounded. Yet again the platoons were reorganised and the men cleaned up as best they could, on 6 November baths were allocated to the battalion and all ranks were able to clean up and de-louse. The weather was wet but this didn't stop the training and the whole battalion practised crossing a river, both by bridge and boat.

On 8 November the training changed to 'forming up at a river crossing', to all ranks it must have been obvious that they were to be the assault battalion for the crossing of the Scheldt. The next morning the battalion set off by route march and moved to an area near the village of Klieneberg, where they were met by the battalion cooks and their mobile cookers and a hot meal was served to the men. While the battalion was eating dinner the news was received that the enemy had withdrawn from the eastern bank of the River Scheldt and as a consequence of this the battalion would move forward and occupy billets at Meersche. The following day they moved further forward and found billets in Schoorisse. On 11 November 1918 the battalion continued to follow the retreating enemy and passed through 123 Brigade, as 124 Brigade took over the lead and 20/Durham LI, the leading battalion became the advance guard. At about 0930 hours the Commanding Officer announced that an armistice had been signed and that at 1100 hours there would be a cease-fire and hostilities would end. The battalion kept pushing forward until at 1100 hours they were some two kilometres west of the small town of Nederbrakel about twelve kilometres from Oudenarde, but instead of halting they pushed through the town and formed an outpost line beyond it. The last casualty occurred when one man was accidentally wounded by one of his comrades. There was no demonstration or cheering by the men when the news was received, the majority were just glad it was all over and soon they would be going home.

23489 Sergeant J A Armstrong MM from Gateshead.

20/787 Private J A Donkin MM, came from Wheatley Hill.

So the war ended for 20/Durham LI, but not the soldiering, for very soon as we will learn they were to be part of the British Army of the Rhine. It is interesting to note that at the end, the three divisions containing the locally raised battalions of the Durham Light Infantry, 31st Division, 35th Division and 41st Division all formed XIX Corps of SECOND Army in what became known as the Battles of Courtrai and at the end they were fighting as hard, if not harder than at any time in their short existence.

20/145 Bugler Gordon Forbes, reputedly the tallest man to serve in the battalion, received his Military Medal in 1919.

Chapter Ten

The Army of the Rhine

WHEN HOSTILITIES CEASED 41st Division were in the line and as such were required to man outpost positions, each battalion in turn was employed in this way. When not on outpost duty the battalion cleaned up and then carried out close order drill and there were a number of inspections, by the commanding officer, the brigade commander and then the GOC 41st Division. Platoon and company drill, sport and other recreational games took place. On 27 November C Company played D Company in the first round of the Divisional Inter Company Football Tournament and D Company came out the winners by two goals to one. The next day in the same round of the tournament, A Company was defeated two goals to nil by B Company.

On the evening of 29 November 'The Crumps', the 41st Division concert party put on a show for the battalion which, we are told, was enjoyed by all attending. The next afternoon saw the next stage of the Divisional Football Tournament when B Company met D Company to decide which team would represent the battalion in the next round. In a very one-sided match D Company came out on top by five goals to one.

December began in cold weather, with a Divine Service for all ranks in the village hall at Bievene. The same pattern of training took place and in the evenings a French language class was started with over sixty men attending. The football tournament continued on 8 December, with D Company 20/Durham LI meeting A Company 26/Royal Fusiliers with the DLI Company

Riehl Pioneer Barracks, Cologne.

20/Durham LI, Battalion sports day, Cologne 1919. Top: the 'Busy Bees' are in the lead. Below: the 'Good Ladies' of C Company cannot believe that they are falling behind.

150

Battalion Quarter Guard in Cologne.

running outright winners by six goals to nil. Further sporting activity occurred when, within the battalion, an inter-platoon football competition was started.

The battalion started moving by route march towards the German border on 12 December when they marched to Enghien, and then the next day to Hal. Still in Belgium, on 14 December they marched to Waterloo where they were accommodated in billets. The following day the men were taken to the Waterloo battlefield at Mont-St-Jean and saw the 'Lion' monument above the

'Turn out the guard', the Provost Sergeant, standing in the centre of the gate, and the barrack guard await the return of the battalion from a parade in the town.

'Dear Mother, this was taken when we were away from the battalion firing on the ranges.' Note the men wearing the ribbons of the British War and Victory Medals and those wearing wound stripes.

battlefield. The next day as they marched to Genappe they were inspected on the line of march by King Albert, the King of the Belgians. The march continued daily, via Ligny, Spy, and Champion until they arrived in Antheit, about fifty miles from the German border, on 20 December. Here each company had its own mess and the village school was taken over for educational purposes. A number of religious services were held, those for the C of E and non conformists were in the village school, whilst Holy Mass for the Roman Catholics was held in the local convent by invitation of the Mother Superior. On Christmas Eve preparations were made for a grand Christmas dinner, but before a number of men could enjoy it they were sent home. The War Diary records that on Christmas Eve a large draft of miners left the battalion for demobilisation.

On Christmas Day each company had a huge Christmas dinner followed by a religious service and then the revelry and rejoicing went on until late in the evening. On Boxing Day, the officers played the non commissioned officers at football, the officers' team winning by four goals to nil. The weather was wet at this time so classes in reading, writing, spelling, arithmetic, grammar, composition and French were started, with sport most afternoons.

New Year's Day was a holiday and on the following days the educational classes continued. On 6 January the battalion marched to Huy (Nord) Station to entrain for Cologne; 41st Division was to relieve the 1st Canadian Division in the Engelskirchen area. 20/Durham LI crossed into

20/Durham LI was reformed as a Pioneer Battalion and wore the Pick and Rifle collar badge.

A Guard found by men of the Durham Light Infantry outside the Hotel Monopole, the Military Governor's residence in the town centre.

Privates Cain and N Coyle at the rear gate of Riehl Pioneer Barracks in Cologne.

Private Scott from Felling on guard.

The battalion band taken in Cologne. They were much in demand for the ceremonial duties and during guard changing in town.

...uary 1920, the Battalion Cadre returns to Sunderland, the last Service Battalion of the Regiment to return home.

Colonel Leather and the Mayor watch the proceedings.

Germany at Herbesthal and eventually detrained at 1030 hours in Hoffungsthal and proceeded by route march to Engelskirchen where it took over duties from the 48th Canadian Highlanders. Once settled in, the education classes started again. Training for those not on outpost duty consisted of close order drill. On 19 January the Divisional Inter Company Football Tournament was revived and D Company met 187 Battery Royal Field Artillery, who they defeated by one goal to nil.

On 28 January a very considerable number of men left for demobilisation. In wet and sometimes snowy weather the battalion continued on outpost duty, by now D Company had reached the semi-final of the football tournament and met 23/Middlesex Regiment and beat them two goals to one, to reach the final. On 3 February the battalion paraded and practised for the ceremonial parade when the colours would be presented. On the following day another rehearsal took place, this time in front of the divisional commander and then on 6 February the final of the football tournament took place; D Company 20/Durham LI met the team from the 41st Divisional Ammunition Column, Royal Field Artillery, and in a close-fought match came out on top by one goal to nil, lifting the trophy on behalf of 20/Durham LI.

On a cold frosty morning on 10 February the SECOND Army Commander, General Sir H Plumer, presented the colour to the battalion. The next day they were relieved in the outpost line and moved back to support positions. Eventually by 26 February the advance party of the battalion moved to Riehl Pioneer Barracks in Cologne to take over from 3/Grenadier Guards; that same day the commanding officer, Lieutenant Colonel A V A Gayer, left the battalion for England

The Colour Party parade in Sunderland.

and demobilisation and command passed back to Major Charles Pannall DSO, MC.

The 41st Division was now renamed the London Division and 20/Durham LI was converted from an infantry battalion into the divisional pioneer battalion. Many of the old soldiers were demobilised and their places taken by young soldiers from 51 and 52/Durham LI. But other warrant officers and NCOs stayed on, wishing to remain with the battalion until disbandment. In September 1919, when there were further changes in the British Army of the Rhine, a new formation named the Independent Division was formed and 20/Durham LI became the pioneer battalion to that formation.

All through 1919, drill, education, sport and inspections were the chief activities of the 20/Durham LI until, in February 1920, news was received that the battalion was to disband. On 20 February all men except the Cadre were sent to the dispersal camp, the Cadre following a few days later on 23 February. By Friday 27 February the Cadre, under the command of Major C Pannal DSO MC, were in Sunderland and the Colour was laid up in Bishopwearmouth Church. Today there is a plaque on the wall which reads as follows:

This colour of the 20th (Wearside) Battalion of the Durham Light Infantry was entrusted to the Rector and Wardens of Bishopwearmouth Parish Church on Friday, February 27th, 1920, for safe keeping for all time.

After the service the Cadre marched to the Palatine Hotel where they were entertained by the Mayor, Alderman Sir Arthur Ritson KCBE JP. Just as in Durham, there was much speech making and farewells until it became the time for the Cadre to entrain for the last time. They were carried from Sunderland station to Newcastle Central station and from there marched up to the Joint Northumberland Fusiliers/Durham Light Infantry Depot at Fenham Barracks. There the last pieces of paperwork were signed and thus the 20th (Service) Battalion, the Durham Light Infantry, (Wearside), came to the end of its career.

Nothing is known or has been traced of an Old Comrades Association – possibly many joined the Regimental Association, whilst others may have just wanted to forget.

Gallantry Awards

The Distinguished Service Order

Major Graham McNicholl 20th Bn   LG 1/1/17
King's New Years Honours- no citation

Lieutenant Colonel Piers William North R Berks Regt Comdg 20th Bn   LG 26/9/17

Temporary Major, Acting Lt Colonel Charlie Pannall MC 20th Bn   LG 4/10/19
On 14–15 October 1918, near Wevelghem, his great gallantry and fine leadership greatly contributed to the success of the battalion under his command. During the attack on 14 October, he directed the attack on the first line personally through dense fog and towards the end of the day placed his men in position on the final objective exposing himself throughout to heavy shell and machine-gun fire. He has at all times shown gallantry and devotion to duty of a high order.

Captain Arnold Pumphrey 20th Bn   LG 4/6/17

Bar to The Distinguished Service Order

Lieutenant Colonel Aubrey Vivian A Gayer Bar to the DSO with 20th Bn   LG 16/9/18
DSO with 32nd Bn Middlesex Regiment   LG 19/11/17
For conspicuous gallantry and devotion to duty while commanding his battalion during an enemy attack. Six times in one morning, owing to his fine example, the battalion repulsed enemy attacks with heavy loss. Next evening when ordered to withdraw he did so skilfully with few casualties. He did fine work.

Lieutenant Colonel Piers William North DSO R Berks Regt Comdg 20th Bn   LG
For conspicuous gallantry and devotion to duty. He led his men to the attack with utter disregard of danger under heavy fire and the dash with which his battalion went forward in the attack and secured a considerable number of prisoners was largely due to his fine personal example. He was shortly afterwards severely wounded in the chest and back.

The Military Cross

Second Lieutenant William Reginald Brooke 20th Bn   LG 25/8/17
For conspicuous gallantry and devotion to duty. He displayed great courage, coolness and good leadership during an attack and afterwards when consolidating the position. On his way to the assembly area he led his men with great skill in pitch darkness and under shellfire, keeping them on the move forward at a time when delay would have been serious.

Second Lieutenant William Cuthbert Brown 20th Bn   LG 25/8/17
For conspicuous gallantry and devotion to duty. He led his company boldly and skillfully to their objective, carrying other troops with him. After reaching the objective under heavy shellfire he at once reorganised not only his own men but men of other regiments.

Second Lieutenant Philip Lys Davies Border Regiment att 20th Bn   LG 18/7/18
For conspicuous gallantry and devotion to duty. He led a patrol in an attempt to cross a river in order to ascertain its depth and if possible to reconnoitre the opposite bank. He made two

attempts at different places and was in the water over two hours. The water was icy cold and the current very swift, and he was repeatedly swept off his feet but did not give up the attempt to cross until he was overcome by the cold. He showed magnificent determination and devotion to duty.

Second Lieutenant, Acting Captain Andrew Sydney Davison 20th Bn LG 16/9/18
For conspicuous gallantry and devotion to duty during an enemy attack. He commanded a company with great coolness and ability and encouraged his men under heavy attacks to hold on to their positions.

Second Lieutenant Frederick Bowler Davison 20th Bn LG 8/3/19
For gallantry and devotion to duty on the night of 14th October, 1918, near Menin, when he took out patrols and gained valuable information. On the morning of the 15th despite heavy machine gun fire, he pushed forward with patrols, and eventually established a line of posts on the River Lys. His conduct was of a very high order throughout the operation.

13769 CSM James Donnelly 20th Bn. DCM & Bar, MM & Bar LG 3/6/19
King's Birthday Honours- no citation

Second Lieutenant Thomas Sydney Duddy DCM 20th Bn LG 16/9/18
For conspicuous gallantry and devotion to duty during an enemy attack. He handled his platoon and later his company with great courage and ability against heavy enemy attacks. He also successfully carried out a reconnaissance under heavy barrage.

Lieutenant Thomas May Fletcher 20th Bn LG 9/1/18
For conspicuous gallantry and devotion to duty. Although wounded in the head on the way to the assembly area, he returned to his company after being dressed, in time to lead them to the attack. This he did with great gallantry until wounded a second time, gaining both his objectives and setting a splendid example of fearlessness and energy to his men.

Second Lieutenant Ronald Monckton Fulljames 20th Bn LG 26/9/16
For conspicuous gallantry in action. He repeatedly reorganised his party, and after evacuating the wounded, led forward the remainder to force a way through the wire.

Lieutenant Harold Goodley 20th Bn LG 16/9/18
For conspicuous gallantry and devotion to duty under heavy shellfire in repeatedly organising communications during very critical periods and enabling touch to be kept when the situation would otherwise have been obscure.

Lieutenant Robert Donald Green 20th Bn LG 4/6/17
King's Birthday Honours no citation

Lieutenant & Quartermaster Arthur Higham Royal Fusiliers att 20th Bn LG 3/6/18
King's Birthday Honours- no citation

Lieutenant C E Hopkinson 20th Bn LG 1/1/19

Second Lieutenant James Gordon Reay Pacy 20th Bn LG 9/1/18
For conspicuous gallantry and devotion to duty. After his company commander had become a

casualty, he led his company with great dash and when concealed snipers proved troublesome, he organised a bombing attack and put them out of action. He subsequently organised the captured ground with great skill and successfully resisted two counter-attacks.

Second Lieutenant (T/Capt) Frank William Paley DCM MM KRRC att 20th Bn.
King's Birthday Honours- no citation   LG 3/6/19

Lieutenant John Edward Rasche 20th Bn   LG 15/10/18
For conspicuous gallantry and devotion to duty during an enemy attack. He was in command of a patrol, and his retreat being cut off by an enemy barrage, he stood off the enemy until their barrage lifted, when he withdrew to his lines, bringing in his whole party, including wounded. During the withdrawal he was wounded himself but remained on duty until ordered to the ambulance at the close of the action.

Lieutenant Scott RAMC attached 20th Bn

Captain Edwin Smith 20th Bn   LG 26/9/17
For conspicuous gallantry and devotion to duty. When his company commander had become a casualty, he led his company forward with the greatest gallantry, organising and personally leading bombing parties to account for snipers, who were firing upon his men from concealed dug-outs. Later he successfully organised his company's defences and repelled two counter-attacks, in the course of which he personally accounted for many of the enemy.

Second Lieutenant Frank Edward Corbitt Douglas Smith 20th Bn   LG 22/3/18
For conspicuous gallantry and devotion to duty during a counter-attack by the enemy he led his platoon forward out of the trenches the better to meet the attack and brought his left flank up so that the enemy were enfiladed and driven back in disorder. He set a fine example to his men throughout the operations.

Second Lieutenant I. W Stephenson 20th Bn

Lieutenant Harold Grieg Thompson Gen List att 20th Bn   LG 3/6/18
King's Birthday Honours- no citation.

Lieutenant James Thompson-Hopper 20th Bn   LG 27/7/16
For conspicuous gallantry when in charge of a party, working in front of our parapet. The enemy opened machine-gun fire and wounded a sergeant. Lieutenant Thompson-Hopper withdrew his party and then went out alone and carried in the sergeant under heavy fire aided by a flare.

Second Lieutenant (T/Capt) Norman Wilson Turnbull 20th Bn   LG 11/7/19
For conspicuous gallantry and devotion to duty. This officer led his company in the attack with such dash that he gained his first objective in 20 minutes in the face of heavy machine-gun fire. Later, when the company on his right was counter-attacked and forced to retire, he formed a defensive flank, which saved a larger withdrawal.

Second Lieutenant Henry Waters DCM 20th Bn   LG 16/9/18
For conspicuous gallantry and devotion to duty during an enemy attack. When his company commander became a casualty he took command and handled his men with great skill and courage against heavy enemy attacks.

Second Lieutenant Fawcitt Wayman 20th Bn   LG 4/6/17
King's Birthday Honours- no citation.

Second Lieutenant Bernard Wilkinson 20th Bn   LG 25/8/17
For conspicuous gallantry and devotion to duty. He led his company to their objective with great ability. Having reached it he at once cleared the enemy dug-outs, organised his prisoners, dug a well sited trench and mounted a machine gun he had captured, as part of the defence.

Captain Hubert Francis Wilson RAMC attached 20th Bn   LG
For conspicuous gallantry and devotion to duty. He repeatedly led his stretcher-bearers under heavy fire, and succeeded in evacuating all the wounded on his front; and when most of the stretcher-bearers had become casualties he organised a party of riflemen, with whom he worked for eight hours in the open under shellfire and continued to clear many wounded. He then returned and led up another large party with which he succeeded in clearing the front, having displayed splendid courage and devotion to duty throughout the day.

Second Lieutenant Frederick Wood 20th Bn   LG 11/1/19
For conspicuous gallantry and devotion to duty. This officer with about forty men, rushed forward to support a company, which was being heavily counter-attacked. Collecting stragglers he organised his men on forward isolated posts, moving amongst them under heavy fire and encouraging them to hold on until almost surrounded. Despite heavy casualties he stood fast until ordered to retire. His conduct throughout the day was most inspiring.

BAR TO THE MILITARY CROSS

Second Lieutenant Ronald Monckton Fulljames MC 20th Bn   LG 25/11/16
For conspicuous gallantry in action, he led three small parties and established them under very heavy fire 200 yards from the enemy's trenches, holding his ground for seven hours until relieved. He has previously done very fine work.

Second Lieutenant L W Stephenson MC 20th Bn

SECOND BAR TO THE MILITARY CROSS

Lieutenant James Wallace Macfarlane MC & Bar RAMC att 18th Bn

MENTIONED IN DESPATCHES

Lieutenant, A/Captain G A Bamlet att 20th Bn   9/7/19

Second Lieutenant T Bassett 20th Bn   9/7/19

Second Lieutenant W Hebron 20th Bn   28/12/18

Captain F H S Le Mesurier Border Regiment att 20th Bn   4/1/17

Captain F W Paley DCM 5th KRRC att 20th Bn   28/12/18
THE DISTINGUISHED CONDUCT MEDAL

20/750 Lance Corporal J W Clark   LG 17/4/18

For conspicuous gallantry and devotion to duty. He has carried out his duties with great skill and energy, and has shown splendid coolness under heavy fire.

245420 Sergeant H Ebbs 20th Bn   LG 5/12/18

For conspicuous gallantry and devotion to duty. When all the officers of his company became casualties he took command moving about among the men and organising them against counter-attack. Owing to heavy casualties he was eventually obliged to withdraw a short distance. He set a fine example to the other non-commissioned officers and men.

16669 Lance Corporal J Foreman 20th Bn   LG 3/9/18

For conspicuous gallantry and devotion to duty. When his company commander was ordered to withdraw to a new position he volunteered to stay behind with his Lewis gun to cover the withdrawal. Alone he mounted his gun in an exposed position, and successfully checked parties of advancing enemy before returning to the company with his gun. He displayed great gallantry and determination.

11596 Lance Sergeant W Fowler 20th Bn   LG 3/9/18

For conspicuous gallantry and devotion to duty. During an intense bombardment of his trench he rallied his platoon and beat off three enemy attacks. Next day he again beat off the enemy. It was due to his skilful regulating of rifle and Lewis-gun fire that the enemy were repulsed with heavy losses. He showed fine courage and leadership.

20/41 Sergeant A Houston   LG 26/1/18

For conspicuous gallantry and devotion to duty. Having led a bombing attack on an enemy sniping post with his company commander, all the party except himself were killed, whereupon he organised a second party and led them on again. When all these men were killed he organised a third party and successfully bombed the enemy out of his position. On the following day he organised a defence against an enemy counter-attack, which was repulsed by his skill and coolness, and throughout the whole operation he set a fine example of fearlessness and initiative to those who were with him.

20/955 CQMS G Potts with 15th Bn   LG 3/9/18

For conspicuous gallantry and devotion to duty on the Yellow Line in March 1918, during operations when acting as CSM. On the occasion of the battalion's counter-attack he became in command of a platoon, which he led forward with great courage and coolness and was the first to reach the objective. Although wounded he remained on duty, displaying the utmost coolness and resource until the withdrawal.

20/821 Sergeant T Robinson   LG 17/4/18

For conspicuous gallantry and devotion to duty as transport sergeant. He continually showed great courage and determination in bringing stores to the line, under heavy fire, and by his coolness and judgement saved many casualties.

20/142 Company Sergeant Major J Sherriff   LG 3/9/19

During the period 25 February to 16 September 1918, he showed a fine example to the men. During the retirement on the Somme he carried out the duties of platoon commander in a highly satisfactory manner. On 4 September his conduct was again of the highest order. He repeatedly exposed himself when encouraging the men and directing fire.

18/1153 Corporal J G Wilkinson with 20th Bn   LG 5/12/18

For conspicuous gallantry and devotion to duty. When two Lewis guns were knocked out, and the enemy were bombing the position, this NCO rushed forward alone and brought one of the guns into action again. He kept it in action until he was severely wounded, both legs being broken. By his timely initiative he saved a critical situation.

THE MILITARY MEDAL

20/163 Corporal F R Abernethy	LG 9/12/16
20/247 Private E Anderson	LG 9/12/16
24795 Corporal G N Armstrong 20th Bn	LG 17/6/19
23489 Sergeant J A Armstrong 20th Bn	LG 17/12/17
21015 Sergeant R Atkinson 20th Bn	LG 11/2/19
18215 Private C Barnes 20th Bn	LG 12/12/17
20/558 Private E Bell	LG 28/9/19
20/660 Private H Bennett	LG 11/2/19
28420 Private E H Best 20th Bn	LG 21/8/17
4/8000 Private J Betteridge 20th Bn	LG 21/8/17
27249 Sergeant J Brough 20th Bn	LG 23/7/19
18/1773 Sergeant J R Brough with 20th Bn History	
12516 Private W Burke 20th Bn	LG 28/9/17
18/430 Lance Corporal G Burns with 20th Bn	LG 12/12/17
250415 Private J G Clarey 20th Bn	LG 6/8/18
93280 Corporal A Cochrane 20th Bn	LG 23/7/19
20/613 Lance Corporal T Cummings	LG 21/9/16
93274 Private Curry W 20th Bn	LG 23/7/19
300090 Corporal F Danforth 20th Bn	LG 23/7/19
9081 Private J M C Darrell 20th Bn	LG 27/10/17
20/407 Lance Sergeant G Dazley	LG 9/12/16
20/929 Private R Dixon	LG 28/9/17
20/787 Private E Donkin	LG 23/7/19
32673 Private R Ellison 20th Bn	LG 28/9/17
20/76 Private B Fenwick	LG 21/8/17
20/145 Private G Forbes	LG 17/6/19
32010 Private J Forbes 20th Bn	LG 17/6/19
20/13 Lance Corporal G Forster	LG 12/12/17
12928 Private C F Grant 20th Bn	LG 23/7/19
20/485 Lance Corporal J Hannah	LG 28/9/17
20/139 Private J T Hardy	LG 9/12/16
45901 Corporal W H Hare	LG 29/8/17
20/1068 Private J Harris	LG 16/8/17
32768 Lance Corporal T Harrison 20th Bn	LG 23/2/18
20/513 Private G Hayes	LG 19/3/18
200979 Private E H Hewitt 20th Bn	LG 6/8/18
23411 Private H Hey 20th Bn	LG 11/2/19
20/981 Private T H Jeffrey	LG 24/1/19
203996 Lance Corporal A E Johnson 20th Bn	LG 19/3/18
44835 Private J Jones 20th Bn	LG 6/8/18
82380 Private J Kearney 20th Bn	LG 23/7/19
327199 Private F Kelly 20th Bn	LG 3/6/19
36935 Private F H Kenworthy 20th Bn	LG 6/8/18
19188 Private L Kingstone 20th Bn	LG 16/8/17

20/44 Private J Kirkup	LG 28/9/17
110672 Sergeant J R Leighton 20th Bn	LG 22/11/19
20/448 Lance Corporal T Liddle	LG 29/8/18
30231 Private H Lockey 20th Bn	LG 9/12/16
44669 Private T M Maider 20th Bn	LG 23/7/19
20/62 Lance Corporal T S Mathieson	LG 21/8/17
20/175 Private T McClumpha	LG 9/12/16
25903 Sergeant W McPherson 20th Bn	LG 21/8/17
203951 Private W Mears 20th Bn	LG 28/9/17
42633 Private W R Moody 20th Bn	LG 17/6/19
20/331 Bugler R Mordey	LG 28/9/17
20/110 Private G Newton with 19th Bn	LG 14/5/19
45800 Lance Corporal A Nicholson 20th Bn	LG 23/7/19
20/249 Private J Parkin	LG 21/8/17
82218 Private R Pope 20th Bn	LG 11/2/19
20/815 Sergeant John Potts (Westgate)	LG 29/8/18
20/220 Sergeant E Priestley 20th Bn	LG 19/2/17
20/634 Private M Quinn	LG 21/8/17
18189 Lance Corporal J Ramsden 20th Bn	LG 28/9/17
202946 Corporal H Ratcliffe 20th Bn	LG 23/7/19
32364 Sergeant H M Ridley with 20th Bn	LG 6/8/18
44834 Lance Corporal W S Rowe 20th Bn	LG 6/8/18
19/866 Sergeant B Scott with 20th Bn	LG 28/9/17
82343 Private O Seabourne 20th Bn	LG 7/10/18
20/142 CSM J W Sherriff DCM	LG 23/7/19
20/441 Private P Smith	LG 12/12/17
27402 Lance Corporal W S Smith 20th Bn	LG 21/9/16
83229 Private J Squirrel 20th Bn	LG 29/3/19
203128 Private H D Taylor 20th Bn	LG 6/8/18
302243 Private F B Thompson 20th Bn	LG 6/8/18
22133 Private J F Thompson 20th Bn	LG 28/9/17
21790 Lance Corporal C Turley 20th Bn	LG 17/6/19
202999 Private A Turnbull 20th Bn	LG 6/3/18
44677 Private W Wilkie 20th Bn	LG 23/7/19
20/566 Sergeant W Wilson	LG 19/3/18
20/502 Lance Sergeant E Winter	LG 6/1/17
42575 Private T Yeomans 20th Bn	LG 28/9/17
44734 Private J Young 20th Bn	LG 11/2/19
32426 Lance Corporal J G Young 20th Bn	LG 6/8/18

BAR TO THE MILITARY MEDAL

10535 Sergeant J Clark MM 20th Bn	LG 6/8/18
9081 Private M Darrell MM 20th Bn	LG 9/11/17
13769 CSM J Donnelly MC DCM & Bar MM 20th Bn	LG 21/8/19
38696 Lance Corporal J W Hall MM 20th Bn	LG 17/6/19
20/62 Lance Corporal T S Mathieson MM with 15th Bn	LG 14/5/19

20/249 Sergeant J Parkin MM	LG 6/8/18
22133 Lance Corporal J F Thompson MM 20th Bn	LG 12/12/17

MERITORIOUS SERVICE MEDAL

20/207 Sergeant W J Bertram	LG 18/1/19
27180 RQMS W Coxon 20th Bn	LG 3/6/19
20/3 CQMS E S Gore	LG 18/1/19
38915 Private A Hind 20th Bn	LG 3/6/19
201358 Private A Kirsop with 20th Bn	LG 3/6/18
20/11 Sergeant A E Miller	LG 3/6/19
20/914 Private W Naugher	LG 3/6/18

FOREIGN DECORATIONS

CROIX DE GUERRE BELGIUM

245420 Sergeant H Ebbs DCM 20th Bn	LG 4/9/19
20/1044 Sergeant T H Greenlees	LG 4/9/19
28104 Private T Slater 20th Bn	LG 4/9/19
Captain N W Turnbull MC 20th Bn	LG 4/9/19

MEDAL MILITAIRE BELGIUM

13769 CSM J Donnelly DCM MM 20th Bn	LG 21/8/19
16660 Lance Corporal E Foreman DCM 20th Bn	LG 5/4/19

CROIX DE GUERRE FRANCE

325383 CSM M Brindle 20th Bn	LG 21/7/19
42230 Private W E Bushby 20th Bn	LG 19/6/19
T/Lt Colonel A V A Gayer 20th Bn	LG 21/7/19
44744 Private T J Hancey 20th Bn	LG 19/6/19
45798 Private F Summerscales 20th Bn	LG 21/7/19
300381 Private J Watson 20th Bn	LG 19/6/19

ORDER OF KARRA-GEORGE (SERBIA)

20/220 Acting Sergeant E Priestley	LG 19/2/17

MENTIONED IN DESPATCHES

44828 Sergeant W Collis 20th Bn	LG 9/7/19
245112 Private A Daft 20th Bn	LG 9/7/19
20/1044 Sergeant T H Greenlees	LG 21/12/17 & 4/9/19
20/78 Private H Noon	LG 9/7/19
20/142 Sergeant J W Sherriff	LG 21/12/17
45798 Private F Summerscales 20th Bn	LG 28/12/18

Alphabetical Roll of Officers that served with the 20th Service Battalion of the Durham Light Infantry 1915-1918

NAME	INITIALS	RANK	CASUALTY
ANDREWS	L W	2nd Lt	TO 22/DLI 23/3/17
APPLETON	J	2nd Lt	WND 21/10/18
ARKLESS	F C	2nd Lt	WND 15/09/16
ARMSTRONG	John W	2nd Lt	KiA 21/10/18
ATKINSON	G	Lt	WND 02/10/18
BAINBRIDGE	J	2nd Lt	
BALLANTYNE	James A	2nd Lt	WND 4/4/17, KiA 01/08/17
BAMBROUGH	Thomas C	2nd Lt	WND 21/09/17, DoW 25/09/17
BAMLET	G A	2nd Lt	
BANNERMAN	W	2nd Lt	
BARKER	J H	2nd Lt	WND 02/06/16
BASSETT	T H	2nd Lt	WND 04/09/18
BLACK	G R	2nd Lt	WND 31/03/18
BLAIR		Lt	WND 02/10/18
BRANT	F	Captain	
BRETTELL	W P M	2nd Lt	
BREWER	H H	Lt	
BRITTON	Edward W	2nd Lt	WND 26/07/16 KiA 31/07/17
BROOKE	W R	2nd Lt	
BROWN	A	2nd Lt	WND 24/03/18
BROWN	W C	2nd Lt	
BROWNE	Archibald T	Captain	WND 17/01/17, KiA 29/09/18
BRUNT	F	Lt	WND 04/09/18
BUDGE	A R V	2nd Lt	
BUTTERFIELD	J W	2nd Lt	WND 10/10/16
CALLOW	E H	2nd Lt	
CANON		2nd Lt	
CARMICHAEL	John	2nd Lt	DoW 25/03/18
CARROLL	J M	Lt	
CARTWRIGHT	Nigel W H	2nd Lt	KiA 21/09/17
CHARLTON	Ralph T	2nd Lt	KiA 20/09/17
CHATT	F C	2nd Lt	
CLARK	W D	2nd Lt	
COLLINS	A F	Lt	WND 11/09/16
CONRATH	P T	2nd Lt	FROM ROYAL FUS KiA 04/09/18
CORBETT	J	2nd Lt	WND 20/09/17
COX	P H	2nd Lt	
CUNNINGHAM	C S	2nd Lt	WND 20/09/17
DAVELL	C G	2nd Lt	
DAVIES	P L	2nd Lt	
DAVISON	A S	2nd Lt	
DAVISON	F B	2nd Lt	
DIXON	J E	2nd Lt	
DOBINSON	P L	Lt	WND 21/09/17
DONNELLY	A	2nd Lt	
DONNELLY	J	2nd Lt	WND 25/10/18
DORMAND	T W	2nd Lt	
DOUTHWAITE	P H	2nd Lt	
DUDDY	T S	2nd Lt	WND 25/03/18
EGGLESTONE	Ernest	2nd Lt	Died 02/06/19
EPPSTEIN	William R	Captain	DoW 04/09/18
FLETCHER	Thomas M	Lt	WND 16/09/16, KiA 01/08/17
FOSTER	Joseph	2nd Lt	DoW 14/10/18
FRISBY	G	2nd Lt	
FULLJAMES	R M	Lt	WND 31/07/17
GARDNER	J H	Lt	WND 20/09/17
GAYER	A V A	Lt Colonel	WND (GAS) 04/09/18
GOODLEY	Harold	Captain	

GOUGH		Lt	
GRAHAM	A	2nd Lt	
GREEN	R D	Lt	
GREW	B	Lt	
GRUBB	J D	Lt	
HALL	R	2nd Lt	
HAND	Moreton	Captain	KiA 31/07/17
HEATHERLEY	Francis	Lt RAMC	
HEBRON	Wm	2nd Lt	KiA 25/10/18
HERBERT	E	2nd Lt	
HIGHAM	A	Lt &QM	
HILLER	W D	Captain	
HILLS	J W	Captain	WND 30/09/16
HOPKINSON	C E	2nd Lt	WND 16/09/16, 30/09/16
IVESON	James H	Captain	KiA 23/03/18
JENNINGS	R	2nd Lt	
JESSOP	D E	2nd Lt	WND 26/07/16, 16/09/16,D36
JOHNSON	G H	2nd Lt	
JOHNSON	W	Captain	
KAY	Robert R	2nd Lt	FROM 5/DLI KiA 23/03/18
KENT	C	Lt & QM	
KIPPS	W H	2nd Lt	WND 07/06/17
LARGE	P F	2nd Lt	WND 28/06/17
LAVELL	C G	2nd Lt	WND 04/09/18
LAX	Donald	2nd Lt	KiA 25/10/18
LE MESURIER	F H S	Major	
LEATHER	K J W	Lt Colonel	WND 22/07/16
LIDDLE	W	2nd Lt	
LISTER	G	2nd Lt	
LITTLE	G M	2nd Lt	WND 03/05/17
LOWELL	C G	2nd Lt	
MacLAREN	W R	2nd Lt	WND 04/09/18
MANSFIELD	J N	2nd Lt	
McDONALD	A	2nd Lt	
McGIBBON	William P	2nd Lt	KiA 23/09/17
McKINLAY		Lt	WND 04/08/18
McNICOLL	David G	Lt Colonel	WND 22/06/17 DoW 20/09/17
MITCHELL	W	2nd Lt	WND 16/09/16
MUNRO	Hugh Mc	Lt	KiA 25/03/18
NEILL	V	2nd Lt	
NICHOL	M	Captain	
NORTH	P W	Lt Colonel	WND 31/07/17
OLIVER	G R	2nd Lt	
OLIVER	W J	Captain	
PACEY	J G	2nd Lt	
PALEY	F W	2nd Lt	
PANNELL	C	Major	
PARKER		2nd Lt	WND 29/09/18
PARSONS	A D	2nd Lt	FROM 5/DL DoW 26/03/18
PEAT	T	2nd Lt	INJURED WHEN DUG OUT COLLAPSED 02/08/18
PENRICE	William G	2nd Lt	KiA 07/06/17
POLLARD	G G	2nd Lt	
PRUDHOE	W S	2nd Lt	WND 21/09/17
PUMPHREY	Arnold	Captain	WND 30/6/16, KiA 21/09/17
RASCHE	E	Captain	SEV BURNED EVAC 31/5/16
RASCHE	J E	2nd Lt	
REAH	A R	2nd Lt	
RICHARDSON	J O	2nd Lt	
RICHWOOD	G	2nd Lt	SICK 17/07/16

RIDLEY	H W	2nd Lt	
RILEY	C L	2nd Lt	
RISDON	H	Lt	WND 16/09/16
ROBERTS	B S	2nd Lt	
ROBINSON	R W	2nd Lt	
ROBSON	H G S	Lt	
RODEN	A G	2nd Lt	WND 20/09/17
RODWELL	W A	2nd Lt	
RUDLAND	H	2nd Lt	
RUFFLE	C J	Lt	WND 31/03/18
RUSSELL	Ernest	2nd Lt	KiA 04/09/18
SAUNDERS	J T	Captain	
SCOTT	W J	2nd Lt	
SHAW	O R	2nd Lt	
SHEPHERDSON	L W	Lt	
SIM	H E H	Captain	
SIMPKIN	J S	Lt & QM	EVAC SICK 23/06/16
SMITH	E	2nd Lt	WND 21/09/17
SMITH	E P	2nd Lt	WND 21/09/17
SMITH	F E C	2nd Lt	
SMITH	R C	Major	
SOUTHWELL	H R	Lt	WND 21/09/17
SPENCER	Percival	Captain	WND 16/09/16
STEPHENSON	W O M	2nd Lt	
STRUTHERS	J A	Lt	WND 12/09/16
TERRY	J	2nd Lt	
THOMPSON	H G	2nd Lt	
THOMPSON-HOPPER	James	Lt	KiA 30/06/16
TURNBULL	N W	Captain	WND 23/03/18
UPTON	Roger M	2nd Lt	KiA 07/06/17
WALTON	William K	Lt	KiA 31/07/17
WARWICK	S W	2nd Lt	WND 21/10/18
WATERS	H	2nd Lt	
WAYMAN	Fawcitt	Captain	WND 2/7/16, KiA 31/07/17
WAYMAN	Myles	Captain	WND 30/06/16
WELFORD	F	2nd Lt	
WHITFIELD	H	2nd Lt	
WILKIN	F	2nd Lt	WND 31/12/16
WILKINSON	B	Captain	WND 25/03/18, 25/10/18
WILLIS	A R	2nd Lt	ATTD FROM 4/HLI KiA 28/07/17
WILLS	John S	Lt	KiA 04/09/18
WILSON	Hubert F	Captain	RAMC ATTD
WOOD	F	2nd Lt	WND 25/10/18
WOOD	J	2nd Lt	WND 21/10/18
YEWDALL	Frederick G	Lt	Died 18/05/18

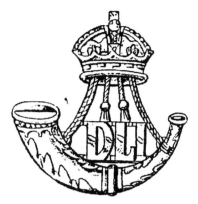

ALPHABETICAL NOMINAL ROLL OF ORIGINAL OTHER RANKS

20th (Service) Battalion
Durham Light Infantry
(Wearside)

1915 – 1919

NAME	INITIALS	RANK	NUMBER	TOWN_VILL	DATE & PLACE, BURIED	TRANSFER - HOSP - NEW REGT NUMBER- PLACE OF BIRTH ETC
ABERNETHY	F K	CPL	/163			
ABLEY	Jos	PTE	/343		21/9/15	KR para 392 5/3/18	TO DEPOT. AGE 25
ADAMS	H	PTE	/665			
ADAMS	Har B	PTE	/181			TO 20th BN, CLASS Z RESERVE. LCPL
ADAMSON	J	PTE	/671		
ADAMSON	M	PTE	/359		
ADAMSON	ThosW	PTE	/256	WILLINGTON	BISHOP AUCKL 27/7/16 TANCREZ FARM CEM
ADEY	John	PTE	/633	SUNDERLAND	19/11/16 RIDGE WOOD MIL CEM
AIRSON	J W	PTE	/1022	
ALDERSON	G	PTE	/934	
ALDERSON	JohnW	PTE	/576	HETTON LE HOLE	HOUGHTON LE 7/6/17 MENIN GATE MEM
ALDERSON	Thos	PTE	/908	SHILDON	BISHOP AUCKL 31/7/17 MENIN GATE MEM	AGE 31, LNER LABOURER SHILDON LOCO SHEDS.
ALDERSON	W	PTE	/909	
ALDERTON	Fred	PTE	/800	WHEATLEY HILL	3/1/15	KR para 392 6/12/18	AGE 22.
ALEXANRA	G	PTE	/972	
ALLAN	Fred	PTE	/385		6/11/15	KR para 392 4/2/19	TO 20th, 20th, 14th BNS, CLASS Z RESERVE.
ALLEN	Robt	PTE	/871			TO 14th, 18th, 4th BNS. AGE 23
ALLINSON	R	PTE	/342	
ANDERSON	Chas	PTE	/234	SEAHAM HARBOUR	SEAHAM HARB 30/6/16 TANCREZ FARM CEM	BORN DIPTON. AGE 24
ANDERSON	Edmnd	PTE	/247	HETTON LE HOLE	HOUGHTON LE 1/10/16 THIEPVAL MEM	BORN EPPLETON.
ANDERSON	RobtW	PTE	/878			TO 19th, 20th BNS, CLASS Z RESERVE.
ANDERSON	W	PTE	/754	
ANGEL	Rich	PTE	/379	WEST HARTLEPOOL	WEST HARTLEP 7/6/17 MENIN GATE MEM	AGE 18.
APPLEBY	Wm	PTE	/417	SOUTH HETTON		TO 18th, 18th, 17th BNS, CLASS Z RESERVE.
APPLEGARTH	Geo	PTE	/824	DARLINGTON		TO CLASS Z RESERVE.
APPLETON	Alf	LSGT	/567	SADBERGE		TO 20th, 20th BN, CLASS Z RESERVE. SGT
ARCHER	Fredk	PTE	/298	DAWDON	SEAHAM HARB 17/9/16	BORN HENDON SUNDERLAND.
ARCHER	John	PTE	/995			TO 19th BN, CLASS Z RESERVE.
ARKLEY	Jas M	PTE	/630	SUNDERLAND	26/6/17 MENIN GATE MEM
ARMSTRONG	F	PTE	/960	
ARMSTRONG	G	BGLR	/294			TO 20th, 20th BN, CLASS Z RESERVE.
ARMSTRONG	Geo F	BGLR	/214			AGE 19 TO 139 F AMB 12/6/16 EVAC 2 CCS SHRAP WND LEG + BACK
ARMSTRONG	N	PTE	/1038	HETTON	HOUGHTON LE 5/10/18 BEAUREVOIR BRIT CEM	TO 10th, 13th, 13th BNS.
ASHCROFT	JohnG	PTE	/748	SUNDERLAND	3/10/16 ETAPLES MIL CEM	ATT YORK & LANCASTER REGIMENT(9th BN), TO 20th DLI. AGE 19
ASHER	Sydn	PTE	/676			KR para 392 25/5/17
ATCHESON	Sam	PTE	/328	
ATKINS	F	LCPL	/505		26/3/18 GOMMECOURT BRIT
ATKINSON	Geo	PTE	/85	NEW SEAHAM	SEAHAM HARB CEM No 2	TO 20th, 9th BNS.
ATKINSON	J	PTE	/414	
ATKINSON	J	PTE	/469	
ATKINSON	John	PTE	/603	
ATKINSON	Smith	PTE	/316		5/10/15	KR para 392 7/12/17	TO 3rd BN. AGE 26
ATKINSON	W	PTE	/421	
AVERRE	ThosL	PTE	/423			KR para 392
AYRE	Thos	BGLR	/670		8/11/15	KR para 392 13/4/18	AGE 24.
AYRES	ArthF	SIG	/803	
BAILEY	S	PTE	/464	
BAILEY	Thos	PTE	/893	HENDON	SUNDERLAND	DIED OF ERYSPELAS, AGE 20.
BAINES	John	PTE	/894	TUNSTALL	24/2/16 BISHOPWEARMOUTH CEM	REGIMENTAL POLICE
BALLANTYNE	J W	PTE	/157	
BAMBOROUGH	R	PTE	/507	
			/810	

172

Surname	Forename	Rank	No.	Born	Enlisted	Date	Fate / Memorial	Notes
BANKS	Fred	PTE	/254	FULWELL		17/9/15	KR para 392 15/9/17	TO 3rd BN. AGE 25
BANKS	Thos	LCPL	/1064			16/11/15	KR para 392	2nd IN BILLIARD COMP B/CASTLE 31/12/15. AGE 21.
BARCLAY	Geo	LSGT	/ 5					TO CLASS Z RESERVE.
BARKLE	W H	LCPL	/ 176					
BARNES	T W	PTE	/ 976					
BARRAT	S	PTE	/ 738					
BARRATCLOUGH	Abt	PTE	/ 33	HENDON	SUNDERLAND		16/9/16 THIEPVAL MEM	TO 4th BN. AGE 25
BARTRAM	R	PTE	/ 928					STILL SERVING 1920.
BATLEY	A	SGT	/1011			2/12/15	KR para 392 15/4/18	LCPL. BORN STANHOPE AGE 21.
BATY	Geo W	PTE	/ 845	ROOKHOPE	BISHOP AUCKL		1/10/16 THIEPVAL MEM	
BEADLE	John	PTE	/ 843					
BEAMSON	W T	PTE	/ 718					
BEATTIE	R	PTE	/ 84					
BEATTIE	J W	PTE	/ 274					
BECK	M	PTE	/ 789					
BECK	D	PTE	/ 790					
BELL	R	PTE	/ 850					TO ARMY RESERVE CLASS P. AGE 23
BELL	Edwd	PTE	/ 558	HASWELL		23/10/15	KR para 392 2/4/19	AGE 23.
BELL	Geo	BGLR	/ 736	DARLINGTON		1/11/15	KR para 392 3/4/19	
BELL	Henry	CPL	/ 246			6/9/15		TO MACHINE GUN CORPS(FEB 18), STILL SERVING 1920.
BELL	James	PTE	/ 559	HASWELL	SUNDERLAND		23/10/18 ST SOUPLET BRIT CEM	TO 10th, 11th, 2nd BNS. AGE 25
BELL	JohnW	PTE	/ 679	EIGHTON BANKS	SUNDERLAND		22/9/17 ZANTVOORDE BRIT CEM	LCPL
BELL	Matt	PTE	/ 284	CROOK	CROOK		31/3/18 ARRAS MEM	TO DEPOT.
BELL	Nich	LCPL	/ 396			3/10/15	WOUNDS 26/2/17	TO DEPOT. AGE 21
BELL	Robt	PTE	/ 943					
BELL	RobtW	PTE	/ 352	DARLINGTON		17/11/15	KR para 392 2/3/18	TO 19th, 20th, 20th BN, CLASS Z RESERVE. BROTHERS IN NAVY AND RFA
BELL	R W	PTE	/ 55		SUNDERLAND		27/2/17 LIJSSENTHOEK MIL CEM	TO 12th, 20th BNS. AGE 27
BELLERBY	Thos	PTE	/1000	SUNDERLAND				TO 20th, 20th BN, CLASS Z RESERVE.
BENNET	Harld	LCPL	/ 660	SUNDERLAND				TO 11th, 20th, 20th, BNS, STILL SERVING 1920.AGE 21 to 139 F AMB 9/5/16-12CCS, 20/6/16-8 CCS IMBETIG
BENNET	Robt	LCPL	/ 625		SUNDERLAND		21/7/16 BOULOGNE EASTERN CEM	BORN TRIMDON GRANGE.
BERRIMAN	Robt	LCPL	/ 112	SHOTTON COLL	SUNDERLAND			FROM 18th BN NF, TO 20th, 20th BN, CLASS Z RES MASTER TAILOR
BERTRAM	Wm T	SGT	/ 207	NORTH SHIELDS				
BEWICK	Geo R	PTE	/ 516	SUNDERLAND	SUNDERLAND	20/10/15	AGE 16YRS 11MNTH 25/11/15	HAWKER AGE 16-11MNTH, 5'4". DIS AT BARNARD CASTLE.
BILTON	J	PTE	/ 514					TO SOUTH- LANCASHIRE REGT. S LANCS No 63238
BIRCH	C H	PTE	/ 53					TO DEPOT.
BLACK	T W	BGLR	/ 323			13/11/15	SICK 8/2/17	
BLAKEWAY	Edwd	PTE	/ 922					TO CLASS Z RESERVE.
BLANCHARD	ThosF	PTE	/ 520					TO 10th, 2rd BNS, CLASS Z RESERVE.
BLENKINSOPP	Fred	LCPL	/ 128					TO 22nd, 17th BNS, CLASS Z RESERVE.
BLENKINSOPP	Wm	LCPL	/ 745					TO 2nd, 15th, 1/7th, 1/7th BNS, CLASS Z RESERVE.
BOGGIE	James	PTE	/ 973					
BOOTH	JohnA	PTE	/ 229	SUNDERLAND	SUNDERLAND		8/6/17 VOORMEZEELE ENCL No 3 CEM	REGIMENTAL POLICE
BOSTOCK	John	PTE	/ 337	MERRINGTON LANE				TO 11th, 19th, 15th BNS, CLASS Z RESERVE.
BOWMAN	W	PTE	/ 251					TO 20th, 20th BN, CLASS Z RESERVE.
BOWRAN	FredJ	PTE	/ 743	RYHOPE VILLAGE				TO 20th, 20th BN, CLASS Z RESERVE.
BRADLEY	Thos	PTE	/ 822	HETTON LE HOLE				TO DEPOT. AGE 33
BRADSHAW	JohnH	PTE	/ 124			28/8/15		TO 20th, 20th, 9th BNS, CLASS Z RESERVE.
BRANDT	Geo	PTE	/ 88				KR para 392 22/8/17	
BREED	John	SGT	/ 439	DURHAM CITY				TO 1/7th BN STILL SERVING 1920.TO 139 FA 15/7/16 OPTICAL TO DUTY.CQMS.COY/BN RUNNING TEAM
BREWER	Nor R	PTE	/ 257	DURHAM CITY	SUNDERLAND		21/9/17 TYNE COT MEM	BORN TOW LAW.

SURNAME	NAME	RANK	No	PLACE	PLACE 2	DATE	MEMORIAL	NOTES
BREWIS	Percy	PTE	/954	SUNDERLAND			BECORDEL BEC	AGE 24.
BREWIS	Thos	PTE	/30	SUNDERLAND				TO SOUTH STAFFORDSHIRE REGT. S STAFFS No 54033
BREWSTER	Abt	PTE	/590	MURTON	SUNDERLAND	21/9/16	HEILLY STATION CEM	SGT.
BRIGGS	Geo	PTE	/861	HEBBURN NEWTOWN				
BROWN	E	BGLR	/384					
BROWN	Ed Wm	SGT	/376	TINDALE CRES	BISHOP AUCKL	29/3/18	POZIERES MEM	TO 19th BN. BORN GARROWS, GLENQUAICH. AGE 21
BROWN	G	PTE	/515					
BROWN	J	PTE	/369					
BROWN	J	PTE	/1027					
BROWN	J	PTE	/1049					TO 139 F AMB 10/7/16 SCABIES EVAC TO 50 CCS.
BROWN	J W	PTE	/766					
BROWN	Robt	PTE	/1041			8/12/15	KR para 392 27/3/18	TO DEPOT. AGE 23
BROWN	T	PTE	/170					
BROWN	Thos	CPL	/530	SUNDERLAND			7/6/17 VOORMEZEELE ENCL No 3	
BROWN	W A	PTE	/273	SUNDERLAND		13/9/15	KR para 392 18/4/16	DID NOT SERVE OVERSEAS.
BROWN	Wm C	PTE	/489	SUNDERLAND	SOUTH SHIELD:		22/6/17 MENIN GATE MEM	LCPL.
BRYCE	Rob Y	PTE	/635	NEWCASTLE			1/7/16 THIEPVAL MEM	TO 20th, CLASS Z RESERVE.
BUCHANAN	Fred A	PTE	/215	FULWELL	SUNDERLAND			TO 15th BN.SGT BORN HALIFAX, NOVA SCOTIA
BUCKLEY	Wm	PTE	/648					TO 20th, 20th BN, CLASS Z RESERVE.
BULLMORE	W E	PTE	/178					TO 20th, 20th BN, CLASS Z RESERVE.
BURDEN	J	PTE	/669					
BURKE	Rich J	PTE	/619				8/6/17 VOORMEZEELE ENCL No 3	AGE 25.
BURN	John	SIG	/859	DARLINGTON	GATESHEAD			BORN DURHAM, AGE 23 SERVED E COY.
BURNISTON	James	PTE	/996	HEBBURN	JARROW		31/07/17 MENIN GATE MEM	TO DEPOT. AGE 24
BURNISTON	W	PTE	/368					TO ARMY RESERVE CLASS P.AGE 24
BURTON	Edwd	PTE	/125			26/8/15	KR para 392 19/2/18	TO 18th, 20th BNS, CLASS Z RESERVE. BRYAN ON MR
BYRON	Robt	PTE	/658			27/10/15	KR para 392 25/5/17	TO DEPOT. AGE 20
BYRON	Wm	SIG	/853					TO 20th, 20th BN, CLASS Z RESERVE.AGE 19 TO 139 F AMB 31/7/16 EVAC 140 FLD AMB
CAHILL	Steph	PTE	/640	HENDON		26/10/15	9/7/18 1/9/16 BISHOPWEARMOUTH CEM	TO 19th, 10th, 15th BNS, CLASS Z RESERVE.
CAIRNS	Jos	PTE	/627					TO 20th, 20th BN, CLASS Z RESERVE.
CALLUM	John	PTE	/930	WEST HARTLEPOOL		7/12/15		AGE 21 TO 139 F AMB 18/8/16 EVAC 70 F AMB FLU.
CALLUM	S	PTE	/1021					TO ARMY RESERVE CLASS W. AGE 27 DID NOT SERVE OVERSEAS
CALVERT	Abt	PTE	/984					TO 20th BN. CLASS Z RESERVE.
CAMPBELL	A	PTE	/991					TO 10th, 20th BNS, CLASS Z RESERVE. AWOII
CAMPBELL	John	SIG	/946				KR para 392 27/11/16	TO CLASS Z RESERVE.
CAMPBELL	T	PTE	/156					TO CLASS Z RESERVE.
CAMPBELL	W	PTE	/230					TO CLASS Z RESERVE.AGE 19 TO 139 F AMB 4/9/16 EVAC 50 CCS SCABIES
CAMSELL	Thos	PTE	/66			23/8/15	MINERS AMBLYOPIA 22/1/19	AGE 24.
CARR	Jos	SIG	/851					TO 139 F AMB 5/8/16 SCABIES TO DUTY.
CARR	Jos M	SGT	/690					TO 19th BN, CLASS Z RESERVE.
CARR	Robt	PTE	/108					TO 20th, 13th BNS, CLASS Z RESERVE.
CARR	Tom W	SGT	/179	LITTE LUMLEY				AGE 25.
CARRAHAR	J L	PTE	/549					
CARTER	Abt	PTE	/550			24/10/15	KR para 392 17/4/18	
CARTER	F	PTE	/574					
CATCHPOLE	Geo	PTE	/896					
CAULFIELD	John T	PTE	/118					
CHAPMAN	Abt	PTE	/832					
CHAPMAN	J	PTE	/334					
CHAPMAN	John T	PTE	/907					TO 20th, 20th BN, CLASS Z RESERVE. TRANSPORT SECTION
CHAPMAN	Leond	PTE	/602	SHOTTON COLL	SUNDERLAND	6/11/15	KR para 392 16/3/18	
CHARLTON	J F	PTE	/741				16/9/16 SERRE ROAD No 2	BORN WORKINGTON AGE 19.

Surname	Name	Rank	No	Place	Birth / 2nd	Date	Cemetery / Fate	Remarks
CHARLTON	John	CPL	/141	SUNDERLAND	DARLINGTON	11/10/15	17/9/16 THIEPVAL MEM	BORN DURHAM. TO ARMY RESERVE CLASS P. LCPL AGE 31
CHARLTON	Wm	PTE	/449	SUNDERLAND			KR para 392 1/4/19	TO 139 F AMB 1/7/16 CONTAGIOUS IMBETIGO TO DUTY.
CHERRETT	Wm	CPL	/999	SUNDERLAND	SUNDERLAND	28/12/15	21/9/17 TYNE COT MEM	TO DEPOT.
CHILTON	Chas	PTE	/791				WOUNDS 30/4/17	
CHIPCHASE	Chris	PTE	/411	DARLINGTON			21/12/16 AIF BURIAL GROUND FLERS	TO 11th BN. AGE 19
CLARK	Aquil	PTE	/697	GATESHEAD			31/7/17 MENIN GATE MEM	LCPL BORN HOUGHTON LE SPRING.
CLARK	Fred	PTE	/626				KR para 392	
CLARK	Geo	PTE	/493	GUILDFORD				ATT 123 BDE HQ. 20th, 20th, 20th, CLASS Z RESERVE.
CLARK	Henry	RSM	/177	PELTON FELL	SUNDERLAND	19/9/16	19/9/16 ST SEVER CEM ROUEN	SERVED 8 YEARS IN INDIA, WOUNDED AT MONS. APPOINTED ACTING ORQMS 10/9/15. LCPL, NO 802 ON AVL.
CLARK	J	PTE	/801	SUNDERLAND				
CLARK	J	PTE	/957	SUNDERLAND				
CLARK	James	PTE	/556	SUNDERLAND	SUNDERLAND	16/9/16	16/9/16 THIEPVAL MEM	AGE 29 TO 139 F AMB 9/7/16 SHELLSHOCK TO DUTY.
CLARK	JohnW	BGLR	/750	EASINGTON COLL				TO 20th, 20th, CLASS Z RESERVE. CPL
CLARKE	Ralph	PTE	/758					TO 20th, 20th, CLASS Z RESERVE.
CLARKE	C	PTE	/401					
CLARKE	W	PTE	/829					
CLEAR	Thos	PTE	/964	SUNDERLAND	SUNDERLAND		24/11/17 ROCLINCOURT MIL CEM	ATT LTM BTY, TO 18th, 18th BN. TO 139 FLD AMB 6/9/16 APPENDICITIS EVAC 1NZ ST HOSP AGE 22
CLEMENTSON	Thos	PTE	/604	MURTON	SEAHAM HARBOUR	14/9/16	14/9/16 THIEPVAL MEM	AGE 18.
CLOSE	Edwd	PTE	/381	ESH				TO ROYAL DUBLIN FUSILIERS(2nd BN).
COARE	J	PTE	/1017				10/10/16 DARTMOOR CEM	
COATES	Geo S	PTE	/327	WESTERTON	BISHOP AUCKL		BECORDEL BEC	AGE 19.
COCKBURN	Morri	SGT	/130	COUNDON				TO CLASS Z RESERVE.
COLDWELL	Robt	SGT	/361	EASINGTON COLL	WEST HARTLE	28/7/16	28/7/16 BAILLEUL COM CEM EXT	BORN PITY ME. AGE 28.
COLE	Fred	PTE	/8	SEAHAM HARBOUR				BORN SEATON VILLAGE, AGE 22.
COLEBY	Geo	PTE	/460	SHERBURN HILL	SUNDERLAND	31/7/17	31/7/17 MENIN GATE MEM	TO 20th BN. CLASS Z RESERVE.
COLLINGWOOD	JohnG	PTE	/148	SUNDERLAND	SUNDERLAND	21/3/18	21/3/18 VAULX HILL CEM	TO 12th, 2nd BNS. AGE 20 TO 139 F AMB 28/8/16 SEPTIC FOOT TO DUTY
COLLINGWOOD	Jos	PTE	/509	TOW LAW	CROOK	26/6/16	26/6/16 TANCREZ FARM CEM	
COLLINS	Rob F	PTE	/698	CROOK			KR para 392 15/8/17	ATT 171 TUN COY RE, TO 10th, 11th BNS, CLASS Z RESERVE.
COMMERFORD	Ernst	PTE	/870		10/11/15		KR para 392	TO 3rd BN. AGE 25
CONNELL	P	PTE	/1016					
COOK	Arth	PTE	/434					TO 2nd, 19th BNS. DESERTED 7/5/19
COOK	Ben	PTE	/67	LANGLEY PARK				TO 20th, 20th BN. CLASS Z RESERVE.
COOK	ThosS	PTE	/39	SUNDERLAND	SUNDERLAND	26/6/17	26/6/17 LIJSSENTHOEK MIL CEM	
COOK	Wm	PTE	/798				KR para 392	TO 1/5th, 19th, 2nd BNS. CLASS Z RESERVE.
COOPER	F	PTE	/782					TO 18th, 14th, 11th BNS. CLASS Z RESERVE.
COOPER	John	PTE	/700		18/8/15			
COPELAND	John	PTE	/849					TO 20th, 20th BN. CLASS Z RESERVE.
COPELAND	Robt	PTE	/319	DAWDON				TO DEPOT. AGE 23
CORBETT	Geo J	BGLR	/237	NORTH BIDDICK		18/10/15	KR para 392 17/3/19	TO 22nd, 10th, 15th BNS.
CORNISH	Wm	PTE	/495			15/9/15	KR para 392 5/12/17	TO 20th, 20th BN. CLASS Z RESERVE.
COSGROVE	Geo W	PTE	/306	CROOK			KR para 392 29/5/18	TO CLASS Z RESERVE. CPL
COULTER	Edwd	PTE	/770	TUNSTALL				
COULTHARD	Emms	LCPL	/842	ST JOHNS CHAPEL				
COVERSTON	W	PTE	/218					
COWANS	J W	PTE	/767					
COWELL	Fred	PTE	/544	SUNDERLAND			8/10/18	TO 20th BN, CLASS Z RESERVE.
COWHOUN	Edwd	PTE	/325	SUNDERLAND				TO ROYAL DUBLIN FUSILIERS(6th BN). 139 FLD AMB 4/11/16 TO 10 CCS FLU, AGE 25 RDF No 29875
COX	Henry	PTE	/18					TO 14th BN, CLASS Z RESERVE.
COXON	Rich	LCPL	/744		1/11/15		KR para 392 3/4/19	AGE 25. TRIED BY FIELD GENERAL COURT MARTIAL 21/2/16.
COXON	W	PTE	/227					
COYLE	Arth	PTE	/387	SUNDERLAND	SUNDERLAND		30/7/17 NIEUPORT MEM	TO MANCHESTER REGT(2/6th BN). MANCHESTER No 44944

Surname	Init	Rank	No	Place	Place 2	Date	Reference	Notes
CRAKE	J	PTE	/504	RYHOPE	SUNDERLAND	31/7/17	MENDINGHEM MIL CEM	ATT 171 TUN COY RE, 20th BN. BORN SEAHAM AGE 24
CRAKE	Ralph	PTE	/979			17/12/15	KR para 392 28/1/17	AGE 32, DID NOT SERVE OVERSEAS.
CRAWFORD	A	PTE	/772			13/9/15	OPTIC ATROPHY 24/1/19	TO ARMY RESERVE CLASS W. AGE 28
CRAWFORD	JohnR	LCPL	/949					AGE 24, SERVED A COY.
CRESWELL	Geo	PTE	/271					TO 3rd BN. AGE 30
CRINSON	JohnH	PTE	/947	SOUTHWICK	SUNDERLAND	14/9/16	THIEPVAL MEM	
CRINSON	Wm S	PTE	/998			29/11/15	KR para 392 6/12/18	
CROFT	C	PTE	/916					
CROSBIE	Wm	SIG	/451	GATESHEAD		22/10/15	KR para 392 29/6/18	TO 20th, 20th, 19th, 20th BNS, CLASS Z RESERVE.
CROWE	John	PTE	/545					TO 3rd BN. AGE 25
CROZIER	Normn	PTE	/631					TO 20th, 20th, CLASS Z RESERVE. AGE 19 TO 139 F AMB 31/7/16 OPTICAL TO DUTY
CUMMINGS	David	PTE	/154	EASINGTON COLL	SUNDERLAND	23/3/18	ARRAS MEM	BORN USWORTH. NAME CUMMINS IN BN ROLL.
CUMMINGS	Tom	CPL	/613	WEST RAINTON	HOUGHTON LE	24/4/18	DUNHALLOW ADS CEM	SGT BORN EPPLETON, IN 8 PLATOON B COMPANY.
CUMMINS	H	PTE	/1005					
CURD	Thos	SGT	/737	SUNDERLAND				TO 4th BN, CLASS Z RESERVE.
DAVEY	Wm	SIG	/240	EASINGTON COLL				TO 20th, 20th BN, CLASS Z RESERVE.
DAVIDSON	Geo	SIG	/160			28/8/15	SICK 4/3/16	TO 21st BN. DID NOT SERVE OVERSEAS
DAVIDSON	Robt	PTE	/143					TO CLASS Z RESERVE. CPL
DAVIES	Ernst	PTE	/330			20/8/15	KR para 392 15/2/18 / 30/10/18 ZANTFOORDE BRIT CEM	TO 3rd BN. AGE 27
DAVISON	RichH	SIG	/524	NORTH BIDDICK	SHINEY ROW		CEM	TO ROYAL ENGINEERS(41st DIV SIG COY). RE No 193165. BORN PELTON FELL.AGE 20
DAVISON	S	PTE	/773					DESERTER? NO MEDALS!
DAWSON	A	PTE	/279					CPL BORN EDMONDSLEY. AGE 24.
DAWSON	M	PTE	/1066	FATFIELD	SHINEY ROW		KR para 392	TO 13th, 20th, 20th BNS, CLASS Z RESERVE.
DAWSON	Sam	LSGT	/235			2/4/18	WIMEREUX COM CEM	TO CLASS Z RESERVE.
DAZLEY	Geo	PTE	/407					
DEFTY	R	PTE	/93					
DENNIS	A	PTE	/1043					TO 20th, 20th, CLASS Z RESERVE.
DICKSON	Abt	PTE	/655					
DICKSON	W	PTE	/473					
DINNING	J	PTE	/490					
DINNING	J W	PTE	/86			24/8/15	KR para 392 22/11/18	TO 3rd BN AGE 38
DINNING	Robt	PTE	/491	BELMONT		26/8/15	KR para 392 29/6/18	TO 1/8th, 1/8th BN, CLASS Z RESERVE.
DINNING	Thos	BGLR	/131			19/8/15	WOUNDS 20/2/17	TO 3rd BN. AGE 21
DINSMORE	Sam J	SGT	/34					TO DEPOT. FROM 140 FAMB TO 139 FAMB 20/7/16 EVAC 2 CCS SHELLSHOCK
DITCHBURN	Abt	PTE	/892					ATT 213 FLD COY RE, TO 15th, 1/9th, 12th BNS. CLASS Z RES
DIXON	Geo	PTE	/828	KELLOE	DEAF HILL	1/11/15	24/3/18 ARRAS MEM	ATT 171 TUN COY RE, 1st AUST TUN COY, 20th, 20th, 20th BN. BORN NEWFIELD
DIXON	JohnG	SGT	/715			10/11/15	KR para 392 2/4/19	TO 4th BN.
DIXON	R	PTE	/862				SICK 15/4/17	TO DEPOT.
DIXON	Robt	CPL	/929	SUNDERLAND		1/11/15	KR para 392 13/11/17	TO 20th, 20th BN, CLASS Z RESERVE.
DIXON	Robt	PTE	/1004					DESERTED 17/3/17, STILL AWOL 15/3/20
DOBINSON	T A	SIG	/725					DID NOT SERVE OVERSEAS.
DODD	Thos	PTE	/485	DAWDON		30/10/15	NYSTAGMUS 27/1/19	TO 22nd, 22nd BN, CLASS Z RESERVE.
DODD	Edwd	PTE	/692	BARNARD CASTLE	BARNARD CAST		24/7/16 HOLY TRINITY STARTFORTH	TO ARMY RESERVE CLASS W. AGE 30, DID NOT SERVE OVERSEAS
DODDS	Bert	PTE	/695			25/10/15	KR para 392 6/3/19	AGE 24, DIED OF SICKNESS.
DODDS	Ernst	PTE	/588					TO ARMY RESERVE CLASS P. AGE 23
DODDS	J	PTE	/32					ATT 123 LIGHT TRENCH MORTAR BATTERY, CLASS Z RESERVE.
DODSWORTH	Thos	LSGT	/672					TO 20th, 20th BN, CLASS Z RESERVE.
DOLAN	Thos	PTE	/232			29/11/15	KR para 392 19/6/16	DID NOT SERVE OVERSEAS.
DOLAN	Thos	PTE	/997					ATT 41st DIV HQ, CLASS Z RESERVE.
DONALD	Wm V	PTE	/794					TO 3rd BN. AGE 24 TO 139 F AMB 11/8/16 EVAC 50 CCS ECZEMA
DONALDSON	Fred	PTE	/248					TO 20th, 1/9th BNS. BORN SOUTH SHIELDS
DONALDSON	Lance	PTE	/920	SOUTHWICK	SUNDERLAND	23/2/16	KR para 392 23/11/18	TO 1/9th BN, CLASS Z RESERVE AGE 31 TO 139 F AMB 4/7/16 EVAC 8 CCS SHRAP WND R EYE
DONALDSON	Thos	PTE	/781	SOUTH HYLTON		28/10/17	TYNE COT MEM	
DONKIN	E	PTE	/729	SUNDERLAND				TO 20th BN, ATT No 2 PoW CAMP, CLASS Z RESERVE.

Surname	Forename	Rank	No.	Place	Date / Cemetery–Memorial	Notes
DONKIN	Ernst	PTE	/787	WHEATLEY HILL		TO 13th, 20th BNS, ATT 123 BDE HQ. CLASS Z RESERVE. IN 4 SECTION 16 PLN D COY
DONKIN	G	PTE	/874			TO 10th, 1/6th BNS, CLASS Z RESERVE,
DONNELL	Geo	PTE	/149			
DONNELLY	T	PTE	/570			TO LABOUR CORPS. LAB CORPS No 614327
DOUGHERTY	Abt	PTE	/138	SHOTTON COLL		AGE 24 TO 139 F AMB 30/7/16 EVAC 8 CCS DEBILITY.
DOWSON	H	PTE	/311			TO 18th, 12th 2nd BNS. 4th SOUTHERN GEN HOSP PLYMOUTH 7/16
DRAINER	R	LCPL	/302			TO 20th, 20th BN, CLASS Z RESERVE.
DRING	Percy	PTE	/974	SUNDERLAND	22/11/15 KR para 392 22/8/19	TO 1/5th BN. 139 FLD AMB 21/11/16 PUO EVAC 2 CANADIAN CCS 21/11/16
DRUMMOND	James	PTE	/258	SUNDERLAND		TO 20th, 20th BN.
DRUMMOND	James	PTE	/923	SUNDERLAND	26/3/18 POZIERES MEM	
DRYSDALE	W	PTE	/120			
DUCK	R	PTE	/98			
DUFFY	Mich	PTE	/312	FENCEHOUSES, HOUGHTON LE	8/6/17 VOORMEZELE ENCL Nc 3	
DUNCAN	Edwd	PTE	/435	SUNDERLAND	24/2/17 KLIEN VIERSTRAAT BRIT CEM	ATT TRENCH MORTAR BTY, CLASS Z RESERVE.
DUNN	E	PTE	/674	SUNDERLAND		TO KINGS OWN YORKSHIRE LI(5th BN). KOYLI No 63807. AGE 32. 7 RUTTERS SQ ESH - 918 AVL
DUNN	J	PTE	/1058			
DUNN	John Simps	PTE	/825	MURTON COLLIERY DURHAM	12/9/18 VIS-EN-ARTOIS MEM	
EBDALE	W	PTE	/456			
EDE	F W	BGLR	/418			
EDMUNDS	E	SGT	/982			TO CLASS Z RESERVE. SHOWN IN WGR & SDGW AS 21/198.
EDMUNDS	JohnS	SGT	/416	TRIMDON		
EDMUNDSON	P	PTE	/198			
EGGLESTONE	Wm H	PTE	/817	DADDRY SHIELD	20/5/18 GWALIA CEM POPERINGHE	ATT 123 BDE HQ. BORN STANHOPE. AGE 24. RES ST JOHNS CHAPE
ELGIE	J	PTE	/282	BISHOP AUCKL		
ELLIOT	Wm	CPL	/317	WESTGATE		TO 20th, 20th BN. CLASS Z RESERVE. LSGT AGE 21.
ELLIOTT	John	SGT	/50	BURNOPFIELD	7/10/16 THIEPVAL MEM	TO CLASS Z RESERVE. 139 FLD AMB 17/11/16 PUO. TO 41 DRS AGE 21 D COY
ELLIOTT	Rich	PTE	/747	NEWBOTTLE, SUNDERLAND		TO 13th BN. AGE 25
EMBLETON	Peter	PTE	/1010	SHOTTON COLL	2/12/15 KR para 392 28/1/19	TO HIGHLAND LIGHT INFANTRY(9th BN). HLI No 333725
EMERY	J	PTE	/113	SEAHAM HARBOUR, SUNDERLAND	KR para 392 6/6/13	REGIMENTAL POLICE, BORN SILVERDALE STAFFORDSHIRE.
EMERY	Wm	PTE	/161		AO 265/17 6/6/13; 12/9/16 THIEPVAL MEM	
EMMERSON	J W	PTE	/735		24/3/16 ST PAULS CHYD HUNWICK	
ENGLISH	Matt	LCPL	/408	WASHINGTON STN, SUNDERLAND		AGE 27, BORN HUNWICK. TO CLASS Z RESERVE.
EVANS	Jos	BGLR	/136			TO 20th, 20th BN, CLASS Z RESERVE. SGT. COY/BN RUNNING TEAM
EVANS	T	PTE	/226			
EYTON	Clive	LCPL	/51	BLAYDON		TO MILITARY FOOT POLICE. LCPL. REGIMENTAL POLICE, MFP Nc P14547
FAIL	J	PTE	/450			TO 20th, 20th BN, CLASS Z RESERVE.
FAIR	Rich	CPL	/24			
FAIRBAIRN	F B	SIG	/97	DAWDON		AGE 29 TO 139 F AMB 17/7/16 EVAC 2 CCS S SHOCK, DESERTED.
FAIRER	Robt	PTE	/701	CROOK		
FAIRISH	Thos	PTE	/83	SPENNYMOOR		
FAIRLESS	T W	PTE	/816			
FAIRLESS	W	PTE	/814			
FAIRLEY	T	PTE	/811			
FALCONAR	T	PTE	/31			
FALCONER	Robt	SGT	/579	SUNDERLAND		TO 20th, BN, CLASS Z RESERVE. AGE 29
FARINA	W L	SIG	/46	SUNDERLAND	13/1/21 RYHOPE ROAD CEM SUNDERLAND	TO LABOUR CORPS. LAB CORPS No 606051
FAWCETT	Teasd	PTE	/483	NEWCASTLE		ATT 171 TUN COY RE.
FAWELL	Hub	PTE	/91		13/1/17 BOULOGNE EASTERN CEM; SUNDERLAND	
FEARN	L H	SIG	/887			TO CLASS Z RESERVE.

Surname	Forename	Rank	Number	Birthplace	Enlisted	Date	Reference / Fate	Notes
FEATHERSTONE	S	SGT	/818				28/7/17 MENIN GATE MEM	
FEENEY	Pat	PTE	/586	SUNDERLAND		23/8/15	KR para 392 20/2/19	TO ARMY RESERVE CLASS P. AGE 34
FENWICK	Bert	PTE	/76				21/2/18 SOUTHWICK CEM	TO DEPOT.
FERGUSON	James	SGT	/28	WASHINGTON	SUNDERLAND			TO 1/5th, 20th, 2nd BNS, CLASS Z RESERVE.
FERRY	Harry	PTE	/263	BISHOPWEARMOUTH				
FINLAY	JohnH	PTE	/764					
FINLEY	J	PTE	/216					
FISHER	M	PTE	/966			10/12/1915	KR para 392 29/8/17	
FLETCHER	Edwd	PTE	/1061	HORDEN COLL				TO 15th, 15th BN, DEPOT. AGE 23
FLETCHER	John	SGT	/71			13/9/15	KR para 392 15/8/17	
FLETCHER	Thos	SGT	/277					TO 3rd BN. AGE 43
FLETT	W	PTE	/797					
FLORENCE	R	SGT	/990					
FLOYD	Les A	SGT	/159	GATESHEAD		22/8/15	RELING COMM 7/4/19	TO 16 OFF CADET BN(4/5/17), COMM Y&L REGT 28/8/17,1 CAN GHOSP. TO UK 7/10/16
FOLEY	Edwd	PTE	/721	SHOTTON COLL				
FORBES	Gordn	BGLR	/145	BISHOP AUCKLAND				TO 20th, 20th BN, CLASS Z RES AGE 19 TO 139 F AMB 28/8/16 SCABIES TO DUTY.WOII 1920
FORD	Geo	PTE	/211			2/9/15	KR para 392 31/3/19	TO 13th, 9th, BNS, ARMY RESERVE CLASS P. AGE 24
FORSTER	R	PTE	/135				8/6/17 VOORMEZEELE ENCL No 3	
FORSTER	ThosJ	SIG	/523	PENSHAW	SHINEY ROW			TO 15th, 18th, 15th, 2nd, 18th BNS, CLASS Z RESERVE.
FORSYTH	John	PTE	/557					TO 139 F AMB 5/7/16 DENTAL TO DUTY.
FOSTER	Fmcs	PTE	/420	SHOTTON COLL		14/10/15		STILL SERVING 1920(FEB).AGE 20 TO 139 F AMB 21/8/16 EVAC 2 CCS TUBERCULOSIS. WOII
FOSTER	Geo	CQMS	/13					TO 3rd BN. DID NOT SERVE OVERSEAS.
FOSTER	James	PTE	/477				SICK 17/6/16	
FOSTER	John	PTE	/476	SHOTTON COLL			17/6/16 ELZEN WALLE BRASSERIE CEM	
FOSTER	Tim	PTE	/188			31/8/15	KR para 392 28/9/18	CPL AGE 31.
FOSTER	Wm	PTE	/535	HENDON	SUNDERLAND		16/6/17 ETAPLES MIL CEM	AGE 32 BORN MONKWEARMOUTH.
FOWLER	F	PTE	/400					
FOWLER	J	CQMS	/1007					TO CLASS Z RESERVE.
FRANCE	Rich	PTE	/724	SHINEY ROW	SHINEY ROW		23/9/17 GODEWAERSVELDE BRIT CEM	BORN BENWELL.AGE 26.
FRATER	John	PTE	/1026	RYHOPE	SUNDERLAND		21/9/17 TYNECOT MEM	
FRENCH	Arth	PTE	/869	SEAHAM	SUNDERLAND		9/10/16 THIEPVAL MEM	
FRENCH	F	PTE	/399					
FRENCH	RobtD	PTE	/641					STILL SERVING 1920.
FRYER	J	PTE	/488					
GAIR	W	PTE	/756					
GALES	J	PTE	/879					
GALLAGHER	Peter	PTE	/503			18/10/15	KR para 392 28/1/19	AGE 21.
GARDENER	Geo t	PTE	/848			10/11/15	WOUNDS 24/3/17	TO DEPOT.
GARDNER	Wilf	PTE	/910	ROOKHOPE				TO 19DLI(No 2 Coy).
GARNHAM	J W	PTE	/526	TRIMDON				
GARRY	J J	PTE	/616					
GARTHWAITE	J	PTE	/571					8 PLATOON FOOTBALL TEAM ALDERSHOT
GIBB	R	PTE	/742					
GIBBON	Wm	PTE	/426	BARNARD CASTLE		6/10/15	KR para 392 6/2/18	TO 18th, 20th, 15th BNS, DEPOT. AGE 23
GIBSON	ChasR	PTE	/777	BLACKHALL COLL				TO 11th BN, CLASS Z RESERVE.
GIBSON	Edgar	PTE	/398					ATT 171 TUN COY RE, 1st AUST TUN COY, 3rd ARMY SCHOOL.
GIBSON	Sam S	SGT	/228					COMMISSIONED 29/1/18. AGE 39 COMS TO 139 FLD AMB EVAC TO 140 FLD AMB FLU 6/7/16
GILES	Wm	PTE	/881			9/11/15	KR para 392 22/4/19	TO 1/5th BN. LCPL AGE 21 TO 139 F AMB 31/7/16 EVAC 140 F AMB DEBILITY
GILLHAM	Fred	PTE	/653			26/10/15	KR para 392 16/3/18	TO 20th, 2nd BNS, DEPOT.AGE 22 TO 139 F AMB 12/8/16 EVAC 50 CCS SCABIES
GILLIGAN	J	PTE	/831					
GLENDINNING	John	PTE	/360			25/9/15	KR para 392 1/7/18	TO DEPOT. AGE 22
GLENDINNING	Matt	PTE	/712			1/11/15	KR para 392 14/12/17	DID NOT SERVE OVERSEAS.

Surname	Forename	Rank	No.	Place	District	Date	Cemetery / KR para	Notes
GLOVER	James	RSM	/152	NORTH BIDDICK	SHINEY ROW			EX REG 2nd DLI, STILL SERVING 1920.AGE 29 TO 139 F AMB 22/7/16 ECZEMA EVAC TO 2CCS
GLOYNE	Rich	SGT	/193	SADBERGE	DARLINGTON		21/9/17 TYNE COT MEM	BORN SPRINGWELL,139 FAMB 21/11/16 EVAC 41 DRS AGE 20 A COY.
GOLDBOROUGH	James	PTE	/568				2/10/16 HEILLY STATION CEM	AGE 20 TO 139 F AMB 27/7/16 DENTAL EVAC 140 F AMB.
GOLDEN	JW	PTE	/534	LANCHESTER				
GOLIGHTLY	ThosF	PTE	/65					TO 13th, 3rd BNS, CLASS Z RESERVE.
GOODWIN	Dan	SGT	/344					TO 20th, 20th, 13th BNS, CLASS Z RESERVE.
GOODWIN	RichH	PTE	/304					TO 20th, 20th BN, CLASS Z RESERVE.
GORE	Edwd	COMS	/3	SUNDERLAND				TO CLASS Z RESERVE.
GOULD	Henry	SGT	/739			1/11/15	KR para 392 4/2/19	TO 4th BN, GOLD ON MR & SWB, AGE 24
GOULDEN	JohnG	PTE	/686	HENDON	SUNDERLAND	22/9/15	31/7/17 MENIN GATE MEM	AGE 22, SERVED C COY.
GOURLEY	Robt	PTE	/345	USWORTH		9/11/15	KR para 392 15/2/19	AGE 22
GOWDY	Em H	SGT	/882	SOUTHWICK				ATT 123 LTMB,OFF CADET BN, COMMIS NORTHBLD FUS(16th BN).
GRADON	E	PTE	/733	EASINGTON COLL				
GRAHAM	John	PTE	/350				KR para 392 27/1/19	TO CLASS Z RESERVE. AGE 21 TO 139 F AMB 26/7/16 EVAC 140 F AMB SHELL WND
GRAHAM	Jos	PTE	/746				20/10/18 HARLEBEKE NEW BRIT CEM	TO 18th, 20th, 2nd, 18th BNS, CLASS Z RESERVE.
GRAINGER	Jos	PTE	/543			21/10/15	KR para 392 27/1/19	DID NOT SERVE OVERSEAS.
GRAY	David	PTE	/375					TO ROYAL DUBLIN FUSILIERS(1st BN). DF No 29707
GRAY	JohnT	PTE	/596	SUNDERLAND		25/10/15	KR para 392 27/1/19	DID NOT SERVE OVERSEAS.
GRAY	Jos	PTE	/310					DESERTED.
GRAY	W	PTE	/728					
GREEN	A	PTE	/951					
GREEN	Alf	BGLR	/92	TUNSTALL		24/8/15	KR para 392 20/2/19	TO 12th BN, ARMY RESERVE CLASS P. AGE 23
GREEN	Clark	PTE	/430	NEW HERRINGTON	HOUGHTON LE		11/9/16 THIEPVAL MEM	BORN SHINEY ROW. AGE 18.
GREEN	JW	PTE	/25					
GREEN	John	PTE	/119			26/8/15	KR para 392 20/2/19	TO ARMY RESERVE CLASS P. AGE 35
GREEN	R	PTE	/925					
GREENER	TE	PTE	/788			26/11/15	KR para 392 28/1/19	
GREENFIELD	Geo W	PTE	/992	PALLION		24/8/15	KR para 392 20/2/17	TO CLASS Z RESERVE. AGE 19 TO 139 F AMB 21/8/16 EVAC 50 CCS SCABIES
GREENLESS	T	CPL	/1044					TO LABOUR CORPS, ARMY RESERVE CLASS P. LCPL AGE 38
GREGSON	James	PTE	/82					
GRENDLE	WJ	PTE	/96					
GRIMES	JohnG	PTE	/481					TO 20th, 20th BN, CLASS Z RESERVE.
GUEST	JohnE	CPL	/836					TO CLASS Z RESERVE. AGE 23 TO 139 F AMB 24/8/16 SCABIES TO DUTY
GUSTARD	Henry	PTE	/837	HENDON		2/11/15	KR para 392 14/5/19	TO 18th, 3rd BNS, 139 FLD AMB 30/11/16 EVAC 41 DRS SEPTIC HEELS, AGE 26 D COY
HAINES	Wm	PTE	/391	SUNDERLAND			16/9/16 HEILLY STATION CEM	BORN NEWPORT MONMOUTH.
HAIR	G W	PTE	/662	SEAHAM HARBOUR	SEAHAM HARB		15/9/16 THIEPVAL MEM	
HAIR	Jerm	PTE	/295					IN B COMPANY AGE 20.
HALL	A B	PTE	/906					
HALL	J	PTE	/552					
HALL	John	PTE	/643	SUNDERLAND				TO 20th, 20th BN, CLASS Z RESERVE. LCPL
HALL	JohnR	PTE	/807					TO 20th, 20th BN, CLASS Z RESERVE.
HALL	Norm	PTE	/950	SUNDERLAND			14/9/16 BULLS RD CEM FLERS	
HALL	Robt	PTE	/780					TO 2nd BN, CLASS Z RESERVE.
HALL	T	PTE	/290					
HALL	Thos	PTE	/334	SKELTON	DURHAM	21/9/15		TO 21st BN. LABOURER AGE 29,5'4". DESERTED 25/8/16 HORNSEA
HALL	ThosH	PTE	/710					ATT 171 TUN COY RE, 20th, 20th 20th BN, CLASS Z RESERVE.
HALL	Wm	PTE	/940					TO CLASS Z RESERVE.
HALLAH	T	PTE	/536					
HALPIN	J	PTE	/100					DID NOT SERVE OVERSEAS.
HALSALL	Wm	PTE	/446			11/10/15	KR para 392 27/1/19	TO 2nd BN.
HAMILTON	C	PTE	/569					
HANBERRY			/259					
HANCOCK	Fred	PTE	/288	BISHOP AUCKLAND	BISHOP AUCKL		24/10/18 VIS EN ARTOIS MEM	TO 18th, 2nd, 15th BNS. SERIOUSLY ILL WITH MENINGITIS 21/2/16 BORN B AUCKLAND
HANLON	John	SGT	/168	SUNDERLAND				TO CLASS Z RESERVE. FOOTBALLER, TRENCH RAID 26/7/16
HANNAH	James	LCPL	/485	SUNDERLAND			25/3/18 ARRAS MEM	CPL

Surname	Forename	Rank	Number	Place	Date / Memorial	Notes
HANNAH	T	PTE	/121			TO 13th BN, CLASS Z RESERVE.
HARDY	JohnT	PTE	/139	TRIMDON GRANGE		BORN CASSOP.
HARLAND	ChasD	SIG	/204	DEAF HILL	1/10/16 THIEPVAL MEM	TO 20th, 20th, ATT 124 LTMB, 20th BN, CLASS Z RESERVE.
HARPER	G		/1059			AGE 44 TO 139 F AMB 27/7/16 GASTRITIS EVAC 138 FLD AMB.
HARRIS	Ernst	PTE	/250	NEW SEAHAM	30/8/18 HAC CEM ECOUST ST MEIN	TO MIDDLESEX REGT(1/7th BN). BORN NEW SEAHAM. MDSEX No G/44793. AGE 31
HARRIS	James	PTE	/1068	SEAHAM HARB	28/09/1914	TO ROYAL BERKSHIRE REGT(5th BN), 20th DURHAM LI. R BERKS No 10576. AGE 23
HARRIS	Rich	PTE	/241	EASINGTON COLL	KR para 392 22/5/18	TO 20th, 20th BN, CLASS Z RESERVE.
HARRISON	D	PTE	/1057			
HARRISON	John	PTE	/475	WHITBURN	30/9/16 THIEPVAL MEM	TO 1/7th BN, CLASS Z RESERVE.
HARRISON	S	LSGT	/1001			AGE 21.
HARTLEY	Wm S	LSGT	/935	SUNDERLAND	18/9/16 HEILLY STATION CEM	TO 19th, 18th BNS. STILL SERVING 1920
HARTLEY	Alf	PTE	/945	SUNDERLAND		
HARTLEY	Wm	PTE	/89		12/6/18 MEREKNOLLS CEM	
HASKETT	JohnF	PTE	/927	SUNDERLAND	SUND/LND	TO DEPOT. AGE 30
HASSELL		PTE	/57			
HASWELL	Dav D	PTE	/1056			TO CLASS Z RESERVE.
HASWELL	J	PTE	/127	SUNDERLAND		
HASWELL	Thos	PTE	/134	SUNDERLAND	22/9/17 TYNE COT MEM	
HAUXBY	W F	BGLR	/245	HETTON LE HOLE		
HAUXWELL	J W	PTE	/184			
HAYES	Geo	PTE	/513	NORTH BIDDICK		TO 20th, 139 FLD AMB 20/11/16 EVAC 41 DRS PUO, AGE 19 BORN HOUGHTON
HEATH	Thos	PTE	/761			TO CLASS Z RESERVE.
HEDGER	J	PTE	/605			
HENDERSON	Jos	SGT	/623	SUNDERLAND	8/10/16 THIEPVAL MEM	
HENDERSON	J	PTE	/905			
HENDERSON	Robt	PTE	/575	PITTINGTON	26/5/17 LIJSSENTHOEK MIL CEM	LCPL AGE 24
HENRY	Matt	PTE	/351			
HENSHAW	T	PTE	/786			TO CLASS Z RESERVE.
HEPPLE	Thos	PTE	/965	SUNDERLAND	24/3/18 ARRAS MEM	TO 20th, 20th BN. 139 FLD AMB 21/11/16 EVAC 41 DRS PUO. AGE 22, D COY
HERBERT	John	LCPL	/985	25/11/15	KR para 392 10/12/18	TO 1st SCOTTISH GHOSP ABERDEEN 7/1/16. AGE 24.
HESLOP	John	PTE	/363			TO 20th, 18th BNS, CLASS Z RESERVE.
HESLOP	Lawr	PTE	/615			TO 1/5th, 20th, 18th, CLASS Z RESERVE.
HETHRINGTON	G F	BGLR	/287	BELMONT		BATTALION BOXER RUNNER UP AT B/CASTLE.
HETHRINGTON	Sam	PTE	/624		KR para 392	ATT 171 TUN COY RE, TO 19th, 12th, 13th BNS, CLASS Z RESERVE
HEWITSON	John	PTE	/860			
HEWITT	Thos	PTE	/709	LEAMSIDE	10/8/17 CALAIS SOUTHERN CEM	AGE 23.
HILL	Geo	BGLR	/286	NORTH BIDDICK	14/9/15 KR para 392 18/11/18	AGE 22.
HINDMARSH	W	PTE	/877			
HIRD	J	SGT	/190			
HOBSON	C	PTE	/1015			
HOCKRIDGE	Rich	PTE	/171	SOUTHWICK	25/3/18	TO 13th, 20th BNS.
HODGES	E	PTE	/582			
HODGSON	P	PTE	/804			
HODGSON	Robt	LCPL	/14	SOUTHWICK	27/5/18 SOISSONS MEM	TO 22nd, 10th, 1/7th BNS. SHOT WHILST TRYING TO ESCAPE FROM THE GERMAN LINES. AGE 24
HODGSON	Robt	LSGT	/890			TO 20th, 20th BN, CLASS Z RESERVE. ASGT
HODGSON	T E	PTE	/266			AGE 29 TO 139 F AMB 31/7/16 EVAC 140 F AMB DEBILITY, SGT.
HODSON	A	PTE	/858			
HOFFMAN	G	PTE	/56			
HOGGETT	Wm G	PTE	/90			TO CLASS Z RESERVE.
HOLBURN	H	PTE	/903			TO CLASS Z RESERVE.
HOLDSWORTH	MarkS	CPL	/506		8/10/15	TO DEPOT.
HOLLYWOOD	Jos	PTE	/433		SICK 8/8/17	

Surname	Forename	Rank	No.	Attested	Place	Died / Disposal	Notes
HOLMES	John	PTE	/751	2/11/15		KR para 392 4/5/17	TO ARMY RESERVE CLASS P. AGE 24
HOLMES	Wm	PTE	/667				TO 20th, 20th, CLASS Z RESERVE. TO 139 F AMB 11/7/16 SCABIES TO DUTY
HOLYOAK	Ford	PTE	/472				TO 20th, 20th BN, CLASS Z RESERVE.
HOOKER	Robt	SGT	/48			12/11/16 CHADDERTON CEM OLDHAM	COMMISSIONED DURHAM LIGHT INFANTRY 30/4/18 BN SIGNALS SERGEANT. SERVED WWII
HOPE	Geo A	PTE	/1036		SUNDERLAND		TO DEPOT. AGE 17
HOPKINS	Walt	SIG	/707				TO 20th, 20th BN, CLASS Z RESERVE.
HOPPER	J R	PTE	/49				5'7". FAIR COMPXN, RED HAIR. DESERTED IN FRANCE 10/10/16.
HOPPER	Thos	PTE	/497	18/10/15		KR para 392 5/3/19	ARMY RESERVE CLASS P. AGE 38
HORLINGTON	W	PTE	/931				TO 139 F AMB 28/6/16 EVAC TO 140 FLD AMB. WND FINGER.
HORN	R	LCPL	/305				
HOUGHTON	E	PTE	/1013				
HOUGHTON	J W	PTE	/599				
HOUSBY	B	PTE	/841				
HOUSTON	Arth	SGT	/41		SUNDERLAND		TO 20th, 20th BN, CLASS Z RESERVE.
HOUSTON	Wm	PTE	/40	20/8/15			LCPL AGE 25.
HOWARD	Ernst	PTE	/681			KR para 392 25/6/18	TO 20th, 20th BN, CLASS Z RESERVE.
HOWARD	J	PTE	/611				
HOWARD	J	PTE	/952				
HUDSON	C	PTE	/1029				TO DEPOT. AGE 23
HUDSON	JohnM	PTE	/595	23/10/15		KR para 392 6/11/17	
HUDSON	W	PTE	/810				
HUGHES	Ben	PTE	/706	30/10/15		KR para 392 25/4/19	TO 2nd, 19th BNS. AGE 33
HUGHES	J	PTE	/422				
HUGHES	Mich	CPL	/911	13/11/15		SICK 13/5/16	TO 21st BN. AGE 22 DID NOT SERVE OVERSEAS
HUGHES	Wm	CPL	/591	25/10/15	MURTON	KR para 392 4/4/19	AGE 24.
HULL	T	PTE	/1055				
HUMBLE	John	PTE	/471				TO 20th, 20th, CLASS Z RES AGE 36 LCPL TO 139 F AMB 31/7/16 DEAFNESS EVAC 140 FLD AMB
HUMPHRYS	Arth	PTE	/589		SUNDERLAND	8/5/17 ARRAS MEM	TO 18th, 15th, 18th BNS. AGE 22
HUNNAM	Her W	COMS	/353		FULWELL		TO 20th, 20th BN, CLASS Z RESERVE.
HUNNUM	Frd J	LCPL	/308				TO 20th, 20th BN, CLASS Z RESERVE.
HUTCHINSON	Geo W	SGT	/322		SPENNYMOOR	11/10/16 DARTMOOR CEM BECORDEL BEC	LNER GOODS CLERK TRENHOLME BAR.
HUTCHINSON	J	PTE	/355				TO 27th BN.
HUTTON	Thos	PTE	/926		SUNDERLAND	27/9/18 ORIVAL WOOD FLESQUIRES	TO WEST YORKSHIRE REGT(1/8th BN). 139 FLD AMB 15/11/16 TO 41 DRS AGE 30, WEST YORKS No 64349 ATT 41st DIVISIONAL SIGNALS SCHOOL, TO CLASS Z RESERVE.
IBINSON	ThosH	PTE	/185		DARLINGTON	20/8/19	TO 20th, 19th BNS. AGE 25
IBINSON	James	PTE	/54	21/8/15	RYHOPE COLLIERY / RYHOPE	KR para 392 6/5/18 / 21/3/18 ARRAS MEM	TO YORK & LANCASTER REGT(2nd BN, A COY). Y&L No 39926, AGE 20
INCHCLIFFE	ThosW	LCPL	/607	23/10/15	SUNDERLAND / CASSOP	8/8/19 / KR para 392 2/4/19	TO ARMY RESERVE CLASS P. CPL AGE 24
INNES	Geo T	PTE	/886	6/11/15	FORRES	10/10/18 FORRES CLUNY HILL CEM	CPL AGE 34.
IRWIN	Berti	SIG	/621				TO 20th, 20th BN, CLASS Z RESERVE.
IRWIN	J	SIG	/402				
JACKSON	E	PTE	/769				TO CLASS Z RESERVE.
JACKSON		PTE	/16				
JACOBS	Stan	PTE	/389		SUNDERLAND	27/9/18 BRIE BRIT CEM	TO YORK & LANCASTER REGT(2nd BN). Y&L No 39924
JAMES	Arth	SGT	/1053				TO BASE BEF, CLASS Z RESERVE. ORDERLY ROOM CSGT AT BASE
JEFFREY	Thos	LCPL	/981		HOUGHTON LE	4/9/18 TYNE COT MEM	TO 20th, 20th BN. BORN CHILTON MOOR, AGE 24 SERVED B COY
JOHNSON	C	PTE	/711		LUMLEY		
JOHNSON	D	PTE	/210				
JOHNSON	John	PTE	/938				TO 20th, 20th BN, CLASS Z RESERVE.
JOHNSON	Nich	PTE	/1018				TO ROYAL DEFENCE CORPS. RDC No 66251. IN FRANCE 5/5/16 - 7/2/17
JOHNSON	Percy	PTE	/808				TO 20th, 20th BN, CLASS Z RESERVE.
JOHNSON	Randl	BGLR	/123	26/8/15		KR para 392 27/10/17	TO DEPOT. AGE 20
JOHNSON	RobtH	PTE	/680				TO 20th, 20th BN, CLASS Z RESERVE.

Surname	Name	Rank	No.	Place	Place 2	Date	KR / Memorial	Notes
JOHNSON	Sam	PTE	/348	EASINGTON COLL				TO 20th, 20th BN.
JOHNSON	T	BGLR	/291	SUNDERLAND				AGE 19 TO 139 F AMB 16/7/16 SCABIES TO DUTY.
JONES	Wm	PTE	/970	SUNDERLAND			KR para 392	
KAVANAGH	W	PTE	/685			SUNDERLAND	29/9/16 THIEPVAL MEM	
KEAVENEY	J	PTE	/397					
KEEGAN	Frank	PTE	/ 36	TUNSTALL				AGE 19 TO 139 F AMB 11/7/16 EVAC 50 CCS SCABIES
KENNEDY	Edwd	PTE	/395			3/10/15	KR para 92 15/3/19	TO 3rd BN. AGE 36
KENNEDY	John	PTE	/404					TO 22nd BN, CLASS Z RESERVE.
KENNEDY	JohnW	LCPL	/ 38					TO 2nd BN, CLASS Z RESERVE.
KENT	Thos	PTE	/301			15/9/15	KR para 392 31/3/19	TO 18th, 15th BNS. LCPL TO 139 FLD AMB 7/8/16 SCABIES TO 50 CCS AGE 26
KIDNEY	T	PTE	/884					TO 3rd BN. AGE 29
KING	Alb E	PTE	/332			20/9/15	KR para 392 24/10/18	
KING	Frank	CSM	/578	SUNDERLAND			21/9/17 TYNE COT MEM	
KING	J	PTE	/983					
KINGHORN	Wm	PTE	/447	SUNDERLAND			16/9/16 THIEPVAL MEM	
KINNERY	Thos	SIG	/203	HORDEN				TO CLASS Z RESERVE. LCPL
KIPLING	ChasE	PTE	/762					TO CLASS Z RESERVE.
KIRBY	ThosR	PTE	/386	MURTON				TO 19th, 12th BNS.
KIRKUP	R	PTE	/ 44					
KIRTON	J	PTE	/164					
LAKE	E	PTE	/303					
LAMB	John	PTE	/180			30/8/15	KR para 392	
LANGLEY	Frien	PTE	/915				KR para 392 6/3/19	TOP ARMY RESERVE CLASS P. AGE 24
LANGSTAFF	J	PTE	/528					
LAURENCE	J	PTE	/895					TO CLASS Z RESERVE. NAME LAWRENCE ON MR
LAWS	Sam	PTE	/459					
LAWSON	Chas	PTE	/759	SUNDERLAND			30/9/16 THIEPVAL MEM	AGE 18.
LAWSON	Wm	PTE	/554			27/10/15	KR para 392 21/9/18	AGE 42
LAYBOURN	W	PTE	/ 58	SOUTHWICK		13/9/15	12/9/18 HERMIES HILL BRIT CEM	TO 1/8th BN. AGE 22
LAYBOURN	Wm	PTE	/289				KR para 392 11/12/17	
LAZZARI	J	PTE	/856					
LEADBITTER	A	BGLR	/167			29/8/15	KR para 392 20/2/18	ATT 123 BDE SIG COY RE, TO 13th, 20th BNS, DEPOT. AGE 19 TO 139 F AMB 22/7/16 SCABIES TO DUTY
LECK	Chris	PTE	/1048	CASTLE EDEN	HOUGHTON LE		1/10/16 BENAFRAY WOOD CEM	TO 2nd, 20th BNS. ***SHOWN IN WGR AS BROWN C**
LEE	J	PTE	/296					AGE 46 TO 139 F AMB 31/7/16 EVAC 140 FLD AMB NEURATHESIA.
LEITH	JohnM	PTE	/1037	SHOTTON COLL	SUNDERLAND		12/9/16 THIEPVAL MEM	AGE 21, BORN SUNDERLAND
LEMON	F	PTE	/453	RYHOPE COLLIERY				
LEMON	Ralph	PTE	/499					TO CLASS Z RESERVE.
LENG	Geo	PTE	/956					TO CLASS Z RESERVE.
LEWIS	Henry	PTE	/900					TO 20th, 20th BN, CLASS Z RESERVE.
LIDDLE	J	PTE	/647					
LIDDLE	Thos	CPL	/448	FULWELL				TO 20th BN, CLASS Z RESERVE LSGT
LILL	Arth	PTE	/212	DARLINGTON			27/7/16 TANCREZ FARM CEM	AGE 21 TO 139 F AMB 27/6/16 SCABIES TO DUTY.
LINDLEY	M	PTE	/863					LCPL AGE 30 TO 139 F AMB 8/8/16 WND L ARM TO 8 CCS.
LINDSAY	H	PTE	/436					
LINDSAY	James	SGT	/206	JARROW			SOUTH SHIELD: 3/10/16 HEILLY STATION CEM	
LINDSAY	R	PTE	/424					
LITTLE	Brit	PTE	/1040	CARRVILLE	HOUGHTON LE		27/7/16 BAILLEUL COM CEM EXT BORN BELMONT.	
LIVAIN	W	PTE	/1014					
LLEWELLYN	J G	PTE	/270					
LONG	John W	PTE	/696	HORDEN				TO LABOUR CORPS, LANCASHIRE FUSILIERS LC No 402122, LF No 49721
LONGSTAFF	D L	PTE	/993					
LONGSTAFF	Robt	SGT	/553	MIDDLESBROUGH	SUNDERLAND		14/2/17 KLIEN VIERSTRAAT BRIT CEM	

Surname	Forename	Rank	Number	Place	Memorial / Date	Notes
LONGSTAFF	Wm	PTE	/876	WASHINGTON		TO 20th, 20th, CLASS Z RESERVE.
LOUGHLIN	L	PTE	/1025			BORN STANHOPE AGE 23.
LOWERY	Herbt	PTE	/847	EASTGATE	BISHOP AUCKL 16/9/16 THIEPVAL MEM	TO 12th BN, CLASS Z RESERVE.
LOWTHER	Sam	PTE	/664			
LOWTHER	D	PTE	/648			
LOWTHER	J	PTE	/969			
LUSHBY	Thos	PTE	/699	HENDON DOCK	31/10/15 KR para 392 21/1/18	TO DEPOT. Age 21
LYALL	Tom	PTE	/15		SUNDERLAND 3/6/16 TANCREZ FARM CEM	AGE 17.
MADDISON	G	PTE	/919			
MADDISON	T	PTE	/854			
MANNERS	Wm	PTE	/539	SUNDERLAND	12/9/16 HEILLY STATION CEM	
MANSON	JohnW	PTE	/1019		5/12/15 KR para 392 28/4/16	AGE 19 DID NOT SERVE OVERSEAS.
MAROONEY	C	PTE	/1050			
MARSHALL	Geo L	PTE	/835	DUNFERMILNE	SUNDERLAND 15/9/16 THIEPVAL MEM	
MARSHALL	H	PTE	/537			
MARTIN	Pat	PTE	/191			STILL SERVING 1920. AGE 21 TO 139 F AMB 10/7/16 SHELLSHOCK TO DUTY
MARTINSCROFT	Geo	PTE	/839	RICHMOND YORKS DARLINGTON	1/10/18 ZANTVOORDE BRIT CEM	TO 19th 20th BNS. BORN BOLTON LANCS AGE 37
MATHIESON	Jos P	PTE	/61			TO 20th, 20th BN, CLASS Z RESERVE.
MATHIESON	ThosH	PTE	/62	HASWELL	WEST HARTLEF 24/10/18 AWOINGT BRIT CEM	TO 19th, 10th 15th BNS. LCPL BORN HARTLEPOOL AGE 29
MAUGHAN	T	PTE	/597			
MAUGHAN	Wm	PTE	/394		2/10/15 KR para 92 11/4/13	TO DEPOT. AGE 24
McANDREW	Henry	LCPL	/540			TO 20th, 20th BN, CLASS Z RESERVE.
McBETH	JohnW	PTE	/636			TO 20th, 20th BN, CLASS Z RESERVE.
McCABE	John	PTE	/378	WEST HARTLEPOOl 28/9/15	KR para 392 10/7/18	TO DEPOT. AGE 21
McCLUMPHA	Edwin	PTE	/390			TO CLASS Z RESERVE.
McCLUMPHA	T	CPL	/175			
McCONNOLLY	N	PTE	/364			AGE 20 TO 139 F AMB 20/6/16 EVAC 50 CCS SCABIES.
McCORRY	Wilf	SGT	/21	MURTON	2/4/17 KLIEN VIERSTRAAT BRIT CEM	TO 11th, 20th BNS, CLASS Z RESERVE.
McCULLAGH	Malc	PTE	/529	SHOTTON COLL	SUNDERLAND	BORN DURHAM.
McDERMOT	Wm	PTE	/468	SUNDERLAND	25/10/16 CITE BON JEAN CEM	TO NORTHUMBERLAND FUSILIERS(26th BN). NORTHBLD FUS No 41271.IN 20th BN AS McDONALD
McDIARMED	Donld	PTE	/137	EDINBURGH	25/3/18 ARRAS MEM	TO 20th, 20th BN.
McELVOQUE	J	SGT	/87			TO CLASS Z RESERVE.
McGAHAN	Barry	PTE	/606	SUNDERLAND	23/8/17 TYNE COT MEM	TO 20th, 20th, 9th BNS. BEST BRAKE IN BILLIARD COMP B/CASTLE 31/12/15
McGORIN	P	PTE	/27			TO 10th BN
McGUIRE		PTE	/581			
McGURRELL	Myles	PTE	/487			TO CLASS Z RESERVE.
McKEAND	JohnG	PTE	/855	SACRISTON	SUNDERLAND BECOURT	BORN CHESTER LE STREET
McKENZIE	Thos	PTE	/722		KR para 392	
McKENZIE	Thos	PTE	/723		2/1/15 KR para 392 25/5/17	TO ARMY RESERVE CLASS P. AGE 24
McLAREN	James	PTE	/371		25/9/15	TO 20th, 20th BN, CLASS Z RESERVE.
McLAREN	Thos	PTE	/1031		9/12/15 KR para 392 15/8/17	TO DEPOT. AGE 19 TO 139 F AMB 4/9/16 SCABIES EVAC 50 CCS
McLEAN	D	PTE	/606			
McMANNERS	T	PTE	/645			
McMILLAN	S	PTE	/547			
McNICHOLAS		PTE	/64			
McPARTLIN	John	PTE	/275	TRIMDON GRANGE SUNDERLAND	22/6/17 MENIN GATE MEM	BORN SUNDERLAND.
McPHEE	Wm J	PTE	/264			TO 15th, 8th BNS, CLASS Z RESERVE. 139 FLD AMB 30/11/16 EVAC 41 DRS DIARRHOEA, AGE 18 A COY
McVINISH	Dunc	SGT	/713			TO 19th, 20th, 20th, 20th BNS, CLASS Z RESERVE.
McWILLIAMS	J	PTE	/517			TO 27th BN, CLASS Z RESERVE.
MEIR	David	PTE	/683	SEAHAM		TO CLASS Z RESERVE.
METCALF	A	PTE	/140		9/12/15 KR para 392 2/12/17	
METCALF	Thos	PTE	/1033			TO 4th BN. AGE 21

Surname	Forename	Rank	No.	Place	Service/Date	Notes
MIDDLEMAS	Robt	CPL	/866		10/11/15 GSW ARM 28/1/19	TO ARMY RESERVE CLASS W. AGE 31
MIDDLETON	JohnW	PTE	/533			TO 20th, 20th BN. CLASS Z RESERVE.
MILBURN	Fenwk	PTE	/873	MURTON	SEAHAM HARB(4/10/17 TYNE COT MEM	TO 15th BN.
MILBURN	J	PTE	/338			AGE 25 TO 139 F AMB 27/8/16 EVAC NZ STAT HOSP NYD.
MILES	Wm	PTE	/1047			TO 12th, 11th BNS, CLASS Z RES AGE 22 TO 139 FAMB 11/5/16 12CCS, 139 FAMB 15/7/16-1 CAN CCS
MILLER	Alf	PTE	/276			TO 20th, 20th, 20th BN, CLASS Z RESERVE. 139 FLD AMB 3/12/16 TRENCH FEVER EVAC 3 CANADIAN CCS,
MILLER	Alf E	SGT	/11			TO 20th, 20th BN, CLASS Z RESERVE. ORDERLY ROOM SGT
MILLER	J	PTE	/1045			
MILLER	Jamps	PTE	/219		5/9/15 KR para 392 8/2/18	TO 3rd BN. REGIMENTAL POLICE.AGE 37
MILLER	Thos	PTE	/438	BLACKHILL	31/1/17 LA CLYTTE MIL CEM	
MILLS	Geo B	COMS	/757		SUNDERLAND	TO 20th, 20th BN, CLASS Z RESERVE.
MILLS	J	PTE	/939			
MINTO	G	PTE	/70	HORDEN	5/10/15	TO LAB CORPS, THEN LANCASHIRE FUSILIERS,139 FLD AMB 3/11/16 - 41 DRS NYD. AGE 23.B COY. LF 60'
MITCHELL	A	PTE	/410	SOUTH SHIELDS	13/11/15 SUNDERLAND	TO 21st BN. MINER AGE 33 5'6", DESERTED 16/5/16 HORNSEA
MITCHELL	Ral S	PTE	/912		KR para 392 18/6/17	TO ARMY RESERVE CLASS P. AGE 22
MOLE	Jos	PTE	/205	WINGATE	DEAF HILL 5/8/17 ETAPLES MIL CEM	BORN HESELDENE.
MONARCH	H	PTE	/313			
MOODEY	J W	PTE	/548			TO CLASS Z RESERVE.
MOON	Harry	PTE	/78	BLAYDON		
MOON	T	PTE	/478			
MOORE	H	PTE	/432			
MOORE	R	PTE	/297			
MOORIN	Mich	SGT	/133			TO CLASS Z RESERVE. PIONEER CORPORAL 1/9/15
MORAN	H	PTE	/309			
MORCAMBE	Normn	PTE	/572	HETTON LE HOLE	HOUGHTON LE 26/6/17 MENIN GATE MEM 11/5/18 PERTH CEM CHINA WALL	AGE 20 TO 139 F AMB 18/7/16 HAND WND EVAC 140 FLD AMB.
MORDEY	ChasA	PTE	/678	SUNDERLAND		TO 20th, 20th BN.
MORDEY	R	PTE	/988			TO ARMY RESERVE CLASS P. AGE ON SWB 58?
MORDEY	Rich	BGLR	/331	SUNDERLAND	23/10/15 KR para 392	TO CLASS Z RESERVE.
MORRIS	Evan	PTE	/565		KR para 392 4/5/17	
MORRISON	Hugh	PTE	/649			
MORRISON	A	PTE	/826			
MORRISON	H	PTE	/584		Dis 2/10/16 Died 14/12/19 MEREKNOLLS CEM	
MORTON	Geo	PTE	/677		28/10/15	TO 10th, ATT NORTHUMBERLAND FUS(26th BN). AGE 20
MOSES	Tom T	PTE	/116	DARLINGTON	29/7/16 BAILLEUL COM CEM EXT AGE 20.	
MOUNTFORD	Wm	CPL	/12			TO CLASS Z RESERVE.
MURPHY	J	PTE	/498			TO YORKSHIRE REGIMENT, LABOUR CORPS, LANCASHIRE FUSILIERS, YR 42925, LC 12906, LF61084
MURRAY	Alex	PTE	/924	MONKWEARMOUTH- SUNDERLAND	10/5/17 ARRAS MEM	TO 10th BN.
MURRAY	Frank	PTE	/512		18/10/15 SICK 21/6/16	TO 21st BN. DID NOT SERVE OVERSEAS
MURRAY	W	PTE	/875			
MUSHENS	H	PTE	/918			
NAISBETT	P	PTE	/479	BLACKHALL COLL		
NAPIER	Andrw	PTE	/221			TO 25th BN. FARRIER
NAUGHER	Wm	PTE	/914		15/8/15 KR para 392 22/12/17	TO CLASS Z RESERVE.
NAYLOR	T	PTE	/52			TO LABOUR CORPS(360 LAB COY). LAB CORPS No 196770
NEAREY	Geo H	PTE	/668	PENSHAW	1/12/15 KR para 392 3/6/16	TO 2nd, 18th, 15th BNS, CLASS Z RESERVE.
NELSON	T A	PTE	/1008			
NESBETT	Alf	PTE	/268		10/9/15 SICK 29/5/17	TO DEPOT. LCPL
NEWMAN	H	PTE	/673		19/10/18 HARLEBEKE NEW BRIT CEM	
NEWTON	Geo	PTE	/110	DARLINGTON	SUNDERLAND	TO 14th, 19th(Y COY) BNS. 22 YORK STREET IN AVL
NICHOL	H	PTE	/372		25/6/15	TO DEPOT. AGE 22
NORTON	Jas E	LSGT	/714		26/10/15 KR para 392 25/12/17	TO DEPOT. AGE 22
NOTON	JohnE	CSM	/708	ROKER	SUNDERLAND 25/3/18 BAC DU SUD BRIT CEM	AGE 32.

Surname	Forename	Rank	No.	Born	Enlisted	Death / Cemetery	Notes
NOVINSKI	Solom	LCPL	/778				TO 20th, 20th BN, CLASS Z RESERVE.
NURSE	Em G	PTE	/719	LONG SUTTON	SUNDERLAND	14/9/16 THIEPVAL MEM	AGE 33 TO 139 F AMB 25/6/16 SCABIES TO DUTY.
O'BRIEN	Nich	PTE	/358	EASINGTON COLL		KR para 392	ATT 8th CORPS HQ, 20th, 15th BNS.
OGLETHORPE	E	PTE	/541				
O'HALLORAN	JohnE	PTE	/155				ATT 171 TUN COY RE. 1st AUST TUN COY, CLASS Z RESERVE.
OLIVER	David	PTE	/806				TO 20th, 14th, 26th BNS, CLASS Z RES TO 139 F AMB 2/7/16 EVAC 1 CAN CCS SPRAINED KNEE AGE 22 DESERTED STILL AWOL 15/3/20.
OLIVER	Jas	PTE	/1009	SPENNYMOOR	FERRYHILL	27/7/16 TANCREZ FARM CEM	BORN DURHAM
OLIVER	JohnE	PTE	/196	SOUTHWICK	SUNDERLAND	4/10/16 HEILLY STATION CEM	ACPL.
OLIVER	Mich	PTE	/ 1			1/10/16 BEAULLENCOURT BRIT CEM	
OLIVER	Thos	PTE	/233	FATFIELD	SHINEY ROW		AGE 25
OLIVER	W	PTE	/864				AGE 23 TO 139 F AMB 9/5/16 TO 12CCS.
ONION	JohnW	PTE	/467	RYHOPE COLLIERY			TO 20th, 20th BN, CLASS Z RESERVE.
ORD	W	PTE	/366				
OWENS	E	LCPL	/128				
OWENS	Wm	PTE	/132	TRIMDON	26/8/15		TO 20th BN, CLASS Z RES AGE 19 TO 139 F AMB 8/8/16 EVAC 140 F AMB SHRAP WND L WRIST
OWSNETT	Chas	PTE	/117	DARLINGTON		KR para 392 2/9/18	TO 20th BN, DEPOT. AGE 22.BROTHER IN 18th BN
OXLEY	J	PTE	/812				
PAGETT	W	PTE	/ 29				
PAIN	Mark	PTE	/917	SUNDERLAND		18/3/17 KLEIN VIERSTRAAT BRIT CEM	
PALLISTER	A	PTE	/717				AGE 22 TO 139 F AMB 10/7/16 DENTAL TO DUTY.
PARKER	Tom H	PTE	/318	USHAW MOOR			ATT 171 TUN COY RE, 20th, 20th, 20th BN, CLASS Z RESERVE.
PARKIN	Jos	SGT	/249				TO 20th BN, CLASS Z RESERVE.
PARKIN	Roger	PTE	/365	EASINGTON COLL	WEST HARTLEF	22/7/16 BAILLEUL COM CEM EXT	BORN BARERHA??
PASSMORE	Flemg	PTE	/280		13/9/15	SICK 24/3/16	TO 3rd BN. DID NOT SERVE OVERSEAS
PATTERSCN	A	PTE	/102				
PATTERSCN	J E	PTE	/913				TO CLASS Z RESERVE.
PATTISON	J E	PTE	/242				REGIMENTAL POLICE
PAXTON	J	PTE	/243				
PAXTON	Ron V	PTE	/1030	SUNDERLAND	SUNDERLAND	10/10/16 HEILLY STATION CEM	AGE 19
PAYNE	Chas	PTE	/805	SUNDERLAND	4/11/15		TO 3rd BN LABOURER AGE 28, 5'7", DESERTED 26/8/16 SOUTH SHIELDS
PAYNE	J	PTE	/779				
PEARSON	A	BGLR	/122				
PEARSON	Jos	BGLR	/727		1/11/15	KR para 392 22/12/17	TO DEPOT. 139 FLD AMB 13/8/16 SCABIES TO DUTY, AGE 18
PEARSON	T	PTE	/445				
PEARSON	Thos	LCPL	/169				TO CLASS Z RESERVE.
PEART	Wm	PTE	/593	MURTON	SEAHAM HARB	1/10/16 HEILLY STATION CEM	
PEMBERTON	O	PTE	/429	MONKWEARMOUTH			1st IN BILLIARD TOURNAMENT B/CASTLE 31/12/15
PENDERGAST	James	PTE	/238	HOUGHTON LE SPR			TO CLASS Z RESERVE.
PETLEY	Percy	SGT	/ 60	HETTON LE HOLE	25/8/15		TO 20th, 20th BN, CLASS Z RESERVE. FAMILY LIVING 40 HIGH NORTHGATE DARLINGTON
PETLEY	Wm Wr	PTE	/114			SICK 17/4/17	TO DEPOT. SGT
PEVERLEY	Wm	BGLR	/150				TO CLASS Z RESERVE.
PICKERING	David	PTE	/ 75	SUNDERLAND	SUNDERLAND	20/1/17 KLIEN VIERSTRAAT BRIT CEM	
PICKERING	Geo W	PTE	/932	SUNDERLAND		17/9/16 HEILLY STATION CEM	TO 20th, 20th BN, CLASS Z RESERVE.
PICKERING	J	PTE	/941				TO 20th, 20th BN, CLASS Z RES AGE 22,NF No 61388,KOYLI No 63226.139 FAMB 10/5/16 TO 12 CCS
PILLANS	Wm	PTE	/ 74				TO CLASS Z RESERVE.
PINDER	Geo W	CQMS	/891				TO 11th BN, CLASS Z RESERVE.
POOL	A	PTE	/792				
POOL	S	PTE	/564				
POTTER	JohnY	PTE	/409	SUNDERLAND		30/9/16 THIEPVAL MEM	139 F AMB 1/8/16 DENTAL TO DUTY.
POTTS	E	PTE	/393	SUNDERLAND			TO 18th, 13th, 12th, 15th BNS. WOII CSM
POTTS	E	PTE	/388				
POTTS	Geo	PTE	/955	SUNDERLAND		24/8/18 REGINA TRENCH CEM	

Surname	Name	Rank	No.	Residence	Enlisted	Date	Cemetery / Fate	Remarks
POTTS	John	SGT	/815	WESTGATE				TO 20th, 20th BN, CLASS Z RESERVE.
POTTS	Wm	PTE	/587					TO 20th, 20th BN, CLASS Z RESERVE.
POUNDER	Ernst	PTE	/987	SUNDERLAND	SUNDERLAND		1/4/17 KLIEN VEIRSTRAAT BRIT CEM	AGE 19 TO 139 F AMB 18/6/16 WND HAND TO DUTY,
POWELL	W	PTE	/192					
PRESTON	W	PTE	/1046				3/11/18 ELSEGEM CHURCH YARD	AGE 26,5'2", DESERTED IN FRANCE.
PRICE	And R	PTE	/617	SUNDERLAND	SUNDERLAND			TO 20th, 20th BN, LCPL, AGE 22
PRICE	Geo	PTE	/20					TO ROYAL DEFENCE CORPS, RDC No 79341
PRICE	W	PTE	/374					
PRIDE	H	PTE	/538	SUNDERLAND	SUNDERLAND		13/8/18 BAGNEUX BRIT CEM	TO 20th BN, AGE 41.
PRIESTLEY	Edwd	SGT	/220					TO 20th, 20th, CLASS Z RESERVE.
PROUD	Went	PTE	/820					ATT TRENCH MORTAR BTY
PROUDFOOT	J	PTE	/975					
PROUDFOOT	John	PTE	/94	SOUTH HETTON	SUNDERLAND		8/6/17 VOORMEZELE ENCL No 3	TO 12th, 20th BNS. BORN SOUTH SHIELDS
PURNELL	Jos	PTE	/883	GRANGETOWN	SUNDERLAND		15/9/16 SERRE ROAD No 2 CEM	BORN GLOUCESTER.
PURVIS	Fred	LCPL	/255	WILLINGTON	BISHOP AUCKL		16/9/16 THIEPVAL MEM	ACPL, AGE 24.
PURVIS	Wm	PTE	/592	MURTON				TO 18th BN, CLASS Z RESERVE.
PURVIS	Wm D	CPL	/153	SUNDERLAND	SUNDERLAND		17/9/16 THIEPVAL MEM	
QUINN	J	PTE	/783					AGE 30 TO 139 F AMB 26/7/16 INFLAMED STOMACH.
QUINN	M	PTE	/634					TO 20th, 20th BN, CLASS Z RESERVE.
RAINE	FredA	PTE	/109					AGE 25, BORN CASSOP.
RAINE	RobtW	SGT	/693	COXHOE	DURHAM CITY		25/6/17 MENIN GATE MEM	
RAMAGE	R	PTE	/419					
RAWNSLEY	JohnW	SGT	/77	HUTTON HENRY	SUNDERLAND		30/5/16 TANCREZ FARM CEM	BORN OTLEY.
REAY	Geo	PTE	/458	HASWELL	HOUGHTON LE		27/7/16 TANCREZ FARM CEM	BORN BRANDON COLLIERY.
REAY	J W	BGLR	/174					ATT 41st DIV HQ, 20th BN.
REAY	Robt	PTE	/1006	LANGLEY MOOR	DURHAM		27/7/16 PLOEGSTEERT MEM	
REED	J	PTE	/650					
REED	James	PTE	/618			19/8/15	KR para 392 6/5/18	
REED	John	CPL	/403					TO 3rd BN. AGE 30
RENNEY	J	PTE	/6					TO 21st BN. DID NOT SERVE OVERSEAS
RENWICK	Phil	PTE	/705			2/11/15	SICK 25/6/16	
REYNOLDS	ThosH	PTE	/760					TO 20th, 20th BN, CLASS Z RESERVE.
RICABY	T	PTE	/492					DID NOT SERVE OVERSEAS.
RICE	Thos	PTE	/314			17/9/15	KR para 392 25/1/19	AGE 28 TO 139 F AMB 23/7/16 EVAC 8 CCS ULCERATED EYE.
RICH	G	SIG	/222					TO LINCOLNSHIRE REGT(1/5th BN).
RICHARDS	J	PTE	/666					TO KINGS OWN YORKSHIRE LI(6th BN),KOYLI No 42296
RICHARDSON	B	PTE	/632	SUNDERLAND	SUNDERLAND		10/4/17 TIGRIS LANE CEM	
RICHARDSON	Frk D	PTE	/702	SILKSWORTH	SUNDERLAND		8/6/17 BRANDHOEK MIL CEM	
RICHARDSON	Geo	CPL	/43	SUNDERLAND	SUNDERLAND		16/9/16 THIEPVAL MEM	
RICHARDSON	Harld	BGLR	/726	TUNSTALL		1/1/15	KR para 392 3/4/19	AGE 23.
RICHARDSON	James	PTE	/486				KR para 392 30/1/19	
RICHARDSON	John	PTE	/563			17/10/15	KR para 392 2/4/19	TO 20th, 14th, 2nd BNS. AGE 20 TO 139 F AMB 10/6/16 EVAC 140 F AMB GSW
RICHARDSON	Thos	PTE	/902	SUNDERLAND		25/10/15	7/1/17 RIDGE WOOD MIL CEM	
RICHARDSON	Wm	PTE	/852					TO ARMY RESERVE CLASS P. AGE 33
RICHES	J	PTE	/500					
RICHMOND	Wm	PTE	/521	DEPTFORD	SUNDERLAND		11/9/16 DARTMOOR CEM BECORDEL BEC	LCPL,AGE 19, TO 139 FLD AMB 6/7 + 4/9/16 SCABIES REALLY 17.
RINGER	James	PTE	/732	TRIMDON			20/10/16 VOORMEZEELE ENCL No 3	BORN THORNLEY.
RITSON	Geo	PTE	/937		DEAF HILL	1/11/15	MYALGIA 27/1/19	TO ARMY RESERVE CLASS W. AGE 42 DID NOT SERVE OVERSEAS
ROBE	Stan	PTE	/612					TO 20th, 20th BN, CLASS Z RESERVE.
ROBERTS	John	PTE	/209	WEST RAINTON				TO ARMY RESERVE CLASS P. AGE 23
ROBINSON	Alf E	PTE		SACRISTON		26/10/15	KR para 392 2/4/19	TO 20th, 20th BN, CLASS Z RESERVE.

Surname	Forename	Rank	Number	Place	Date	Cemetery / Memorial	Notes
ROBINSON	FrcsC	PTE	/656	SOUTHWICK		SUNDERLAND 19/8/17 SOUTHWICK CEM	TO LINCOLNSHIRE REGT(1/5th BN);LINCOLNS No 41420. AGE 20
ROBINSON	J	PTE	/802		15/11/15		
ROBINSON	John	PTE	/933			SICK 28/7/16	TO 3rd BN. AGE 39 DID NOT SERVE OVERSEAS
ROBINSON	R S	PTE	/10			15/9/18 SUNKEN RD CEM	
ROBINSON	Robt	PTE	/594	MURTON		SEAHAM HARB(BOISLEUX	TO 3rd BN(5 COY), KINGS OWN YORKSHIRE LI(5th BN), KOYLI No 63812
ROBINSON	Thos	SGT	/821	WEARHEAD			TO CLASS Z RESERVE. TRANSPORT SECTION
ROBINSON	W	PTE	/819				
ROBSON	Chas	PTE	/980	DAWDON	18/10/15	KR para 392 27/1/19	TO 20th, 20th BN. CLASS Z RESERVE.
ROBSON	Chris	PTE	/494		31/8/15	KR para 392 27/9/18	DID NOT SERVE OVERSEAS.
ROBSON	Edwd	PTE	/186				TO 20th BN. AGE 22
ROBSON	J	PTE	/546				BORN GATESHEAD.
ROBSON	Ralph	PTE	/752	EASINGTON COLL		WEST HARTLEF 30/9/16 THIEPVAL MEM	
ROBSON	T	PTE	/600				TO 25th BN(C COY). 139 F AMB 29/6 SCABIES, 17/11/16 TO 41 DRS.LCPL AGE 19 C COY
ROBSON	Wm M	PTE	/341	EASINGTON COLL		KR para 392	TO 20th, 20th BN. CLASS Z RESERVE. ASGT
ROE	Albt	CPL	/452				TO YORK & LANCASTER REGT(2nd BN).
ROGERS	D	PTE	/1034				
ROKES	R	PTE	/795			KR para 392	
ROOKS	Fmcs	LCPL	/622				
ROSE	R	PTE	/265				
ROSS	Jos	PTE	/808	KELLOE	25/10/15	KR para 392 25/10/18	AGE 19 TO 139 F AMB 31/7/16 EVAC 140 FLD AMB CONTUSIONS.
ROSS	ThosR	PTE	/642	SUNDERLAND		17/9/16 DARTMOOR CEM BECORDEL-BEC	AGE 36
ROUSE	Chris	PTE	/704				TO 20th, 20th BN. CLASS Z RESERVE.
ROUTLEDGE	T	PTE	/267				
ROWELL	Normn	PTE	/637	NEW SEAHAM		SUNDERLAND 31/7/17 MENIN GATE MEM	AGE 21.
ROWLAND	Frcs	PTE	/740				TO 20th, 20th BN, CLASS Z RESERVE.
ROWLANDS	Chas	PTE	/208				ATT YORK & LANCASTER REGT, TO 14th BN DLI. CLASS Z RESERVE.
RUBBIN	J L	LCPL	/868				
RUDDOCK	Geo	PTE	/106	HETTON LE HOLE			TO LABOUR CORPS, KO SCOTTISH BORDERERS.LAB CORPS No 382361, KOSB No 47202
RUSHWORTH	A	PTE	/785				BROTHER IN WEST YORKS
RUSSEL	J	PTE	/865	NEWBOTTLE			
RUSSELL	J	SIG	/428	EASINGTON COLL			TO 4th BN, CLASS Z RESERVE.
RUTHERFORD	Thos	LCPL	/315				TO 3rd, 20th, 15th BNS, CLASS Z RESERVE.
SAMPLE	Wm	PTE	/357				
SANDERS	T	PTE	/1051				
SANDERSON	W	PTE	/844				
SCORER	Ralph	PTE	/377	STANLEY			TO 19th, 12th, 12th BNS, CLASS Z RES, AGE 23 TO 139 F AMB 8/8/16 SHRAP WND R BUT K EVAC 8 CCS
SCOTT	Edwd	PTE	/415	TRIMDON	25/8/15	SUNDERLAND 28/9/17 ZUYDCOOTE MIL CEM	ATTACHED ROYAL FUSILIERS. AGE 28
SCOTT	Frank	PTE	/37	SUNDERLAND		FLAT FOOT 24/1/19	TO ARMY RESERVE CLASS W.AGE 25. DID NOT SERVE OVERSEAS
SCOTT	G	PTE	/107				
SCOTT	John	PTE	/158				
SCOTT	John	PTE	/944	SUNDERLAND	29/10/15	SUNDERLAND 8/10/16 THIEPVAL MEM	AGE 24 TO 139 F AMB 15/8/16 EVAC 8 CCS OTITIS MEDIA.
SCOTT	JohnJ	PTE	/684			KR para 392 27/1/19	TO ARMY RESERVE CLASS W. AGE 33, DID NOT SERVE OVERSEAS
SEAGO	Fred	CSM	/776				TO 19th, 20th, 19th BNS, CLASS Z RESERVE.
SEAMAN	John	PTE	/19	WINGATE			TO 20th BN, CLASS Z RESERVE.
SEAMLER	C	PTE	/901				
SEARY	James	PTE	/560				TO 20th, 20th BN, CLASS Z RESERVE.
SEERY	Mich	PTE	/370		25/9/15	KR para 392 16/9/18	AGE 24.
SETTINGS	R	PTE	/577				
SEWELL	Jas	SGT	/833	BISHOP AUCKLAND SUNDERLAND		1/4/18 ETAPLES MIL CEM	TO CLASS Z RES. 139 FLD AMB 9/8/16 EVAC 50 CCS SCABIES,19/11/16 EVAC 41DRS
SHARP	Fred	SIG	/501				LCPL, 139 FLD AMB 19/11/16 EVAC 41 DRS ICT WRIST, D COY.
SHAW	C D	PTE	/166				
SHAW	J G	PTE	/346				
SHAW	James	PTE	/967				

Surname	Forename	Rank	No.	Place	Date	Reference	Notes
SHEAVILLE	John	PTE	/601	SHOTTON		26/10/15 SUNDE 27/7/16	26/10/15 BAILLEUL COM CEM EXT MINER AGE 19, CANADIAN CCS 27/7/16 DIED WHILST A PATIENT.
SHELDON	R	CPL	/172				
SHEPHERD	J	PTE	/474				
SHERAN	J	PTE	/880				
SHERIDAN	J	PTE	/480				
SHERIFF	JohnW	SGT	/142	BIRTLEY			STILL SERVING 1920. WOII
SHIELDS	C	SGT	/347				TO 25th BN(C COY), 20th BNS.
SHIELDS	Hend	PTE	/838	HOUGHTON LE SPC	8/11/15	HOUGHTON LE SP	TO DEPOT, 20th BN, ATT TRENCH MORTAR BTY. MINER AGE 20, 5'2", DESERTED 28/10/16 NEWCASTLE
SHIELDS	W	PTE	/688				
SHILLAW	Rich	SIG	/349	EASINGTON COLL		KR para 392	TO 2/7th BN.
SIMMONS	Ambr	PTE	/187				TO 15th, 20th, 15th, 15th BNS, CLASS Z RESERVE.
SIMPSON	C	PTE	/231				
SIMPSON	J	PTE	/189				
SIMPSON	JohnB	CPL	/2				
SINCLAIR	F	PTE	/532				TO MACHINE GUN CORPS.
SKILLET	J G	PTE	/382				
SLATER	Robt	PTE	/857		10/11/15	KR para 392 22/4/19	AGE 26.
SLY	Matt	PTE	/1035	SUNDERLAND		12/9/16 THIEPVAL MEM	LNER ASSISTANT FITTER SUNDERLAND LOCO SHEDS.
SMAILES	W	PTE	/99	HETTON LE HOLE			TO 20th, 19th, 20th, 20th, 10th BNS, CLASS Z RESERVE.
SMILES	Jas A	PTE	/244				TO ARMY RESERVE CLASS P. AGE 23
SMITH	F K	PTE	/519				
SMITH	Hugh	PTE	/639		26/10/15	KR para 392 3/4/17	
SMITH	J	PTE	/356				
SMITH	J R	SIG	/1060				TO CLASS Z RESERVE.
SMITH	James	PTE	/111				
SMITH	James	PTE	/261				
SMITH	John	CPL	/26	EAST HARTLEPOOL SUNDERLAND		8/8/16 BAILLEUL COM CEM	TO 20th BN, CLASS Z RESERVE.
SMITH	JohnP	LCPL	/661				TO CLASS Z RESERVE.
SMITH	Pat	PTE	/441	TRIMDON			
SMITH	R	PTE	/921				
SMITH	R E	SIG	/223				ATT 171 TUN COY RE, 20th, 20th, 20th BNS, CLASS Z RESERVE. LCPL
SMITH	Robt	PTE	/437				TO 20th, 20th BN, CLASS Z RESERVE.
SMITH	T	PTE	/329				
SMITH	W	PTE	/731				TO 20th, 14th, 20th BNS. AGE 23.IN C COY AGE 24
SMITH	Wm Ed	PTE	/629	LANGLEY PARK	21/9/15	KR para 392 19/3/19	
SMITH	Wm W	PTE	/340		19/8/15	KR para 392 6/12/18	
SMURTHWAITE	Wm R	PTE	/17				TO 20th, 20th BN, CLASS Z RESERVE.
SNAITH	Madd	PTE	/260				TO 25th BN.
SNAITH	T T	PTE	/225				
SNOWDEN	H	SIG	/443				
SNOWDON	T	CPL	/80				
SOUTHERN	John	PTE	/144		27/8/15	KR para 392 6/12/17	TO 3rd BN. AGE22
SPALDING	Ernst	CPL	/531	SUNDERLAND		30/3/18 MONT HUON MIL CEM	TO 20th, 22nd, 20th BN. AGE 20
SPENCE	Wm	PTE	/272		13/9/15	KR para 392 10/2/19	TO 18th, 20th BNS. AGE 22
SPENCER	Tim	PTE	/508				TO CLASS Z RESERVE.
SPENDLEY	Percy	PTE	/774				TO 20th, 20th BN, CLASS Z RESERVE.
SPOONER	John	PTE	/324		17/9/15	KR para 392 21/9/17	TO DEPOT. AGE 30
SPRUCE	E	PTE	/703				
SPRUTH	E	SGT	/165				
STABLER	Geo	PTE	/573	HETTON LE HOLE	25/10/15	KR para 392 29/6/18	AGE 29 TO 139 FLD AMB 15/11/16 EVAC 41 DRS SAME DAY.
STAMPS	Leon	PTE	/899	SOUTH SHIELDS	JARROW	29/9/16 ANCOURT BRIT CEM	TO 3rd BN. AGE 19 TO 139 F AMB 20/9/16 EVAC 2 CCS ABCESS
STEEDMAN	John	PTE	/103	CONSETT	JARROW	27/7/16 PLOEGSTEERT MEM	AGE 24 TO 139 F AMB 9/8/16 SCABIES TO DUTY.AGE 26 IN WGR. IN V PLTN B COY.BORN HEBBURN AGE 24.
STEEL	Mann	PTE	/598				TO 12th, 15th BNS, CLASS Z RESERVE.
STEPHENSON	Albt	PTE	/948				TO ROYAL DEFENCE CORPS. RDC No 65416, IN FRANCE 4/5/16 - 4/10/16
STEPHENSON	John	PTE	/195				TO CLASS Z RESERVE.

Surname	Forename	Rank	No.	Place	Date	Casualty / Death	Notes
STEPHENSON	Percy	PTE	/555				ATT TRENCH MORTAR BTY, 20th BN, CLASS Z RESERVE.
STEPHENSON	Rich	PTE	/763				TO 2nd BN, CLASS Z RESERVE.
STEPHENSON	W S	PTE	/79				TO CLASS Z RESERVE.
STEPHENSON	Wm	PTE	/59	LEASINGTHORNE	23/8/15	KR para 392 20/2/19	TO 20th, 11th, 1/7th BNS, CLASS P RESERVE. AGE 32
STEVENSON	Fred	PTE	/691	FENCEHOUSES		1/10/16 THIEPVAL MEM	AGE26
STODDART	W J	PTE	/217				
STOKELL	O S	PTE	/45				DID NOT SERVE OVERSEAS.
STOKER	C	PTE	/889				AGE 24.
STOKER	J	PTE	/775				TO 20th, 20th BN, CLASS Z RESERVE.
STOKOE	John	PTE	/994	LANCHESTER	27/11/15	KR para 392 21/6/16	BORN HASWELL
STOREY	Newtn	SGT	/444	NORTH BIDDICK		DURHAM CITY 27/7/16 PLOEGSTEERT MEM	
STRANGROOM	Jas K	LCPL	/236				TO 20th BN, CLASS Z RESERVE.
STUBBS	Wm	PTE	/362	EASINGTON COLL		WEST HARTLEF 27/7/16 TANCREZ FARM CEM	
STUDHOLME	Wilsn	PTE	/146				TO 20th BN, CLASS Z RESERVE.
SUDDES	A	PTE	/326				AGE 28,5'4". DESERTED IN FRANCE 7/8/16. FAIR COMPLEXION, BROAD BUILD, VERY SLOVENLY
SUDDES	Jas M	PTE	/784	ESH VILLAGE			TO 3rd BN.
SURTEES	Jas M	PTE	/1012				TO 3rd BN. AGE 21
SUTHERLAND	W	PTE	/755				TO 19th, 12th BNS, ATT 1 AUST TUNN COY, CLASS Z RESERVE.
SWAINSTON	Geo	PTE	/320		18/9/15	GSW 14/8/16	TO ARMY RESERVE CLASS W. AGE 24
SWALES	Sid	CPL	/442		10/10/15	KR para 392 5/11/17	NAME VALENTINE IN BN HISTORY
SWINDLES	P	PTE	/239			DAH 22/1/19	AGE 20
SYKES	Ben H	PTE	/101	SHILDON	24/8/15	KR para 392 2/2/18	TO CLASS Z RESERVE.
SYKES	JohnT	PTE	/455		6/12/15	SICK 17/7/17	TO CLASS Z RESERVE. ACPL
SYKES	Rob T	PTE	/1024		27/11/15	AO 265/17 9/1/16	TO NORTHUMBERLAND FUSILIERS, KINGS OWN YORKSHIRE LI.
TALLENTIRE	Geo F	PTE	/716				AGE 20 TO 139 F AMB 10/7/16 EVAC 2 CCS SCABIES.
TANSEY	Jos L	CPL	/95				TO DEPOT. AGE 31
TANSEY	Jos S	CPL	/22	SUNDERLAND	28/8/15	17/1/17 LA CLYTTE MIL CEM	
TATE	Chas	PTE	/614	SOUTHWICK			TO 18th, 20th BNS, ARMY RESERVE CLASS P. AGE 27
TATE	JohnJ	PTE	/1054	HETTON LE HOLE			AGE 22.
TATTERS	C	PTE	/4				
TAYLOR	A	PTE	/73				
TAYLOR	A	PTE	/197				
TAYLOR	A N	PTE	/963				
TAYLOR	Alf B	PTE	/1065				
TAYLOR	J	PTE	/1063				
TAYLOR	Jas W	PTE	/638		26/10/15	KR para 392 15/11/16	
TAYLOR	John	LCPL	/69		23/8/15	KR para 392 20/2/19	
TAYLOR	P	PTE	/644				
TAYLOR	Percy	PTE	/834		6/11/15	KR para 392 8/2/19	
TAYLOR	W	PTE	/1042				
TAYLOR	Wlf	PTE	/269	BRANDON	19/10/15	KR para 392 4/3/18	TO 20th, 20th BN, CLASS Z RESERVE
TAYLOR	Wm A	SIG	/527				TO COMMAND DEPOT RIPON. AGE 21
TEASDALE	W	PTE	/867				
TEESDALE		PTE	/1002				
TELFER	Robt	PTE	/989	HEATON		JARROW 27/7/16 TANCREZ FARM CEM	BORN SUNDERLAND BOOT SHOP MANAGER AGE 32.
THOMAS	S	PTE	/283				
THOMPSON	ArthT	PTE	/35				TO CLASS Z RESERVE.
THOMPSON	G	PTE	/462				SGT AGE 40,5'4". DESERTED IN FRANCE.
THOMPSON	Jos	PTE	/959	WEARHEAD			TO 14th BN(B COY), CLASS Z RESERVE.
THOMPSON	R	PTE	/200				
THOMPSON	R	PTE	/687				
THOMPSON	Ralph	PTE	/904	MONKWEARMOUTH SUNDERLAND		31/7/17 MENIN GATE MEM	
THUBRON	Thos	CPL	/151				TO 18th BN, CLASS Z RESERVE.
TIERNEY	G	PTE	/431				ACPL
TINAILES	N	PTE	/68				
TINAILES	J R	PTE	/720				

Surname	Forename	Rank	No.	Residence	Enlisted/Loc.	Fate / Cemetery	Remarks
TINKLER	Henry	PTE	/162	TRIMDON			TO ROYAL FUSILIERS. R FUS No GS/112260, 139FLD AMB 20/11/16 EVAC 41 DRS PUO
TIVENAN	J	PTE	/830				TO 19th BN. CLASS Z RESERVE.
TODD	Peter	LCPL	/561	SPENNYMOOR			
TODD	R Wm	PTE	/962				
TODD	RobtW	PTE	/651	CASSOP COLL	DEAF HILL	27/6/17 BUS HOUSE CEM YPRES	BORN WEST STANLEY. AGE 32.
TODD	Wm	PTE	/609			KR para 392	TO 18th, 14th BNS.
TOMSETT	Edwd	PTE	/872				ATT 257 TUN COY RE, TO 18th, 15th, 11th BNS, CLASS Z RESERVE
TONKS	Edwd	PTE	/827				TO 18th BN, CLASS Z RESERVE.
TRACEY	J	PTE	/81				TO LABOUR CORPS. LAB CORPS No 371678
TRAYNOR	John	PTE	/253	DAWDON	3/10/15	SICK 3/5/17	TO 12th BN(D COY).
TROTTER	Harld	PTE	/406		20/8/15	KR para 392 18/4/16	TO DEPOT.
TROTTER	James	PTE	/42				AGE 34 DID NOT SERVE OVERSEAS.
TURNBULL	J M	PTE	/321	WEST HARTLEPOOl	SUNDERLAND	21/10/17 TYNE COT MEM	TO CLASS Z RESERVE.
TURNBULL	John	PTE	/518			3/6/17 DICKEBUSCH NEW MIL EXT	TO 19th, 13th BNS.
TURNER	ChasR	PTE	/1067	DUBLIN	DUBLIN		FROM 36th (ULSTER) DIV CYC COY. ACYCLIST No 6855.AGE 19
TURNER	G	PTE	/551				
TUTT	J	PTE	/354				
TYRELS	W	PTE	/293				
URQUAHART	JohnF	SGT	/682		24/11/15	SICK 19/6/16	TO 21st BN. DID NOT SERVE OVERSEAS
URWIN	James	PTE	/654	NORTH BIDDICK			TO 20th, 20th BN, CLASS Z RESERVE.
URWIN	Thos	CPL	/252				TO CLASS Z RESERVE.
USHER	Hen S	BGLR	/525				TO 20th, 20th BN, CLASS Z RESERVE. 139 FLD AMB 2/12/16 EVAC 41 DRS PUO, AGE 19 B COY
USHER	R	PTE	/958				
USHER	Ralph	PTE	/961				TO 20th, 20th BN, CLASS Z RESERVE.
USHER	W	PTE	/628				
VARVILL	J	PTE	/425				COMMISSIONED YORKSHIRE REGT(3rd BN). SERVED WWII
VASEY	Wm	SGT	/971				
VAUGHAN		PTE	/470				
VEASEY	HerbE	LSGT	/620	HENDON	SUNDERLAND	27/3/18 FONQUEVILLERS MIL CEM	TO 20th, 20th BN. AGE 22
VEITCH	Jos	SGT	/659				TO 20th, 20th BN, CLASS Z RESERVE.
VEST	Fred	PTE	/23				TO DEPOT.
VICKERS	J H	PTE	/1003	SUNDERLAND	10/11/15	SICK 22/2/17	TO 12th, 6th, 20th, 2nd BNS, CLASS Z RES. AGE 19 TO 139 F AMB 21/7/16 INFLAMED EYE TO DUTY
VICKERS	Wm	PTE	/846				
VITTY	Geo	PTE	/129			9/2/17 BOULOGNE EASTERN CEM	
VOUT	Hen G	PTE	/542	SEAHAM HARBOUR	SUNDERLAND	22/11/16 RIDGE WOOD CEM	AGE 25.
WAITER	Robt	PTE	/936	ROKER	SUNDERLAND		DID NOT SERVE OVERSEAS.
WALDREN	Fr	PTE	/461	FULWELL			TO MACHINE GUN CORPS(123 Coy). MGC No 72125
WALKER	A	PTE	/675		2/9/15		AGE 27.
WALKER	Robt	PTE	/213	TRIMDON	DEAF HILL	KR para 392 12/12/16	
WALKER	Thos	PTE	/522	SUNDERLAND		1/8/17 MENIN GATE MEM	
WALLACE	Alex	PTE	/580	SUNDERLAND		31/7/17 MENIN GATE MEM	BORN ESH WINNING
WALSHAW	Geo F	PTE	/336	HASWELL PLOUGH	SUNDERLAND	12/9/16 HEILLY STATION CEM	TO 4th BN. AGE26
WANDLESS	Thos	PTE	/47		SUNDERLAND	6/11/16 MENIN GATE MEM	
WARDLE	Geo	PTE	/373		25/9/15	KR para 392 19/9/17	AGE 26
WARDLE	J	PTE	/466				
WARDLE	Wm	PTE	/796	MONKWEARMOUTH	SUNDERLAND	4/9/18 ZANTVOORDE BRIT CEM	TO 20th, 20th BN, CLASS Z RESERVE.
WARLOW	Thos	CSM	/63	NEW BRANCEPETH			TO 2nd, 15th BNS, CLASS Z RESERVE.
WARREN	John	PTE	/427				
WARREN	W	PTE	/1032				
WASS	Thos	PTE	/496		18/10/15	KR para 392 27/1/19	TO 10th BN, ATT NORTHUMBERLAND FUS(26th BN).
WATSON	Chris	PTE	/657	RYHOPE COLLIERY			TO 15th, 15th BN, CLASS Z RESERVE.AGE 21 TO 139 F AMB 21/6/16 EVAC 50 CCS SCABIES
WATSON	John	PTE	/333				

Surname	Forename	Rank	No	Place	Place 2	Date	Memorial / KR	Notes
WATSON	John	CSM	/339					COMMISSIONED 25/7/17.
WATSON	Jos	PTE	/694					TO 18th, 15th BNS, CLASS Z RESERVE. AGE 20 TO 139 F AMB 28/8/16 SCABIES TO DUTY
WATSON	Sam	PTE	/793					AGE 34
WATSON	T	PTE	/1039	DURHAM CITY	SUNDERLAND		30/9/16 THIEPVAL MEM	
WATSON	Thos	PTE	/183	EASINGTON COLL	DURHAM		16/9/17 ST PATRICK'S CEM / LOOS	TO 18th, 14th BNS TO 139 FAMB 25/6 138 FAMB DENTAL-139 FA 19/8/16 TO 1 CAN CCS
WATSON	W	PTE	/1062					TO 19th BN, CLASS Z RESERVE.
WAUGH	J R	PTE	/199					TO KINGS OWN YORKSHIRE LI(6th BN). BORN HART, KOYLI No 42300
WAYMAN	Harry	PTE	/1052	WEST HARTLEPOOl	SUNDERLAND		24/8/17 TYNE COT MEM / WOUNDS 5/11/16	TO DEPOT.
WEAR	Wm	PTE	/182			25/10/15		
WEBSTER	Jos	PTE	/413	MONKWEARMOUTH	SUNDERLAND		22/8/17 MEREKNOLLS CEM / SUND/LND	AGE 21.
WEBSTER	Nich	PTE	/813					TO 20th BN, CLASS Z RESERVE. LEFT BEHIND ON HOME SERVICE WHEN BN EMBARKE
WEBSTER	Robt	SGT	/9					TO 20th, 20th BN. CLASS Z RESERVE.
WEIGHTMAN	Wm	LCPL	/978					TO DEPOT. 139 FLD AMB 5/11/16, SHRAP ARM WRIST LEG. AGE 41 TO 41 DRS
WEST	Edwd	PTE	/484					TO 20th BN, CLASS Z RESERVE. CPL
WHATCOTT	Geo W	PTE	/986	MORTON GRANGE		16/10/15	KR para 392 19/12/17	TO CLASS Z RESERVE. CPL
WHEALANDS	Henry	PTE	/823					TO 20th, 18th, 15th BNS.
WHELAN	J	SGT	/307					TO CLASS Z RESERVE.
WHITE	ChasW	SIG	/482					COMMISSIONED 9/10/15.
WHITE	JohnH	SIG	/363					
WHITLEY	A W	PTE	/977					139 FLD AMB 29/11/16 EVAC 41 DRS, B COY AGE 25.
WHITTON	G M	PTE	/510					
WIGHAM	R W	PTE	/652					DESERTED 2/1/16, STILL ABSENT 9/3/20.
WIGHAM	James	PTE	/202					
WILCOX	John	PTE	/194				KR para 392 31/3/19	REGIMENTAL POLICE.
WILCOX	T	PTE	/285			31/8/15		DISTRICT COURT MARTIAL 17/12/15 PERSISTANT TROUBLEMAKER. 54 PREVIOUS CONVICTIONS
WILKINSON	Arth	PTE	/968					
WILKINSON	E	PTE	/224					
WILKINSON	J	PTE	/104					TO 20th BN, CLASS Z RESERVE.
WILKINSON	John	PTE	/585				WITH IGNOMY 17/12/15	DID NOT SERVE OVERSEAS.
WILKINSON	R	PTE	/771					AGE 28, BORN LUDWORTH.
WILKINSON	T	PTE	/885					TO 19th, 18th BN(A COY 1 PLTN).AGE 29 TO 139 F AMB 14/7/16 DENTAL TO DUTY
WILLIAMS	Jas	PTE	/72			12/10/15	KR para 392 10/6/16	TO 12th BN. 139 FLD AMB 1/8/16 SCABIES TO DUTY.19/11 TO 41 DRS. AGE 19
WILLIAMS	Thos	PTE	/457				20/2/16 MEREKNOLLS CEM / SUNDERLAND	
WILLIAMSON	Henry	PTE	/173	SOUTHWICK				TO 20th BN, CLASS Z RESERVE.
WILLIAMSON	Matt	PTE	/730	GRANGETOWN	SUNDERLAND		19/7/18 PLOEGSTEERT MEM	AGE 29, BORN GREAT LUMLEY.IN 1 PLTN A COY.
WILLIAMSON	W	PTE	/392				KR para 392	
WILLIS	ChasE	PTE	/201	MERRINGTON LANE			4/9/18 VOORMEZEELE / ENCLOSURE No 3	
WILLIS	Wm	SGT	/689					AGE 28.
WILLOUGHBY	J	PTE	/1028	FENCEHOUSES	HOUGHTON LE			TO CLASS Z RESERVE.
WILSON	Bert	SGT	/440			3/12/15	KR para 392 11/3/19	
WILSON	Geo	CPL	/281					
WILSON	Geo	SGT	/562	CASSOP COLLIERY	DEAF HILL	23/10/15	25/8/17 GODWAERSVELDE BRIT CEM	
WILSON	Geo	LSGT	/563	CASSOP		15/11/15	KR para 392 2/4/19	AGE 24.
WILSON	Gordn	PTE	/888				KR para 392 10/10/18	TO 4th BN, ARMY RESERVE CLASS P. AGE 23
WILSON	J G	PTE	/300					TO 10th, 14th, 22rd BNS. AGE 22
WILSON	James	PTE	/454	SEAHAM		9/10/15	KR para 392 1/4/19	TO ARMY RESERVE CLASS P. AGE 25
WILSON	John	PTE	/115	SALFORD	SUNDERLAND	8/11/15	22/3/18 POZIERES MEM	TO 15th BN. BORN DURHAM RESIDENT MANCHESTER
WILSON	JohnR	PTE	/897			14/9/15	KR para 392 26/12/17	
WILSON	JosW	PTE	/299				SICK 2/6/16	TO DEPOT. CFL, AGE 33
WILSON	W	PTE	/147					DID NOT SERVE OVERSEAS.
WILSON	Wm	CPL	/566	COXHOE	DEAF HILL		25/3/18 ARRAS MEM	TO 20th, 20th BN. SGT, BORN SOUTH HYLTON.

NAME	INITIALS	RANK	NUMBER	TOWN_VILL	DATE & PLCACE ENL	DATE & CAUSE_DIS, DIED BURIED	TRANSFER NEW NUMBER DESERTED ETC
WOODS	James	CSM	/ 21	HARTLEPOOL	WEST HARTLEPOOL	2/7/17 BELGIAN BATTERY CORNER CEM	AGE 25.
WRIGHT	Rob H	PTE	/ 17	GATESHEAD	GATESHEAD	16/7/16 CAMBRIN CH YD EXT	
WRIGHT	Wm	PTE	/ 707				TO CLASS Z RESERVE.
WRIGHT	Rich	PTE	/ 836	HEBBURN COLLIERY			TO CLASS Z RESERVE.
WRIGHT	John	PTE	/ 983				TO CLASS Z RESERVE.
YOUDALE	John	PTE	/1108	HAVERTON HILL			TO 18th, 15th, 20th, 2nd BNS, CLASS Z RESERVE.
YOUNG	James	PTE	/ 510				TO 1/7th BN, CLASS Z RESERVE.
YOUNG	Wm	PTE	/ 242				TO CLASS Z RESERVE.